ENGLISH MASTERPIEC

IMAGINATIVE LITERA'

T. S. ELIOT · UNDER THE GENERAL EDITOR-

SHIP OF MAYNARD MACK, YALE UNIVERSITY

Romantic and Victorian

Poetry

edited by

WILLIAM FROST

Associate Professor of English,
University of California, Santa Barbara

Second Edition

PRENTICE-HALL, INC.

Englewood Cliffs, N. J.

Romantic and Victorian Poetry

TO THE READER

These volumes present a carefully proportioned collection of writings in English, from Chaucer to the present, which are primarily valuable as literary works of art. Writings in the less imaginative modes have been almost entirely excluded, and complete works have been preferred to excerpts. Where cutting or selection was necessary, an effort has been made to preserve what is crucial for an understanding of the artistic value of the whole piece. Since novels cannot be condensed or excerpted satisfactorily, they have been omitted. Separate reprints of prose fiction may be used to supplement the last two volumes of this set. The introductions try to focus the reader's attention on what is imaginatively interesting and valuable in the various selections. If they succeed, they will at the same time provide the justification for this anthology and distinguish it from the many other anthologies that are available.

SECOND PRINTING .. .. DECEMBER, 1952

THIRD PRINTING .... SEPTEMBER, 1953

FOURTH PRINTING .. . . JANUARY, 1955

FIFTH PRINTING ... ... JUNE, 1956

SIXTH PRINTING .. .. JULY, 1958

SEVENTH PRINTING .... SEPTEMBER, 1959

EIGHTH PRINTING .... APRIL, 1960

SECOND EDITION

NINTH PRINTING .... FEBRUARY, 1961

TENTH PRINTING .... AUGUST, 1961

LIBRARY OF CONGRESS
CATALOG CARD NO.: 61-9352

28140-C

Contents

THE ROMANTICS

THE VICTORIANS

A Note on Chronology
and the Historical Background

Most, but not all, of the poetry included in this volume appeared during the nineteenth century. Its authors can be conveniently grouped as follows:

1. *Preromantics:* Akenside, Thomson, Collins, Gray, Smart, Burns, and Blake. Of these the most important are Burns and Blake. Practically all the preromantic poetry included here appeared during the eighteenth century.

2. *Romantics.* Romanticism covers roughly the first quarter of the nineteenth century (1800-1825). The romantic poets can be divided into two groups, earlier and later. The major poets of the first group were Wordsworth and Coleridge, whose best poetry was written in the decade or so following 1798, when their *Lyrical Ballads* appeared (it contained "The Ancient Mariner" and "Tintern Abbey," among other poems). The second group consists of Byron, Shelley, and Keats, whose major poetry appeared during the fifteen-year period 1810-25. (By 1824 all three were dead.)

3. *Victorians.* The rest of the poetry in the volume, with the exception of "The Lotos-Eaters" and "The Lady of Shalott" (1832), came out during the Victorian era. (Queen Victoria came to the throne in 1837 and reigned till the end of the century.)

The chief poem not strictly covered by the above scheme is Wordsworth's *Prelude,* published after its author's death in 1850. It was written, however, in substantially its present form, before the end of the first decade of the nineteenth century.

The period during which the romantic sensibility was created and came to dominate English poetry (roughly, 1775-1910) was the period that ushered in modern times. During it England was industrialized; political power shifted within the nation; and scientific rationalism became increasingly important and influential. By 1800 a workable steam engine had been perfected; during the first two decades of the nineteenth century the textile industry moved from

"cottage production" like the clothes-making described in Words-
worth's "Michael" to a centralized system of factories and power
looms; during the 1840's occurred the widespread introduction of
railroads; by 1871, 55 per cent of the population lived in villages,
towns, or cities (as compared to 40 per cent in 1800). In 1789 the
French Revolution began; in 1832 the English Parliament was re-
constituted so as to give heavier representation to the new urban
bourgeois and less power to a group of privileged landowners; and
throughout the last half of the century the English franchise was
being continually extended. Scientific rationalism invaded social stud-
ies with the theories of *laissez-faire* economists such as Smith and util-
itarian philosophers such as the Mills; while such philosophers laid
increasing emphasis on the satisfaction of man's animal needs, the
theories of Darwin and his predecessors dramatized the animality of
man's nature. In general, then, the period was one of increasing
urbanization, mechanization, collectivization, and accumulation of
financial power; it saw the weakening of degree as a factor in a
society becoming progressively more fluid and less stable, as a com-
parison of *Tom Jones* (1749) and *Vanity Fair* (1847-8) would sug-
gest; and it was marked by a general decline of traditional attitudes
and beliefs together with an increase in scientific skepticism, curi-
osity, and discovery.

    This ferment and these changes affected imaginative literature in
two markedly different ways. In the novel, which during the nine-
teenth century assumed major importance as a literary form, a power-
ful effort was made to symbolize, to comprehend, and to interpret in
terms of value the increasing complexities of modern society, both
in respect to individuals and to wide areas of relationship between
individuals. The scope of the novel became vast, as *Bleak House* and
Middlemarch demonstrate; though simpler and more limited in tex-
ture than the greatest poetry, nevertheless in imaginative reach and
fecundity such works compare with *Lear* or the *Canterbury Tales*.

    The important poets of the period—who were never the same
people as the important novelists—reacted otherwise to their age.
In general it may be said that they reacted *away from* most of
the historical tendencies described above. Frequently the age drove
them either inward, to sensitive analyses of the individual soul, or
outward to remote and exotic nations or centuries. To urbanization
and the factory they opposed a natural landscape and rural country-
side valued as never before; to collectivization, they opposed an in-
dividualism almost anarchic in some of its forms; to animalism
they opposed the spirit; to rationalism, the creative imagination;
to skepticism, faith. By contrast to the contemporary novelists and
to the poets of earlier centuries—Pope, Dryden, or Chaucer—they

seem to have sought less to understand their world than to understand themselves. All my works, said the most famous poet of the era, are fragments of a great confession.

◦◦

Nature

Much of the poetry in this volume, whether preromantic, romantic, or Victorian, has to do with the world of external nature: rivers, mountains, trees, plants, the sky, the wind, night and day, the seasons, animals, the ocean. As a recent critic remarks, such poetry, in general, reads meanings into the landscape. This is true whether the poet be Gray, who sees the dark unfathomed caves of ocean as an emblem of the obscurity of village life; or Arnold, to whom the night tide retreating down the pebbly beach suggests the ebbing away of religious faith during his own scientifically minded epoch. The long day wanes as Ulysses, his life almost at an end, prepares to set forth on his final voyage; while on the unchanging Grecian urn the happy boughs can never shed their leaves, nor the heifer lowing at the skies ever reach the green altar where he is to be sacrificed. We might compare, in earlier poetry, the festal scene briefly painted in the opening lines of the *Canterbury Tales;* or Adam and Eve's unfallen world in Milton, with its "flowers of all hue, and without thorn the rose."

Earlier poetry, however, can give no clear idea of the peculiarly nineteenth-century ways of handling nature. Since some of these began making their appearance among the preromantics, we may begin their study with a comparison of two eighteenth-century poems, Akenside's "Ode on the Winter Solstice" and Collins's "Ode to Evening."

Akenside's ode, in its central structure, is logical and explicit. Winter is unfavorable to human activities; the poet therefore looks forward to the return of spring, season of young love. The first proposition is illustrated in a number of specific ways (by an ironical excess of heat in the opening stanza, for example); the contrast between seasons is bridged by the philosophic seventh stanza, which asserts an ultimate meaning behind life's unpleasanter aspects; and in the last four stanzas, winter now disposed of, the poet turns to consider his own human gratifications—literature, companionship, and love—to which nature forms merely an appropriate incidental background. The pattern of the poem is a series of contrasts (between England and Bolivia, city and country, solitude and friendship); and just enough detail is given to sharpen each. "Flowers and dews and streaming light" is sufficiently evocative of spring for Akenside's purpose; he is not embarking on a full-dress characterization of the season, and the speaker's state of mind (disciplined exuberance) is not complex. Eudora, of course, might be anyone; the reader's imagination is deliberately left at liberty to provide her with such dimensions and attributes as he deems most appropriate.

Collins's heroine, Evening, is presented with infinitely more particularity. The poet's subject is the transitional hour of twilight, personified as a maiden whose temperament is related to the mood induced in the speaker by that period of the day, and whose attributes spring from the concrete experience of a landscape perceived through the half-lights of sundown. Instead of the pointed contrasts of Akenside, Collins evokes a mixture of qualities (neither light nor dark, neither noise nor silence) and sense-impressions which range from the vividly immediate ("short shrill shriek") to the blurred and remote ("hamlets brown and dim-discover'd spires"). The whole scene is poised on the edge of disappearance ("upland fallows grey / Reflect its last cool gleam"). The poet appears in the poem as a spectator; as the recipient of impressions mainly emotional; and his statements form no logical pattern but merely pass from one sort of evening, one set of impressions, to another. By comparison to the "social ease" and "learned toil" of the Solstice ode, the abstractions in the last stanza of "Evening" are fairly gratuitous, what relation they have to the rest of the poem never being made explicit. How little the poem's appeal depends on gratifying a reader's logical powers may be also inferred from the way one stanza, grammatically speaking, often melts into the next, so that by the time the end of a long sentence is reached its original structure may have slipped one's mind; in Akenside, stanzas and statements are co-terminous.

In Akenside, then, certain general aspects of nature are so arranged as to create an orderly effect and reinforce a chain of ideas; in Collins, sharp natural details are blended with hazier suggestive ones to build up, in cumulative fashion, a complex of emotions. The contrast, of course, is not exclusive: it would be wrong to say that Akenside had no feelings and Collins no ideas; but there is a contrast nevertheless. Akenside's method, it can be said in general, is closer to Milton's and Pope's; Collins's to that of Wordsworth, Keats, Shelley, and Tennyson. Milton's Garden of Eden, for example, represents a kind of circumscribed perfection; its details are chosen and arranged to make that perfection explicit; they are followed by a series of comparisons to other, less perfect Paradises. The Garden, like Pope's rose that causes aromatic pain, is in the poem to serve a hard logical underlying purpose, however many immediate emotional nuances it may evoke.

Furthermore, the reader is placed at one remove from Milton's Garden: Milton does not present it as it burst on *his* eyes, but on Satan's. Whereas the typical nineteenth-century poet, like Collins and even more than Collins, places himself (and us) in the immediate center of any natural scene, sacrificing dramatic or ironic detachment to direct, imperative appeal.

We can see this appeal at work, for example, in Wordsworth's "Tintern Abbey," in which the poet's sister, whom he addresses in the final paragraph, is a sort of surrogate for the reader. The poem is cast in the form of a meditative soliloquy in which we are invited to stand with the speaker "on the banks of this delightful stream," to retrace the steps in his emotional development, and to share in his concluding exhortations. So much that nature represented to the poets of this epoch is concentrated in the hundred and fifty lines of "Tintern Abbey" that the poem provides a convenient epitome of several important meanings that in those days could be, and often were, read into landscape.

1. In the first place, there is the sense of returning to an earlier world. For the past two centuries at least, the most striking movement of peoples in the Western nations has been from country to city, as industrialism increases and draws population more and more into the urban vortex; and it is probably no accident that much very popular poetry has associated the country, the village, the out-of-doors with childhood and with nostalgia for early youth.

> Such, such were the joys
> When we all, girls & boys,
> In our youth-time were seen
> On the Ecchoing Green.

So Blake, in his *Songs of Innocence.* If the poet himself happened to have been, like Coleridge, city-bred, he could still imagine a country childhood and promise one to his own offspring—as Coleridge does in "Frost at Midnight," a poem parallel in several respects to "Tintern Abbey." Wordsworth's *Prelude* is the great exemplar of the childhood-landscape relation, its theme being essentially the effect on a sensitive man's total life of early years spent among mountains and lakes remote from any metropolis.

Childhood is generally a time of fresh and vivid impressions, good health, and unreflecting spontaneity—a time of "glad animal movements," "aching joys," and "dizzy raptures," as "Tintern Abbey" puts it. The sense of a return to nature as a turning-back to something that can never be quite recaptured, some haunting quality never vouchsafed "save to the pure, and in their purest hour," enriches the perception of nature in Wordsworth's Intimations Ode and, to some extent, in Coleridge's "Dejection." It is probably related to the emotions felt by many romantic writers for symbols of the unrecoverable past in general: such symbols as the "time-hallowed pile" in the "Ode to Evening."

2. Connected with such feelings about nature and early youth in "Tintern Abbey" is the further conception of external nature as an environment in close, deep, and harmonious affinity with man. "How often," says Wordsworth addressing the river, "how often has my spirit turned to thee." Without such a conception much of the finest 19th-century poetry could never have been written. Nature's education of Wordsworth's Lucy by "silent sympathy" is a dramatic instance:

> She shall be sportive as the fawn
> That wild with glee across the lawn
> Or up the mountain springs;
> And hers shall be the breathing balm,
> And hers the silence and the calm
> Of mute insensate things.
>
> The floating clouds their state shall lend
> To her; for her the willow bend;
> Nor shall she fail to see
> Even in the motions of the storm
> Grace that shall mould the maiden's form
> By silent sympathy.
>
> The stars of midnight shall be dear
> To her; and she shall lean her ear
> In many a secret place
> Where rivulets dance their wayward round,
> And beauty born of murmuring sound
> Shall pass into her face.

The variety of this catalogue implies completeness; surely no phase or feature of the outer natural world is without its appropriate counterpart in the inner world of human personality. Nature, then, can be all things to all men. To the revolutionary Shelley, the rough wind wails, like the poet himself, for the world's wrong; or it lifts his own thoughts to scatter them like leaves, like glowing ashes, over the world in an apocalyptic prophecy of the coming Utopian spring. To Keats, beset by longing and heart-ache, the happiness of the nightingale's song intensifies an unbearable consciousness of unattainable pleasures. To the grief-stricken Tennyson, the transient blossoms of the graveyard yew-tree correspond to the transience of his own momentary relief from sorrow:

> Thy gloom is kindled at the tips,
> And passes into gloom again.

Such a relationship is often dramatized, some character created by the poet engaging in a dialogue with some aspect of his natural environment. An example from the preromantics is the half-humorous, half-human affection of Burns's auld farmer for one of his work-animals. Tennyson's mariners find their own world-weariness reflected and embodied in a land "in which it seemed always afternoon," a land where "like a downward smoke, the slender stream / Along the cliff to fall and pause and fall did seem." Browning's lover, in "Two in the Campagna," searches for his own half-forgotten thought among the yellowing fennel and feathery grasses of the slope on which he sits. A unity, even a mating, between human and cosmic nature is strikingly exemplified in the figure of Tennyson's Tithonus, the successful wooer of Aurora, goddess of Dawn. An older poet—Ovid or Spenser—would have treated such a subject by first wholly personifying and humanizing the goddess. Tennyson allows dawn to remain dawn, but his human protagonist to describe how he

> . . . felt my blood
> Glow with the glow that slowly crimsoned all
> Thy presence and thy portals, while I lay,
> Mouth, forehead, eyelids growing dewy-warm
> With kisses balmier than half-opening buds
> Of April, and could hear the lips that kissed
> Whispering I knew not what of wild and sweet . . .

Man and morning dissolve in a love-embrace.

Nature as a harmonious setting for human nature sometimes evokes, by way of contrast, unhappy reflections about less favorable climates and atmospheres. Wordsworth in "Tintern Abbey" has left "lonely rooms" and "the din / Of towns and cities" to return to his sylvan Wye; Arnold's wandering scholar-gipsy sits "upon the river bank o'ergrown," "Where black-winged swallows haunt the glittering Thames," and owes his imagined immortality to the fact that "tired of knocking at preferment's door" he has abandoned forever the intellectual and spiritual bafflements of "the world." Keats's nightingale, "not born for death," is in a similar condition; and the Ode gives us a glimpse of what specifically such bafflements consisted of in the line "No hungry generations tread thee down," a reference to Malthus's theory, propounded in the early nineteenth century, that since population always tends to outrun food supply, human poverty and famine can never be ultimately alleviated. A rural landscape (pastoral farms, green to the very door; some lone ale-house in the Berkshire moors; or the grass, the thicket, and the fruit-tree wild) offered a refuge from the teeming city and the bad dreams bred or begotten there.

And more than a refuge. One corollary of the theory that rural nature is inherently attuned to human nature is the conception of a regenerative process, a source in the out-of-doors for the reintegration of one's personality. This is a particularly important theme in poems like Wordsworth's "Resolution and Independence," where the metaphors comparing the leech-gatherer to a rock and a sea-beast help convey the sense of revitalizing power; or Arnold's "Thyrsis," where still the haunt beloved a virtue yields. In other poems the very failure or absence of such regenerative power sometimes provides a subject, as in Coleridge's "Dejection: an Ode" or Shelley's "Stanzas Written in Dejection near Naples." The implication of poems like these latter two is that there *ought* to be a reciprocal communion, a reinvigorating harmony, between man and his surroundings, but that the human speaker is incapacitated to enter into it:

> My genial spirits fail;
> And what can these avail
> To lift the smothering weight from off my breast?
> It were a vain endeavor,
> Though I should gaze forever
> On that green light that lingers in the west:
> I may not hope from outward forms to win
> The passion and the life, whose fountains are within.

3. "Tintern Abbey" also embodies yet another conception of nature important to many nineteenth-century poets and philosophers—nature as a source and center of order, knowledge, certainty, stability—as an emanation, indeed, of God, of Eternal Mind. Wordsworth says, in lines as famous as any printed in this volume, that he is "a lover of the mountains and the woods" because he finds in them "a sense sublime / Of something far more deeply interfused" that "rolls through all things." Nature in this view can be a guide and source of wisdom for human life, or an implicit assurance of life's ultimate significance.

The origins of this conception, which arose chiefly during the two hundred years before the publication of the *Lyrical Ballads,* are partly religious and partly scientific. An older poet like Milton, if he asked ultimate questions about life, turned chiefly to two sources for answers: faith and reason, the Scripture in the Book and the Scripture in the Breast. So also the Canterbury Pilgrims usually base their convictions on authority (ancient writings, sacred or profane) and philosophical debate. The Wife of Bath, however, begins her own discourse by citing "experience"; and during the seventeenth and eighteenth centuries, as a body of scientific knowledge accumulated in several fields, experience, taking the form of hypothesis, experiment, and observation of the physical world, became as influential as theology in forming the conceptions of the universe held by educated people. It was sometimes combined with theology, as in the writings of the great scientists Newton and Priestley; if so, the newly found natural laws were cited in illustration of the wisdom of nature's creator. In other thinkers the initial scepticism which is a part of the scientific method undermined traditional beliefs in God, redemption, or immortality. But in either case intense attention was devoted to the workings and the details of the natural universe itself.

Both points of view emerge among the romantic poets. Wordsworth found in the skylark the soul of a "pilgrim," and took the bird for an emblem of traditional moral wisdom; in "Tintern Abbey" he predicts that nature will feed his sister with "lofty thoughts." Shelley, who early in his career devoted a pamphlet to "The Necessity for Atheism," finds a source of intense joy in man's increasing knowledge of and power over the universe:

> The lightening is his slave; heaven's utmost deep
> Gives up her stars, and like a flock of sheep
> They pass before his eye, are numbered, and roll on!
> The tempest is his steed, he strides the air;
> And the abyss shouts from her depth laid bare,
> "Heaven, hast thou secrets? Man unveils me; I have none."

The more cynical Byron attributed cosmic speculations, when his callow here Don Juan indulged in them, to the force of puberty and awakening desire. Later, in the Victorian age, with its new theories about the natural origin of man and of life itself, joy in the advantages of natural knowledge for man decreased, although nature remained a major element in poetry. The stars in Meredith's sonnet may be an "army of unalterable law"; but to Tennyson the evidences of unalterable law in actual operation are the reverse of comforting: man who "trusted God was love indeed / And love Creation's final law" seems destined only to "Be blown about the desert dust / Or sealed within the iron hills."

4. The problem of immortality, which Tennyson considers in "In Memoriam" and resolves eventually by means of faith in a Being beyond and outside of nature, is also a central problem in Shelley's "Adonais." The forty-seventh stanza of this elegy, with its "Spirit's plastic stress" which "sweeps through the dull dense world" recalls strongly Wordsworth's "something far more deeply interfused" in "Tintern Abbey." But nine stanzas later Shelley is speaking of how

> Life, like a dome of many-colored glass
> Stains the white radiance of Eternity,

and we are carried above, beyond, or behind the natural universe of sense-experience. A like extinction of the universe is implied in

"Tintern Abbey" ("we are laid asleep / In body, and become a living soul") and asserted very explicitly in the passage of Wordsworth's *Prelude* devoted to the crossing of the Alps. To such apparently mystic experiences, as well as to the doctrine that nature itself is essentially a key to some eternal, nonnatural essence, the name of transcendentalism is sometimes given. According to this doctrine, as Coleridge put it in "Frost at Midnight," nature is an "eternal language" uttered by God.

Man

Transcendentalism, at least among the important poets, did not survive the Romantic movement; but while it flourished it contributed largely to the conception of the hieratic function of the poet, a conception with which much writing of this period is concerned. A preromantic example is Blake:

> Hear the voice of the Bard!
> Who Present Past & Future sees . . .

or

> Bring me my Bow of burning gold
> Bring me my arrows of desire . . .

In "Adonais" Shelley speaks of Keats as semi-divine:

> A godlike mind soars forth, in its delight
> Making earth bare and veiling heaven . . .

and in a later stanza suggests a parallel between himself and Christ. His appeals to the muse Urania in this poem remind us of Milton's invocations, and of the fact that the romantics were not the first poets to look upon prophecy or special insight as one feature of their art. It was a cardinal belief among them that they had reintroduced the shaping spirit of imagination into English poetry after the prosaic age of the eighteenth century (all except Byron united in attacking the poetic techniques of the Augustan masters). Wordsworth in particular felt strongly his own affinity with Milton in respect to prophecy and law-giving. The Snowdon section of his *Prelude*, a passage ringing with echoes of *Paradise Lost*, leads up to a description of "a majestic mind" (undoubtedly the poet's mind whose growth the *Prelude* as a whole delineates)—

> . . . a mind
> That feeds upon infinity, that broods
> Over the dark abyss, intent to hear
> Its voices issuing forth to silent light
> In one continuous stream; a mind sustained
> By recognitions of transcendent power . . .

The passage, too long to quote here in full, goes on to suggest that such godlike minds can send forth "mutations from themselves" and, in simple terms, create a better world. Such a world, in romantic ideology generally, could evidently be either an internal one, brought about by regeneration of individual personality, or an external one, brought about by reform of existing social institutions—or, of course, both.

Milton had lived during an English revolution, which he advocated and supported. A fact contributing to make the romantics feel they were his spiritual heirs was that they saw themselves, with some justification, as living in a period of world revolution: of Greeks against Turks, Italians against Austrians, Negroes against whites, Americans against British, and, of course, Frenchmen against Frenchmen. Wordsworth interested himself in the abolition of the slave trade, Coleridge once dreamed of founding a Utopian community in the New World, Blake saw existing European churches and governments as the engines of Satan, Shelley and Byron envisioned a new Hellas arising out of the ashes of the old Greece, and Byron himself, after aiding for some time the Italian underground, died in Greece trying to bring the new Hellas about.

Nor did their ardor exhaust itself on politics. Shelley at one time advocated vegetarianism; Shelley and Byron, each in his different way, attacked the institution of marriage as shackling the individual personality; Wordsworth hoped that his poetry would check what he saw as the disintegration of the British family.

Along with such endeavors went two widely held attitudes toward man: a belief in his perfectibility—or at least in the ultimate perfectibility of the individual—and a sense of disillusion arising out of the contrast between what man might be and what he is.

Wordsworth, for example, was in France during the early years of the revolution there; he had friends among one revolutionary party (the idealistic Girondists), and for a time greeted the movement with enthusiasm. But when France and England went to war, and when the extremists of the Terror replaced the moderates within France, Wordsworth was faced with a spiritual crisis from which his comparatively conservative later beliefs ultimately emerged.

Other romantics followed other patterns of development; but in romantic poetry generally it can be said that high hopes of human greatness and melancholy disappointment in human shortcomings are two recurrent themes. In many of the poems reprinted here—such as Wordsworth's "The world is too much with us," Coleridge's Dejection ode, Shelley's "Stanzas near Naples," more than one of Keats's odes, several digressions in Byron's "Don Juan"—the melancholy (which also lives on into Victorian poetry) is more predominant than the hopes. When explicitly accounted for at all it often arises out of unfulfilled longings for an ideal perfection, some internal sense of inadequacy in the poet himself, or a feeling of spiritual isolation which is probably a corollary of the strong romantic emphasis on individualism.

This latter emphasis accounts for the highly personal tone of some of the poems. Wordsworth once defined poetry itself as "the spontaneous overflow of powerful feelings"; we have seen how, in Collins's Ode, the central subject is the delineation by images of a complex mood in the poet himself. The personal lyric is one important vehicle for the treatment of man in nineteenth-century poetry. A second is the short vignette which suggests the emotional core of some situation without recounting its peripheral detail (Shelley's "Away, the moor is dark beneath the moon"; Browning's "Meeting at Night" and "Parting at Morning"). A third is the full-dress presentation of a situation in a poem of medium length—that is, a poem as short as Browning's "My Last Duchess" or as long as the first canto (originally published as a unit) of "Don Juan."

It is in these medium-length poems of human life that the nineteenth-century objectified most successfully, perhaps, its pervading sense of the dilemma within man's nature. "Michael," "The Eve of St. Agnes," "Andrea del Sarto"—each in its different way presents an ideal confronted by circumscribing limitations: the half-built sheepfold now a pile of stones, the sharp sleet against the windowpane breaking off the embraces of lovers who "fled away into the storm," the painter whose very faultlessness is itself a fault. Not all the poems in this general category are equally effective, of course. "The Eve of St. Agnes" dramatizes perfectly both elements in its contrast (the palsy-twitched beldame and icy coats-of-mail set against the lucent syrups tinct with cinnamon); but in "The Scholar-Gipsy" one might object that the strange disease of modern life remains a series of abstract assertions uncrystallized into imagery, by comparison with the sensuously rendered environment of the scholar's wanderings; or that the young lighthearted masters of the waves in the final metaphor seem an odd parallel to the sick fatigue and languid doubt from which the scholar has so fortunately fled. But in general the record of achievement in this kind of poetry is impressive.

What was peculiar to the nineteenth-century sensibility in such poetry can be inferred from a comparison of two poems more than a half-century apart: Burns's "Death and Dr. Hornbook" and Browning's "A Toccata of Galluppi's." These poems are alike in that each is ironic—i.e., the central figure in each is not all that he appears to be, and is thus set at a little distance from both the poet and the reader. Hornbook is a quack physician who, we are told, has had such immense success that he is able by his medical skill to outwit and frustrate Death itself. We are first made suspicious of him by the rowdy burlesque account of his methods (the catalogue of his pharmacopeia, his technique of long-distance diagnosis, etc.), and then by the melancholy and startling disclosure that although Hornbook can preserve the life of whomever he likes, he himself is a greater scourge upon the human race than Death ever was.

> Whare I kill'd ane, a fair strae-death,
> By loss o' blood or want of breath,
> This night I'm free to tak my aith
> That Hornbook's skill
> Has clad a score i' their last daith,
> By drap an' pill.

There follow, in three brilliant stanzas, particular illustrations of Hornbook's destructive powers, illustrations which also insinuate the venality of the physician's motives. There is even a suggestion that the narrator of the episode himself has been involved through moral laxity in the unhappy fate of one of the Doctor's victims. The poem then concludes with a brief prediction of Death's eventual victory over Hornbook.

Three figures are sketched in the poem—Death, the narrator, and Hornbook—each ironically. The narrator is a reeling toper who elaborately vouches for the veracity of his fantastic anecdote; Death, far from playing his usual role as the King of Terrors, is a frustrated spectre of wry pathos; and Hornbook, at first a comic benefactor, turns out to be an underhanded murderer.

Browning's "A Toccata of Galuppi's" presents only one character, the speaker. He is an Englishman, a geologist and mathematician who wrings secrets from nature's close reserve, a lover of music who has a mathematician's command over its technical terminology, and something of an antiquarian. The poem is an account of his mixed emotions as he listens to the music of Galuppi, an eighteenth-century Venetian composer, the light sparkle of whose rhythms is suggested by the three-syllable foot of the poem's meter. At first the Englishman speaks of Galuppi's "old music," which makes him muse on the sensuous attractiveness of young love in the elegant Italy of that day —a reverie which then passes to the thoughts of how brittle such an existence must have been. Galuppi's melodies now become "your cold music." The speaker assures himself that compared to those butter-flies of Venice he leads a higher, worthier life in his researches, that he at least has a soul to become immortal (if souls do). But the as-surance is somewhat hollow, and the music's final effect is "I feel chilly and grown old." Irony is present in the speaker's scientific pre-tensions (there are some secrets—that of death, for example—he has not yet wrung from nature's close reserve); and in his double feelings about Venice: Venice is trivial, yet he would almost like to leave Eng-land and go there; Venice was foolish, yet he calls her women dear.

The outstanding difference between the two poems lies in the atti-tudes they invite us to take toward the two central figures. Each is individualized, each is contemplated from the outside by poet and reader, but we are invited into the English music-lover's heart; about Hornbook's emotions we know and care nothing. Burns's poem, in spirit somewhat outside the romantic tradition, is a comic-satiric fling at overweening human ambitions; Browning's is a compound of longing and regret. The point Burns is making about science is that it ministers dangerously to human pride and corruptibility; Brown-ing's point is merely that it leaves untouched and unsatisfied certain regions of the soul. In so far as each poem succeeds, we agree with Burns as a diagnostician, and draw back from Hornbook; we admire Browning's sensitivity to the nuances of art and life, and feel almost caught up in his character's dilemma.

※

Myth

To recapture in verse their own emotions, to delineate imaginary human situations, and to establish a multiform concept of the natural world did not entirely satisfy the nineteenth-century poets. Looking back on the literature, and especially the poetry, of earlier ages, they felt that their own rational and materialist epoch lived too much in the prosaic light of common day, that there had passed away a glory from the earth. They wanted to hear voices and see visions; "Great God!" cried Wordsworth—

> Great God! I'd rather be
> A Pagan suckled in a creed outworn;
> So might I, standing on this pleasant lea,
> Have glimpses that would make me less forlorn;
> Have sight of Proteus rising from the sea;
> Or hear old Triton blow his wreathèd horn.

Coleridge said that if he could only recapture a glimpse of his Abyssinian maid, then

> . . . with music loud and long
> I would build that dome in air,
> That sunny dome! those caves of ice!
> And all who heard should see them there,
> And all should cry, Beware! Beware!
> His flashing eyes, his floating hair!
> Weave a circle round him thrice,
> And close your eyes with holy dread
> For he on honey-dew has fed,
> And drunk the milk of Paradise.

And Keats pledged himself to Psyche in a similar rapture:

> So let me be thy choir, and make a moan
> Upon the midnight hours;
> Thy voice, thy lute, thy pipe, thy incense sweet
> From swingèd censer teeming;
> Thy shrine, thy grove, thy oracle, thy heat
> Of pale-mouthed prophet dreaming.

From such dreams, from such impulses, arose a body of visionary poetry: legendary enchantresses, strange spells, and the gods or heroes of classical antiquity found enthusiastic chroniclers.

In this the romantics and Victorians had had their preromantic predecessors. Burns, when he dealt with the supernatural, generally affected the jocular air of one who takes for granted an audience whose disbelief is anything but suspended. But Blake devoted himself in complete seriousness to the complications of a private religion (with roots, however, in Biblical, Miltonic, and other sacred poetry), a citadel from which he could attack the skeptics of his age, denounce the abuses of society, or hymn the creation of the tiger with an energy worthy of Old Testament prophesy. And Christopher Smart, from the confines of an asylum to which he had been apparently relegated for praying in public, produced on the inspiration of the Old Testament itself one of the most remarkable long poems of the later eighteenth century, the "Song to David."

Besides predecessors in this kind of poetry, the romantics also had followers. Tennyson turned to Greek and Arthurian myth for poetic subject matter, and Arnold to the more believing seventeenth century for the symbolic figure of his Scholar-Gipsy. To see why all this was so, we must revert for a moment to the subject of nature.

In the seventeenth century, two views of nature struggled for ascendancy in the minds of educated people. According to more traditional ideas, the world around us was pervaded with the supernatural, which might at any moment manifest itself, even in apparitions that involved the suspension of natural (physical) laws—such things as the ghost in *Hamlet,* the witches in *Macbeth,* the omens in *The Scarlet Letter.* According to the ideas of a growing body of natural scientists, however, nature invariably operated according to strict laws, intelligible, rational, observable; and phenomena which had been interpreted (in life or literature) as incursions of the supernatural were really the subjective phantasms of delusion and hallucination. There grew up then, and increased during the eighteenth century, a body of opinion hostile to the human imagination and inclined to exalt in its stead the mind's powers of logic. An illustration is the passage in *Tom Jones* (1749) in which Fielding explains that the modern novelist (i.e., creative writer) cannot introduce the supernatural into his narrative and expect to have his audience take him seriously. If a ghost appears, the novelist must make it show itself only to an ignorant, superstitious lout, and afterwards turn out to have been merely a white-faced calf the lout stumbled against in a dark alley.*

Now the romantics, as we have seen, set out to rehabilitate the imagination as a faculty of the human soul; to reawaken an attitude of wonder, awe, and reverence toward the universe; and to take advantage in literature of emotions which they felt had been starved by eighteenth-century rationalists who looked on the solar system as a gigantic clock, set in motion by its maker eons ago, and now ticking impersonally on. Thus nature in "Tintern Abbey" or "Adonais" is an embodiment of spirit (whether, metaphysically speaking, the spirit be pantheistic, platonic, or something else is of less importance); and poets turned with sympathetic delight to past ages when man perceived a nature alive with supernatural beings, when the god of ocean could say to the god of the sun:

> The loud deep calls me home even now to feed it
> With azure calm out of the emerald urns
> Which stand forever full beside my throne.
> Behold the Nereids under the green sea,
> Their wavering limbs borne on the wind-like stream
> Their white arms lifted o'er their streaming hair . . .

Or when, to quote from Smart's latter-day psalm,

> All scenes of painting crowd the map
> Of nature; to the mermaid's pap
> The scalèd infant clings.

---

* Similarly in Burns's "Address to the Deil," Satan turns out to have been a waterfowl making strange noises at night in the marshes.

The shift in sensibility from eighteenth to nineteenth century can be illustrated from two poems which contain within themselves indications of the spirit in which they are to be read. Compare the opening stanzas of "Death and Dr. Hornbook" with the figure of the wedding guest in "The Rime of the Ancient Mariner." Burns introduces us to a narrator whose sense-perceptions are amusingly befuddled by drink (whether the moon's horns were triple or quadruple "I cou'd na tell") and whose temper is superstitious anyway (he states that he was quite able to distinguish between stones and brushes on the one hand, and "ghaists an' witches" on the other). His hearers, then, will know what to think when he describes an encounter with Death. In "The Rime of the Ancient Mariner" Coleridge introduces an auditor for his mariner's narrative (a proceeding unusual in the older ballads he was imitating); and by means of the wedding guest's rapt, hynotized attitude, interruptions at crucial points, and final departure "a sadder and a wiser man," he builds a dramatic frame of unquestioning acceptance around his wandering hero's tale. Whatever a reader's final interpretations, allegoric or symbolic, of the poem may be, there is no question that the initial response demanded differs crucially from that sought by Burns.

In this respect "The Scholar-Gypsy," in which the poet affirms, denies, and then half reaffirms his protagonist's immortality, falls somewhere between the "Rime" and "Dr. Hornbook." The paragraph from Glanvil, however, which Arnold placed at the beginning of the poem, suggests what the nineteenth-century poets hoped to accomplish in literature through the use of such materials. The scholar-gipsy tells his academic friends

> that the people he went with were not such imposters as they were taken for, but that they had a traditional kind of learning among them, and could do wonders by the power of imagination, their fancy binding that of others . . .

Society

To summarize—the romantics and their followers liked to contemplate man viewed as an individual in relation to nature viewed as an embodiment of, or veil concealing, something beyond nature. Encounters between man and man in their poetry, like Wordsworth's meeting with the old soldier in the *Prelude,* are frequently steeped in an unearthly light, fraught with mysterious significance transcending everyday life. Because of such preoccupations their best poetry tends to be at once intense in feeling and limited in scope.

Its limitation can be seen if we recall how great an interest Chaucer, Shakespeare, and Pope took in man as a social animal, man living in a complex, man-created milieu. The largest social unit dealt with concretely and fully in the poems of this volume is the family, whose ties Byron mocked and Wordsworth hallowed; *Lear* and the Prologue to the *Canterbury Tales* embrace wider ranges of human relationships. Contrast the satiric thrust of "Don Juan" with that of the "Epistle to Augustus." Byron's laughter is at the expense of social institutions, which he portrays as too weak and artificial to dam the turbulence of human blood; Pope takes for granted the institution of monarchy (i.e., the unity of society) and directs his laughter against the inadequacy of the particular king who happens to be reigning. His grossness and stupidity made George, in Pope's eyes, unfit to be a king; her warm affections made Julia, in Byron's eyes, unfit to be a wife. In the first case, the institution is too big for the person; in the second, the person is too big for the institution. (It is noteworthy that in Byron's catalogue of the ingredients in human nature—"blood, bone, marrow, passion, feeling"—reason is not included). Pope's satire, then, points in the direction of a kind of order; Byron's in the direction of a kind of anarchy. (No doubt one outcome of the Byronic trend is the sense of isolation communicated by a poem like Arnold's "Yes, in the sea of life enisled.") Shelley and Blake saw social institutions as conspiracies to perpetuate tyranny.

The interest in social complexities we find reflected in "The Rape of the Lock" or "The Franklin's Tale" did not, of course, vanish among the nineteenth-century public. It was the novelists, however, rather than the poets, who undertook to purvey such material in imaginative form; and in this respect Scott or Thackeray is more truly in the tradition of Shakespeare than Keats or Tennyson. Of all nineteenth-century poets, Byron and Browning come nearest to success in this vein; the rest could not compete (though they occasionally tried) with the novelists.

❧

Metaphor and Image

Our discussion so far has aimed to isolate certain characteristic strains in the subject-matter of nineteenth-century poetry, and also, incidentally, to indicate some of the methods by which the subject-matter got embodied in the verse. One such method deserves special illustration.

If we compare two poems about death, Gray's "Elegy in a Country Churchyard," published in 1751, and Swinburne's "Garden of Proserpine," published in 1866, it becomes at once apparent that the relation between idea and image in the two poems is not at all similar. To leave metaphor aside for the moment, what is the scene of each poem, where is each speaker placed? In the "Elegy," the question is readily answered: Gray (or whoever is supposed to be saying the lines) stands at evening in a country churchyard, contemplates its elms and heaps of turf, listens to the pastoral sounds of droning beetle and tinkling flock, and voices the thoughts that his surroundings occasion. Swinburne's speaker, in the first stanza, watches the green field growing from some spot referred to as "Here" and never fully specified except by paradoxical details ("Here life has death for neighbor" . . . "fruitless fields of corn"). The spot is, of course, the Garden of Proserpine itself, the classical underworld on the far side of the grave; but since the main characteristic of the grave is said to be "sleep eternal / In an eternal night," it is evidently only by a poetic fiction, a metaphor or symbol, that the speaker can be imagined as speaking at all, or the garden as existing. In other words, the concrete details in Gray are partly metaphor and partly literal description; in Swinburne they are entirely nonliteral.

The next point to be noticed is the structure of the metaphors. When Gray uses figurative language—"Full many a flower is born to blush unseen / And waste its sweetness on the desert air"—the concrete details are meant to correspond, in a general but perfectly definite way, to a thought—in this case, the ideas about the obscurity of village life expressed in the stanzas preceding and following the lines quoted. Critics may (and in this case do) differ as to the precise shade of meaning the image is meant to convey; but as to its relation to the general point Gray is making there can be no question.

When we come to Swinburne's images, the same thing is only partly true. In the general context of the poem it is clear that the poppies (the "calm leaves" with which the goddess is crowned) stand for forgetfulness; and that the sea to which even the weariest river finally winds stands for oblivion. But about the morn that comes out of darkness—or even about the "red strays of ruined springs"—we cannot be sure. If "dead men rise up never," morn (however much "by cloud and mist abated") seems an incongruous occurrence in the Garden; the "strays" may be human beings who have died in youth (if we put the emphasis on "springs") or in old age (if we suppose the strays to be leaves turned red by autumn).

There is no point in pushing such analysis further; a poem is not a proposition in logic. There are degrees of distance from logic, however; and Swinburne is certainly at a further remove than Gray. What has happened here—and it was happening throughout the nineteenth century—is that the image as Swinburne created it seems to have broken loose from its moorings and taken on a life of its own, gathering to itself details whose poetic value can be accounted for only in terms of suggestiveness, of nuances, of atmosphere. There is, of course, a residuum of explicit rational statement in "The Garden of Proserpine"; an image more completely unmoored results in such a poem as Yeats's "The Wild Swans at Coole" (see Volume VII).

In estimating the success of a poem like Swinburne's, then, one must assay the richness and complexity of the overtones set vibrating by the images, as well as by the sound and structure of the language (metrical devices, rhetorical arrangements, choice of words, and so forth). In these respects "Proserpine," though a competent and even an interesting achievement, cannot stand comparison with such poems as "The Lotus-eaters" or the "Ode to Autumn," both of which it resembles in certain details. The lanquid lengthening of the line in Tennyson's

> Here are cool mosses deep,
> And through the moss the ivies creep,
> And in the stream the long-leaved flowers weep,
> And from the craggy ledge the poppy hangs in sleep,

or the bee-like hum of Keats's

> Summer has o'erbrimm'd their clammy cells,

make Swinburne's best effects seem relatively plain or tame by comparison. The point is, however, that such comparisons are only possible at all because Swinburne, Tennyson, and Keats are all working within the same poetic convention.

Verse-forms

Renaissance and Augustan English poets worked within a critical tradition which stressed the importance of certain molds into which the lava of poetic inspiration might be poured: the epic, the mock-epic, tragedy, the verse-epistle, the ode, the verse-satire, the pastoral idyll, the lyric, the elegy, and others. Many of these, like the ode and the epic, derived ultimately from the literature of ancient Greece and Rome; others, such as the sonnet and the masque, were of more recent

Continental origin. The forms carried with them certain implications as to content (an elegy, for example, normally had a funeral procession in it), or as to arrangement of parts (an epic generally opened *in medias res*—that is, in the middle of the plot—with a flash-back later), or as to style (the verse-satire called for a more colloquial vocabulary than the pastoral idyll). Poets varied, of course, in the uses they made of the tradition; Milton's epic is much closer to the form of ancient epic than Shakespeare's tragedies are to that of Greek tragedies; but that it was possible to produce highly successful original poetry in close relation to traditional models is shown by Pope's imitations of Horace.

Though the romantics felt themselves to be in revolt against tradition, literary or extra-literary, it would be incorrect to say that they simply jettisoned the older conventions wholesale. The sonnet, the ode, the ballad, the lyric, and the elegy are examples of forms which they modified but continued to practise. Instances of their using past literature in general to help shape both style (Wordsworth's echoes of Milton) and content (Shelley's use of Aeschylus in his "Prometheus Unbound") are not uncommon. They also, however, experimented freely, with the result that the nineteenth century produced a substantial body of poetry not easily classifiable by reference to literary tradition. "Don Juan" is a kind of picaresque novel in verse; the *Prelude* a meditative spiritual autobiography; "In Memoriam" a collection of elegiac lyrics.

In two particular respects, the romantics broke sharply with the immediate past. The best poetry of Pope and Dryden, whose practice tended to dominate the eighteenth century, is written in heroic couplets, a form almost wholly abandoned by the great romantics and Victorians. As we have seen in comparing Akenside and Collins, sharp contrasts and precise arrangements gave way in preromantic verse to the more fluid structures needed for conveying nuances of moods or emotions; and for such purposes the nineteenth-century poets preferred to vary their metrical and stanzaic forms as widely as possible. This practice also accorded with the strong romantic emphasis on individuality and originality. Tennyson, for example, had read no previous poetry in the "In Memoriam" stanza, which he believed that he had invented.

In their choice of vocabulary—particularly in the language they applied to external nature—the romantics also effected innovations. The ancient classical poets, and Homer in particular, had frequently applied recurrent conventional adjectives to aspects of nature: the "wine-dark" sea of the Odyssey is an example. Pope's translation of Homer, an influential eighteenth-century poem, reflects this tradition (which can be seen in the "cavern's *horrid* shade" of Akenside's Ode).

The romantic exaltation of nature into a central subject matter, metaphor, or symbol of much poetry, caused them to set a premium on precise observation and highly individual diction (Coleridge's evening sky "with its peculiar tint of yellow green," for example). The contrast must not be pushed to extremes; there is finely precise observation of nature in the "Essay on Man," and conventional poetic diction in the odes of Keats; but there was a genuine shift in emphasis and in technique. Romantic tendencies toward individuality, both in diction and in the observation that lies behind the diction, can be seen in extreme form in the poems of G. M. Hopkins (see Volume VII).

Romantic innovations in poetic devices, together with occasional romantic leftist sympathies in politics, brought the movement under strong hostile fire from many contemporary book reviewers. Shelley's belief (not strictly accurate) that an anonymous disparaging reviewer had caused or helped cause the actual death of Keats is reflected in the passionate denunciations that occur in "Adonais" (with which may be compared the briefer invective against corrupt clergy in Milton's "Lycidas"). For one reason or another, most of the major nineteenth-century poets had a hard struggle to win public recognition; and the modern popular stereotype of the artist as an iconoclastic, maladjusted, highly individualistic person, in revolt against his age and misunderstood by family, friends, and public alike dates from the romantic movement. It is not a conception that can be made to fit the known facts about the lives of all great poets—Virgil, Chaucer, and Shakespeare are among those who appear to be salient exceptions to it—but it applies with reasonable accuracy to Byron and Shelley.

◆◆◆

A Note on the Texts

Texts of the poems in this volume follow (except for occasional minor changes in spelling) either standard modern editions or editions which appeared during the lifetime of the author. In the case of a poem like the *Prelude*, for which more than one text is extant, the later has generally been given preference.

The Preromantics

The Preromantics

James Thomson

From *Winter*
THE FROZEN NORTH
(1726)

There, through the prison of unbounded wilds,
Barred by the hand of nature from escape,
Wide-roams the Russian exile. Nought around
Strikes his sad eye, but deserts lost in snow;
And heavy-loaded groves; and solid floods,   5
That stretch, athwart the solitary vast,
Their icy horrors to the frozen main;
And cheerless towns far-distant, never blessed,
Save when its annual course the caravan
Bends to the golden coast of rich Cathay,   10
With news of human-kind. Yet there life glows;
Yet cherished there, beneath the shining waste,
The furry nations harbour: tipt with jet,
Fair ermines, spotless as the snows they press;
Sables, of glossy black; and dark-embrowned,   15
Or beauteous freakt with many a mingled hue,
Thousands besides, the costly pride of courts.
There, warm together pressed, the trooping deer

THE FROZEN NORTH: 10. *Cathay:* China.

23

Sleep on the new-fallen snows; and, scarce his head
Raised o'er the heapy wreath, the branching elk   20
Lies slumbering sullen in the white abyss.
Nor dogs, nor toils, they want; nor with the dread
Of sounding bows the ruthless hunter drives
The fearful-flying race; with ponderous clubs,
As weak against the mountain-heaps they push   25
Their beating breast in vain, and piteous bray,
He lays them quivering on the ensanguined snows,
And with loud shouts rejoicing bears them home.
There through the piny forest half-absorpt,
Rough tenant of these shades, the shapeless bear,   30
With dangling ice all horrid, stalks forlorn;
Slow-paced, and sourer as the storms increase,
He makes his bed beneath the inclement drift,
And, with stern patience, scorning weak complaint,
Hardens his heart against assailing want.   35

    .   .   .   .

    Still pressing on, beyond Tornea's lake,
And Hecla flaming through a waste of snow,
And farthest Greenland, to the Pole itself,
Where failing gradual life at length goes out,
The Muse expands her solitary flight;   40
And, hovering o'er the wild stupendous scene,
Beholds new seas beneath another sky.
Throned in his palace of cerulean ice,
Here Winter holds his unrejoicing court;
And through his airy hall the loud misrule   45
Of driving tempest is for ever heard:
Here the grim tyrant meditates his wrath;
Here arms his winds with all-subduing frost;
Moulds his fierce hail, and treasures up his snows,
With which he now oppresses half the globe.   50
               —ll. 799-833; 887-901.

                      ∾

---

36. *Tornea:* river in NE Sweden. 37. *Hecla:* volcano in SW Iceland.

Mark Akenside

ODE ON THE WINTER SOLSTICE
(1740, 1745, 1772)

I

The radiant ruler of the year
At length his wintry goal attains;
Soon to reverse the long career,
And northward bend his steady reins.
Now, piercing half Potosi's height,   5
Prone rush the fiery floods of light,
Ripening the mountain's silver stores:
While, in some cavern's horrid shade,
The panting Indian hides his head,
And oft the approach of eve implores.   10

II

But lo, on this deserted coast
How pale the sun! how thick the air!
Mustering his storms, a sordid host,
Lo, Winter desolates the year.
The fields resign their latest bloom;   15
No more the breezes waft perfume,
No more the streams in music roll:
But snows fall dark, or rains resound;
And while great Nature mourns around,
Her griefs infect the human soul.   20

III

Hence the loud city's busy throngs
Urge the warm bowl and splendid fire:
Harmonious dances, festive songs,
Against the spiteful heaven conspire.
Meantime, perhaps, with tender fears,   25
Some village dame the curfew hears,
While round the hearth her children play:

ODE: 5. *Potosi:* Bolivian mountain, rich in silver. 7. *Ripening . . . stores.*
(it was believed sunlight generated minerals). 11. *this:* (England's).

At morn their father went abroad;
The moon is sunk, and deep the road;
She sighs, and wonders at his stay.   30

IV

But thou, my lyre, awake, arise,
And hail the sun's returning force:
Even now he climbs the northern skies,
And health and hope attend his course.
Then louder howl the aerial waste,   35
Be earth with keener cold embraced,
Yet gentle hours advance their wing;
And Fancy, mocking Winter's might,
With flowers and dews and streaming light
Already decks the new-born spring.   40

V

O fountain of the golden day,
Could mortal vows promote thy speed,
How soon before thy vernal ray
Should each unkindly damp recede!
How soon each hovering tempest fly,   45
Whose stores for mischief arm the sky,
Prompt on our heads to burst amain,
To rend the forest from the steep,
Or, thundering o'er the Baltic deep,
To whelm the merchant's hopes of gain!   50

VI

But let not man's unequal views
Presume o'er Nature and her laws:
'Tis his with grateful joy to use
The indulgence of the Sovereign Cause;
Secure that health and beauty springs   55
Through this majestic frame of things,
Beyond what he can reach to know;
And that Heaven's all-subduing will,
With good, the progeny of ill,
Attempereth every state below.   60

VII

How pleasing wears the wintry night,
Spent with the old illustrious dead!

While, by the taper's trembling light,
I seem those awful scenes to tread
Where chiefs or legislators lie,   65
Whose triumphs move before my eye
In arms and antique pomp arrayed;
While now I taste the Ionian song,
Now bend to Plato's godlike tongue
Resounding through the olive shade.   70

VIII

But should some cheerful, equal friend
Bid leave the studious page awhile,
Let mirth on wisdom then attend,
And social ease on learned toil.
Then while, at love's uncareful shrine,   75
Each dictates to the god of wine
Her name whom all his hopes obey,
What flattering dreams each bosom warm,
While absence, heightening every charm,
Invokes the slow-returning May!   80

IX

May, thou delight of heaven and earth,
When will thy genial star arise?
The auspicious morn, which gives thee birth,
Shall bring Eudora to my eyes.
Within her sylvan haunt behold,   85
As in the happy garden old,
She moves like that primeval fair:
Thither, ye silver-sounding lyres,
Ye tender smiles, ye chaste desires,
Fond hope and mutual faith, repair.   90

X

And if believing love can read
His better omens in her eye,
Then shall my fears, O charming maid,
And every pain of absence die:
Then shall my jocund harp, attun'd   95
To thy true ear, with sweeter sound
Pursue the free Horatian song;

---

68. *Ionian song:* Homer's epics.

Old Tyne shall listen to my tale,
And Echo, down the bordering vale,
The liquid melody prolong.   100

ॐ

William Collins

HOW SLEEP THE BRAVE
(1746)

How sleep the brave, who sink to rest
By all their country's wishes blest!
When Spring, with dewy fingers cold,
Returns to deck their hallowed mould,
She there shall dress a sweeter sod   5
Than Fancy's feet have ever trod.

By fairy hands their knell is rung;
By forms unseen their dirge is sung;
There Honour comes, a pilgrim grey,
To bless the turf that wraps their clay;   10
And Freedom shall awhile repair
To dwell, a weeping hermit, there!

ॐ

ODE TO EVENING
(1746)

If ought of oaten stop, or pastoral song,
May hope, chaste Eve, to sooth thy modest ear,
    Like thy own solemn springs,
    Thy springs and dying gales,
O nymph reserved, while now the bright-haired sun   5
Sits in yon western tent, whose cloudy skirts,
    With brede ethereal wove,
    O'erhang his wavy bed:
Now air is hushed, save where the weak-eyed bat,

---

98. *Tyne:* (Akenside was born in Newcastle upon Tyne).
    ODE TO EVENING: 1. *oaten stop:* (the shepherd's pipe).

With short shrill shriek, flits by on leathern wing,   10
  Or where the beetle winds,
  His small but sullen horn,
As oft he rises 'midst the twilight path,
Against the pilgrim borne in heedless hum:
  Now teach me, maid composed,   15
  To breathe some softened strain,
Whose numbers, stealing through thy darkening vale,
May not unseemly with its stillness suit,
  As, musing slow, I hail
  Thy genial loved return!   20
For when thy folding-star arising shews
His paly circlet, at his warning lamp
  The fragrant hours, and elves
  Who slept in flowers the day,
And many a nymph who wreaths her brows with sedge,   25
And sheds the freshening dew, and lovelier still,
  The pensive Pleasures sweet,
  Prepare thy shadowy car.
Then lead, calm votress, where some sheety lake
Cheers the lone heath, or some time-hallowed pile   3c
  Or upland fallows grey
  Reflect its last cool gleam.
But when chill blustering winds, or driving rain,
Forbid my willing feet, be mine the hut
  That from the mountain's side,   35
  Views wilds, and swelling floods,
And hamlets brown, and dim-discovered spires,
And hears their simple bell, and marks o'er all
  Thy dewy fingers draw
  The gradual dusky veil.   40
While Spring shall pour his showers, as oft he wont,
And bathe thy breathing tresses, meekest Eve!
  While Summer loves to sport
  Beneath thy lingering light;
While sallow Autumn fills thy lap with leaves;   45
Or Winter yelling through the troublous air,
  Affrights thy shrinking train,
  And rudely rends thy robes;
So long, sure-found beneath the sylvan shed,
Shall Fancy, Friendship, Science, rose-lipped Health, 50
  Thy greatest influence own,
  And hymn thy favorite name!

Thomas Gray

ELEGY WRITTEN IN A COUNTRY CHURCH YARD
(1751)

The Curfew tolls the knell of parting day,
    The lowing herd winds slowly o'er the lea,
The plowman homeward plods his weary way,
    And leaves the world to darkness and to me.

Now fades the glimmering landscape on the sight,   5
    And all the air a solemn stillness holds,
Save where the beetle wheels his droning flight,
    And drowsy tinklings lull the distant folds;

Save that from yonder ivy-mantled tower
    The moping owl does to the moon complain   10
Of such, as wandering near her secret bower,
    Molest her ancient solitary reign.

Beneath those rugged elms, that yew-tree's shade,
    Where heaves the turf in many a moldering heap,
Each in his narrow cell for ever laid,   15
    The rude forefathers of the hamlet sleep.

The breezy call of incense-breathing Morn,
    The swallow twittering from the straw-built shed,
The cock's shrill clarion, or the echoing horn,
    No more shall rouse them from their lowly bed.   20

For them no more the blazing hearth shall burn,
    Or busy housewife ply her evening care:
No children run to lisp their sire's return,
    Or climb his knees the envied kiss to share.

Oft did the harvest to their sickle yield,   25
    Their furrow oft the stubborn glebe has broke;
How jocund did they drive their team afield!
    How bowed the woods beneath their sturdy stroke!

Let not Ambition mock their useful toil,
    Their homely joys, and destiny obscure;   30

Nor Grandeur hear with a disdainful smile,
　　The short and simple annals of the poor.

The boast of heraldry, the pomp of power,
　　And all that beauty, all that wealth e'er gave,
Awaits alike the inevitable hour.　　　　　　　　　　　　　35
　　The paths of glory lead but to the grave.

Nor you, ye proud, impute to these the fault,
　　If Memory o'er their tomb no trophies raise,
Where through the long-drawn isle and fretted vault
　　The pealing anthem swells the note of praise.　　　　　40

Can storied urn or animated bust
　　Back to its mansion call the fleeting breath?
Can Honour's voice provoke the silent dust,
　　Or Flattery sooth the dull cold ear of Death?

Perhaps in this neglected spot is laid　　　　　　　　　45
　　Some heart once pregnant with celestial fire,
Hands, that the rod of empire might have swayed,
　　Or waked to extasy the living lyre.

But Knowledge to their eyes her ample page
　　Rich with the spoils of time did ne'er unroll;　　　　　50
Chill Penury repressed their noble rage,
　　And froze the genial current of the soul.

Full many a gem of purest ray serene,
　　The dark unfathomed caves of ocean bear:
Full many a flower is born to blush unseen,　　　　　　55
　　And waste its sweetness on the desert air.

Some village-Hampden, that with dauntless breast
　　The little Tyrant of his fields withstood;
Some mute inglorious Milton here may rest,
　　Some Cromwell guiltless of his country's blood.　　　　60

The applause of listening senates to command,
　　The threats of pain and ruin to despise,
To scatter plenty o'er a smiling land,
　　And read their History in a nation's eyes

ELEGY: 57. *Hampden:* John Hampden, who defied Charles I in the dis-
putes that led to the English Civil Wars.

Their lot forbad: nor circumscribed alone   65
    Their growing virtues, but their crimes confined;
Forbad to wade through slaughter to a throne,
    And shut the gates of mercy on mankind,

The struggling pangs of conscious truth to hide,
    To quench the blushes of ingenuous shame,   70
Or heap the shrine of Luxury and Pride
    With incense kindled at the Muse's flame.

Far from the madding crowd's ignoble strife,
    Their sober wishes never learned to stray;
Along the cool sequestered vale of life   75
    They kept the noiseless tenour of their way.

Yet even these bones from insult to protect
    Some frail memorial still erected nigh,
With uncouth rhymes and shapeless sculpture decked,
    Implores the passing tribute of a sigh.   80

Their names, their years, spelt by the unlettered Muse,
    The place of fame and elegy supply:
And many a holy text around she strews,
    That teach the rustic moralist to die.

For who to dumb forgetfulness a prey,   85
    This pleasing anxious being e'er resigned,
Left the warm precincts of the cheerful day,
    Nor cast one longing lingering look behind?

On some fond breast the parting soul relies,
    Some pious drops the closing eye requires;   90
Even from the tomb the voice of Nature cries,
    Even in our ashes live their wonted fires.

For thee, who mindful of the unhonoured dead
    Dost in these lines their artless tale relate;
If chance, by lonely contemplation led,
    Some kindred spirit shall inquire thy fate,   95

Haply some hoary-headed swain may say,
    "Oft have we seen him at the peep of dawn
Brushing with hasty steps the dews away
    To meet the sun upon the upland lawn.   100

"There, at the foot of yonder nodding beech
   That wreathes its old fantastic roots so high,
His listless length at noontide would he stretch,
   And pore upon the brook that babbles by.

"Hard by yon wood, now smiling as in scorn,   105
   Muttering his wayward fancies he would rove,
Now drooping, woeful wan, like one forlorn,
   Or crazed with care, or crossed in hopeless love.

"One morn I missed him on the customed hill,
   Along the heath and near his favorite tree;   110
Another came; nor yet beside the rill,
   Nor up the lawn, nor at the wood was he;

"The next with dirges due in sad array
   Slow through the church-way path we saw him born.
Approach and read (for thou canst read) the lay,   115
   Graved on the stone beneath yon aged thorn."

The Epitaph

Here rests his head upon the lap of Earth
   A youth to Fortune and to Fame unknown:
Fair Science frowned not on his humble birth,
   And Melancholy marked him for her own.   120

Large was his bounty, and his soul sincere,
   Heaven did a recompence as largely send:
He gave to Misery all he had, a tear,
   He gained from Heaven ('twas all he wished) a friend.

No farther seek his merits to disclose,   125
   Or draw his frailties from their dread abode,
(There they alike in trembling hope repose)
   The bosom of his Father and his God.

Oliver Goldsmith

SONG
From *The Vicar of Wakefield*
(1766)

When lovely woman stoops to folly,
    And finds too late that men betray,
What charm can soothe her melancholy,
    What art can wash her guilt away?

The only art her guilt to cover,   5
    To hide her shame from every eye,
To give repentance to her lover,
    And wring his bosom—is to die.

❧

Christopher Smart

From A SONG TO DAVID
(*written* 1763)

.   .   .   .

O David, highest in the list
Of worthies, on God's ways insist,   290
    The genuine word repeat:
Vain are the documents of men,
And vain the flourish of the pen
    That keeps the fool's conceit.

Praise above all—for praise prevails;   295
Heap up the measure, load the scales,
    And good to goodness add:
The generous soul her Saviour aids,
But peevish obloquy degrades;
    The Lord is great and glad.   300

For adoration all the ranks
Of angels yield eternal thanks,

And David in the midst;
With God's good poor, which, last and least
In man's esteem, thou to thy feast,   305
    O blessed bride-groom, bidst.

For adoration seasons change,
And order, truth, and beauty range,
    Adjust, attract, and fill:
The grass the polyanthus checks;   310
And polished porphyry reflects,
    By the descending rill.

Rich almonds colour to the prime
For adoration; tendrils climb,
    And fruit trees pledge their gems;   315
And Ivis with her gorgeous vest
Builds for her eggs her cunning nest,
    And bell-flowers bow their stems.

With vinous syrups cedars spout;
From rocks pure honey gushing out,   320
    For adoration springs:
All scenes of painting crowd the map
Of nature; to the mermaid's pap
    The scalèd infant clings.

The spotted ounce and playsome cubs   325
Run rustling 'mongst the flowering shrubs,
    And lizards feed the moss;
For adoration beasts embark,
While waves upholding halcyon's ark
    No longer roar and toss.   330

While Israel sits beneath his fig,
With coral root and amber sprig
    The weaned adventurer sports;
Where to the palm the jasmin cleaves,
For adoration 'mongst the leaves   335
    The gale his peace reports.

SONG TO DAVID: 316. *Ivis:* the hummingbird. 320. *rocks . . . out:*
(promised in 81st Psalm). 325. *ounce:* leopard. 329. *halcyon:* bird (king-
fisher) thought to nest on surface of ocean. 331. *Israel . . . fig:* each
citizen was promised his own fig-tree (Micah IV : 4). 333. *adventurer:*
adventuresome child.

Increasing days their reign exalt,
Nor in the pink and mottled vault
   The opposing spirits tilt;
And, by the coasting reader spied, 340
The silverlings and crusions glide
   For adoration gilt.

For adoration ripening canes
And cocoa's purest milk detains
   The western pilgrim's staff; 345
Where rain in clasping boughs inclosed,
And vines with oranges disposed,
   Embower the social laugh.

Now labour his reward receives,
For adoration counts his sheaves 350
   To peace, her bounteous prince;
The nectarine his strong tint imbibes,
And apples of ten thousand tribes,
   And quick peculiar quince.

The wealthy crops of whitening rice, 355
'Mongst thyine woods and groves of spice,
   For adoration grow;
And, marshalled in the fencèd land,
The peaches and pomegranates stand,
   Where wild carnations blow. 360

The laurels with the winter strive;
The crocus burnishes alive
   Upon the snow-clad earth:
For adoration myrtles stay
To keep the garden from dismay, 365
   And bless the sight from dearth.

The pheasant shows his pompous neck;
And ermine, jealous of a speck,
   With fear eludes offence:
The sable, with his glossy pride,
For adoration is descried, 370
   Where frosts the wave condense.

---

341. *silverlings:* tarpons. *crusions:* carp. 356. *thyine woods:* (mentioned in
Revelations XVIII : 12).

The cheerful holly, pensive yew,
And holy thorn, their trim renew;
  The squirrel hoards his nuts: 375
All creatures batten o'er their stores,
And careful nature all her doors
  For adoration shuts.

For adoration, David's psalms
Lift up the heart to deeds of alms; 380
  And he who kneels and chants,
Prevails his passions to control,
Finds meat and medicine to the soul,
  Which for translation pants . . .

             —288-384.

❧

Robert Burns

HOLY WILLIE'S PRAYER
(1799; *written* 1785?)

O Thou, wha in the Heavens dost dwell,
Wha, as it pleases best thysel',
Sends ane to heaven and ten to hell,
    A' for thy glory,
And no for ony guid or ill 5
    They've done afore thee!

I bless and praise thy matchless might,
Whan thousands thou hast left in night,
That I am here afore thy sight,
    For gifts an' grace 10
A burnin' an' a shinin' light,
    To a' this place.

What was I, or my generation,
That I should get sic exaltation?
I, wha deserve most just damnation, 15
    For broken laws,

---

384. *translation:* (to another world).
   HOLY WILLIE'S PRAYER: 3. *ane:* one. 4. *A':* all. 5. *guid:* good. 13. *generation:* origin.

Sax thousand years 'fore my creation,
        Thro' Adam's cause.

When frae my mither's womb I fell,
Thou might hae plungèd me in hell,   20
To gnash my gums, to weep and wail,
        In burnin' lakes,
Where damnèd devils roar and yell,
        Chain'd to their stakes;

Yet I am here a chosen sample,   25
To show thy grace is great and ample;
I'm here a pillar in thy temple,
        Strong as a rock,
A guide, a buckler, an example
        To a' thy flock.   30

O Lord, thou kens what zeal I bear,
When drinkers drink, and swearers swear,
And singin' there and dancin' here,
        Wi' great an' sma':
For I am keepit by thy fear   35
        Free frae them a'.

But yet, O Lord! confess I must
At times I'm fash'd wi' fleshy lust;
An' sometimes too, in warldly trust,
        Vile self gets in;   40
But thou remembers we are dust,
        Defil'd in sin.

O Lord! yestreen, thou kens, wi' Meg—
Thy pardon I sincerely beg;
O! may 't ne'er be a livin' plague   45
        To my dishonour,
An' I'll ne'er lift a lawless leg
        Again upon her.

Besides, I farther maun allow,
Wi' Leezie's lass, three times I trow—   50

---

17. *Sax:* six (allusion to the traditional date of Creation: 4004 B.C.). 29. *buckler:* shield worn on arm. 31. *kens:* know. 34. *sma':* small. 36. *frae:* from. 38. *fash'd:* bothered (by). 43. *yestreen:* last night. 49. *maun:* must. 50. *trow:* believe.

But Lord, that Friday I was fou,
  When I cam near her;
Or else, Thou kens, Thy servant true
  Wad never steer her.

Maybe Thou lets this fleshy thorn   55
Buffet Thy servant e'en and morn,
Lest he owre proud and high shou'd turn,
  That he's sae gifted:
If sae, Thy han' maun e'en be borne,
  Until Thou lift it.   60

Lord, bless Thy chosen in this place,
For here Thou has a chosen race:
But God confound their stubborn face,
  An' blast their name,
Wha bring Thy elders to disgrace   65
  An' public shame.

Lord, mind Gaw'n Hamilton's deserts;
He drinks, an' swears, an' plays at cartes,
Yet has sae mony takin arts,
  Wi' great and sma',   70
Frae God's ain priest the people's hearts
  He steals awa.

An' when we chasten'd him therefor,
Thou kens how he bred sic a splore,
An' set the warld in a roar   75
    O' laughing at us;—
Curse Thou his basket and his store,
  Kail an' potatoes.

Lord, hear my earnest cry and pray'r,
Against that Presbyt'ry o' Ayr;   80

51. *fou:* full (of liquor). 54. *steer:* molest. 56. *e'en:* evening. 57. *owre:* overly. 58. *gifted:* (with God's favor). 59. *e'en:* even. 65. *elders:* (in real life, Holy Willie [William Fisher] was an elder in the local Presbyterian church). 67. *Gaw'n Hamilton:* Gavin Hamilton, a friend of Burns'. 69. *takin:* bewitching. 72. *awa:* away. 73. *chasten'd:* (Fisher brought suit against Hamilton, for immorality, in ecclesiastical court). 74. *bred . . . splore:* stirred up so much amusement (at Willie's expense). 78. *kail:* greens. 80. *Presbyt'ry . . . Ayr:* the church body which tried the case (and acquitted Hamilton).

Thy strong right hand, Lord, make it bare
Upo' their heads;
Lord, visit them, an' dinna spare,
For their misdeeds.

O Lord my God, that glib-tongu'd Aiken,   85
My very heart and soul are quakin',
To think how we stood sweatin', shakin',
An' piss'd wi' dread,
While he, wi' hingin' lips and snakin',
Held up his head.   90

Lord, in the day of vengeance try him;
Lord, visit them wha did employ him,
And pass not in thy mercy by them,
Nor hear their pray'r:
But, for thy people's sake, destroy them,   95
And dinna spare.

But, Lord, remember me and mine
Wi' mercies temp'ral and divine,
That I for gear and grace may shine
Excell'd by nane,   100
And a' the glory shall be thine,
Amen, Amen!

≈

THE AULD FARMER'S NEW-YEAR-MORNING
SALUTATION TO HIS AULD MARE, MAGGIE
On Giving Her the Accustomed Ripp of Corn
to Hansel in the New-Year.

(1786)

A guid New-year I wish thee, Maggie!
Hae, there's a ripp to thy auld baggie:
Tho' thou's howe-backit now, an' knaggie,
I've seen the day

83. *dinna:* do not. 85. *Aiken:* Hamilton's lawyer. 89. *snakin:* sneering. 99.
gear: wealth. 100. *nane:* none.
THE AULD FARMER: *Ripp:* handful. *to Hansel:* as a special present (for).
1. *Guid:* good. 2. *baggie:* stomach. 3. *howe-backit:* hollow-backed.
knaggie: bony.

Thou could hae gaen like ony staggie,   5
  Out-owre the lay.

Tho' now thou's dowie, stiff an' crazy,
An' thy auld hide as white's a daisie,
I've seen thee dappl't, sleek an' glazie,
    A bonie gray;   10
He should been tight that daur't to raize thee,
    Ance in a day.

Thou ance was i' the foremost rank,
A filly buirdly, steeve an' swank;
An' set weel down a shapely shank,   15
    As e'er tread yird;
An' could hae flown out-owre a stank,
    Like ony bird.

It's now some nine-an'-twenty year,
Sin' thou was my guid-father's mear;   20
He gied me thee, o' tocher clear,
    An' fifty mark;
Tho' it was sma', 'twas weel-won gear,
    An' thou was stark.

When first I gaed to woo my Jenny,   25
Ye then was trotting wi' your minnie:
Tho' ye was trickie, slee, an funnie,
    Ye ne'er was donsie;
But hamely, tawie, quiet, an' cannie,
    An' unco sonsie.   30

That day, ye pranc'd wi' muckle pride,
When ye bure hame my bonie bride:
An' sweet an' gracefu' she did ride,
    Wi' maiden air!

---

5. *staggie:* colt. 6. *Out-owre:* over. *lay:* meadow. 7. *dowie:* spiritless.
crazy: worn out. 9. *dappl't:* dappled. *glaizie:* glossy. 11. *tight:* in good
shape. *daur't:* dared. *raize:* rouse. 12. *ance . . . day:* in former times. 14.
buirdly: stately. *steeve:* firm. *swank:* agile. 16. *yird:* earth. 17. *stank:*
ditch. 20. *guid-father's:* father-in-law's. *mear:* mare. 21. *gied:* gave. *o' . . .
clear:* besides the (regular) dowry. 22. *fifty mark:* about $13. 23. *gear:*
money. 24. *stark:* strong. 25. *gaed:* went. 26. *minnie:* dam (mother). 27.
slee: sly. 28. *donsie:* mischievous. 29. *tawie:* tractable. *cannie:* gentle. 30.
unco sonsie: in excellent shape. 31. *muckle:* much. 32. *bure:* bore.

Kyle-Stewart I could bragged wide   35
    For sic a pair.

Tho' now ye dow but hoyte and hobble,
An' wintle like a saumont coble,
That day, ye was a jinker noble,
    For heels an' win'!   40
An' ran them till they a' did wauble,
    Far, far, behin'!

When thou an' I were young an' skeigh
An' stable-meals at fairs were dreigh,
How thou wad prance, and snore, an' skreigh   45
    An' tak the road!
Town's-bodies ran, an' stood abeigh,
    An' ca't thee mad.

When thou was corn't, an' I was mellow,
We took the road aye like a swallow: 50
At brooses thou had ne'er a fellow,
    For pith an' speed;
But ev'ry tail thou pay't them hollow,
    Whare'er thou gaed.

The sma', droop-rumpl't, hunter cattle   55
Might aiblins waurt thee for a brattle;
But sax Scotch mile, thou try't their mettle,
    An' gar't them whaizle:
Nae whip nor spur, but just a wattle
    O' saugh or hazel.   60

Thou was a noble fittie-lan',
As e'er in tug or tow was drawn!
Aft thee an' I, in aught hours' gaun,

---

35. *Kyle-Stewart:* (name of county). 36. *sic:* such. 37. *dow:* can. *hoyte:* limp. 38. *wintle:* rock. *saumont coble:* salmon-fishing boat. 39. *jinker:* runner. 40. *heels:* (i.e., speed). 41. *wauble:* reel. 43. *skeigh:* proud. 44. *stable-meal:* last drink before bringing horse from stable, "night-cap." *dreigh:* long-continuing. 45. *skreigh:* whinny. 47. *abeigh:* out of the way. 48. *ca't:* called. 49. *corn't:* full of oats. 51. *brooses:* cross-country races. 53. *pay't:* beat. 54. *gaed:* went. 55. *droop-rumpl't:* drooping at the rump. *cattle:* (horses). 56. *aiblins:* perhaps. *waurt:* beat. *brattle:* dash. 58. *gar't:* made. *whaizle:* wheeze. 59. *wattle:* wand. 60. *saugh:* willow. 61. *fittie-lan':* plough-horse. 62. *tug:* trace. *tow:* rope. 63. *aught:* eight. *gaun:* going (plowing).

In guid March-weather,
Hae turn'd sax rood beside our han',   65
For days thegither.

Thou never braindg't, an' fetch't, an' fliskit,
But thy auld tail thou wad hae whiskit,
An' spread abreed thy weel-fill'd brisket,
Wi' pith an' pow'r,   70
Till spritty knowes wad rair't and riskit,
An' slypet owre.

When frosts lay lang, an' snaws were deep,
An' threaten'd labour back to keep,
I gied thy cog a wee bit heap   75
Aboon the timmer;
I kenn'd my Maggie wad na sleep
For that, or simmer.

In cart or car thou never reestit;
The steyest brae thou wad hae faced it;   80
Thou never lap, an' stenned, and breastit,
Then stood to blaw;
But, just thy step a wee thing hastit,
Thou snoov't awa.

My pleugh is now thy bairn-time a',   85
Four gallant brutes as e'er did draw;
Forbye sax mae I've sell't awa
That thou hast nurst:
They drew me thretteen pund an' twa,
The very warst.   90

Mony a sair darg we twa hae wrought,
An' wi' the weary warl' fought!

---

65. *turn'd . . . han':* ploughed six roods. 66. *thegither:* together. 67. *braindg't:* plunged. *fetch't:* shied. *fliskit:* fretted. 68. *whiskit:* whisked. 69. *abreed:* abroad. *brisket:* breast. 71-72. *spritty . . . owre:* knolls covered with rushes would roar and crackle (as they were torn up), and (the clods) fall smoothly over. 75. *cog:* feed-dish. 76. *Aboon:* above. *timmer:* wooden edge. 77. *kenn'd:* knew. *wad . . . sleep:* i.e., would work hard (in gratitude). 78. *or simmer:* before summer (i.e., next spring). 79. *reestit:* balked. 80. *steyest brae:* steepest hill. 81. *lap:* leaped. *stenned:* strained. *breastit:* plunged. 84. *snoov't awa:* went smoothly on. 85. *My . . . a':* all my (four) plough-horses are your progeny. 87. *Forbye:* not to mention. *sax mae:* six more. *sell't awa:* sold off. 89. *thretteen . . . twa:* £15. 90. *The . . . warst:* at the very least. 91. *sair darg:* hard day's work. 92. *warl':* world.

An' mony an anxious day I thought
          We wad be beat!
Yet here to crazy age we're brought,   95
          Wi' something yet.

And think na, my auld trusty servan',
That now perhaps thou 's less deservin',
An' thy auld days may end in starvin';
          For my last fou,   100
A heapit stimpart I'll reserve ane
          Laid by for you.

We've worn to crazy years thegither;
We'll toyte about wi' ane anither;
Wi' tentie care I'll flit thy tether   105
          To some hain'd rig,
Whare ye may nobly rax your leather,
          Wi' sma' fatigue.

TO A LOUSE

On Seeing One on a Lady's Bonnet at Church
(1786)

Ha! wh'are ye gaun, ye crowlin' ferlie!
Your impudence protects you sairly:
I canna say but ye strunt rarely,
          Owre gauze and lace;
Tho' faith! I fear ye dine but sparely   5
          On sic a place.

Ye ugly, creepin', blastit wonner,
Detested, shunn'd by saunt an' sinner!
How dare ye set your fit upon her,

---

97. *na:* not. 100. *fou:* bushel. 101. *stimpart:* third of a bushel. 104. *toyte:* totter. *ane anither:* one another. 105. *tentie:* watchful. *flit:* move. 106. *hain'd:* reserved. *rig:* ridge. 107. *rax . . . leather:* stretch your skin.

TO A LOUSE: 1. *wh':* where. *gaun:* going. *crowlin':* crawling. *ferlie:* wonder. 2. *sairly:* surprisingly well. 3. *canna:* cannot. *strunt:* strut. 4. *Owre:* over. 6. *sic:* such. 7. *blastit:* blasted. *wonner:* imp. 8. *saunt:* saint. 9. *fit:* foot.

Sae fine a lady?   10

Gae somewhere else, and seek your dinner
On some poor body.

Swith, in some beggar's haffet squattle;
There ye may creep, and sprawl, and sprattle
Wi' ither kindred jumping cattle,   15
    In shoals and nations;
Where horn nor bane ne'er dare unsettle
    Your thick plantations.

Now haud ye there, ye're out o' sight,
Below the fatt'rels, snug an' tight;   20
Na, faith ye yet! ye'll no be right
    Till ye've got on it,
The very tapmost tow'ring height
    O' Miss's bonnet.

My sooth! right bauld ye set your nose out,   25
As plump and gray as onie grozet;
O for some rank mercurial rozet,
    Or fell red smeddum!
I'd gie you sic a hearty doze o't,
    Wad dress your droddum!   30

I wad na been surpris'd to spy
You on an auld wife's flannen toy;
Or aiblins some bit duddie boy,
    On 's wyliecoat;
But Miss's fine Lunardi! fie,   35
    How daur ye do't?

O Jenny, dinna toss your head,
An' set your beauties a' abread!
Ye little ken what cursèd speed

---

10. *Sae:* so. 11. *Gae:* go. 13. *Swith:* scram! *haffet:* sideburns. *squattle:* nestle. 14. *sprattle:* scramble. 15. *Wi' ither:* with other. *cattle:* animal life. 17. *horn . . . bane:* horn or bone (combs). 18. *plantations:* colonies. 19. *haud . . . there:* stay where you are. 20. *fatt'rels:* ribbon-ends. 21. *faith . . . yet:* hang you! 25. *bauld:* bold. 26. *groset:* gooseberry. 27. *roset:* ointment. 28. *fell:* deadly. *smeddum:* ointment. 29. *gie:* give. 30. *droddum:* breech. 32. *flannen toy:* flannel cap. 33. *aiblins:* perhaps. *bit:* (of a). *duddie:* ragged. 34. *wyliecoat:* underjacket. 35. *Lunardi:* (hat named for first balloonist in Britain). 36. *daur:* dare. 39. *ken:* know.

The blastie's makin'! 40
Thae winks and finger-ends, I dread,
Are notice takin'!

O wad some Pow'r the giftie gie us
To see oursels as others see us!
It wad frae mony a blunder free us, 45
And foolish notion:
What airs in dress an' gait wad lea'e us,
And ev'n devotion!

~~

DEATH AND DR. HORNBOOK

(1781)

Some books are lies frae end to end,
And some great lies were never penn'd:
Ev'n ministers, they hae been kenn'd,
In holy rapture,
A rousing whid at times to vend, 5
And nail't wi' Scripture.

But this that I am gaun to tell,
Which lately on a night befell,
Is just as true 's the Deil 's in hell
Or Dublin city: 10
That e'er he nearer comes oursel
'S a muckle pity.

The clachan yill had made me canty,
I wasna fou, but just had plenty;
I stacher'd whyles, but yet took tent aye 15
To free the ditches;
An' hillocks, stanes, an' bushes kent aye
Frae ghaists an' witches.

---

40. *blastie:* little imp. 41. *Thae:* those. 43. *wad:* would. *giftie:* gift. *gie:*
give. 45. *frae:* from. 47. *lea'e:* leave.
   DEATH AND DR. HORNBOOK: 1. *frae:* from. 3. *kenn'd:* known. 5. *rousing:*
startling. *whid:* fib. 6. *nail't:* confirm it. 7. *gaun:* going. 9. *Deil:* devil. 11.
oursel: to us. 12. *muckle:* great. 13. *clachan:* village. *yill:* ale. *canty:*
happy. 14. *fou:* full. 15. *stacher'd:* staggered. *whyles:* at times. *tent:* care.
aye: always. 16. *free:* avoid. 17. *kent:* distinguished. 18. *Frae:* from.

The rising moon began to glowre
The distant Cumnock hills out-owre: 20
To count her horns, wi' a' my pow'r,
    I set mysel;
But whether she had three or four
    I cou'd na tell.

I was come round about the hill,   25
And todlin' down on Willie's mill,
Setting my staff, wi' a' my skill,
    To keep me sicker;
Tho' leeward whyles, against my will,
    I took a bicker.   30

I there wi' Something did forgather,
That pat me in an eerie swither;
An awfu' scythe, out-owre ae shouther,
    Clear-dangling, hang;
A three-tae'd leister on the ither   35
    Lay large an' lang.

Its stature seem'd lang Scotch ells twa,
The queerest shape that e'er I saw,
For fient a wame it had ava;
    And then its shanks,   40
They were as thin, as sharp an' sma'
    As cheeks o' branks.

'Guid-een,' quo' I; 'Friend! hae ye been mawin,
'When ither folk are busy sawin?'
It seem'd to mak a kind o' stan',   45
    But naething spak;
At length says I, 'Friend, wh'are ye gaun?
    'Will ye go back?'

---

19. *glowre:* glare. 20. *out-owre:* over the top of. 24. *na:* not. 26. *todlin':* tottering. 28. *sicker:* steady. 30. *took . . . bicker:* gave a lurch. 31. *forgather:* encounter. 32. *eerie:* dismal. *swither:* hesitation. 33. *ae shouther:* one shoulder. 35. *-tae'd:* -pronged. *leister:* salmon-spear. *ither:* other. 39. *fient:* the devil a (i.e., no). *wame:* belly. *ava:* at all. 42. *branks:* wooden bridles. 43. *Guid-een:* good evening. *mawin:* mowing (allusion to the scythe). 44. *sawin:* sowing ("This rencontre happened in seed-time, 1785." —Burns). 47. *gaun:* going.

It spak right howe—'My name is Death,
'But be na fley'd.'—Quoth I, 'Guid faith,   50
'Ye're maybe come to stap my breath;
            'But tent me, billie:
'I red ye weel, tak care o' skaith,
            'See, there's a gully!'

'Gudeman,' quo' he, 'put up your whittle,   55
'I'm no designed to try its mettle;
'But if I did, I wad be kittle
            'To be mislear'd;
'I wad na mind it, no that spittle
            'Out-owre my beard.'   60

'Weel, weel!' says I, 'a bargain be't;
'Come, gie's your hand, an' sae we're gree't;
'We'll ease our shanks an' tak a seat—
            'Come, gie's your news;
'This while ye hae been mony a gate,   65
            'At mony a house.'

'Ay, ay!' quo' he, and shook his head,
'It's e'en a lang, lang time indeed
'Sin' I began to nick the thread,
            'An' choke the breath: 70
'Folk maun dae something for their bread,
            'An' sae maun Death.

'Sax thousand years are near-hand fled
'Sin' I was to the butching bred,
'An' mony a scheme in vain's been laid,   75
            'To stap or scar me;
'Till ane Hornbook's ta'en up the trade,
            'And faith! he'll waur me.

'Ye ken Jock Hornbook i' the clachan;
'Deil mak his king's-hood in a spleuchan!   80

---

49. *howe:* hollowly. 50. *fley'd:* alarmed. 52. *tent:* listen to. *billie:* friend.
53. *red:* advise. *skaith:* harm. 54. *gully:* clasp-knife. 55. *whittle:* knife. 57.
kittle: dangerously apt. 58. *mislear'd:* mischievous. 59. *no:* no more than.
62. *sae:* so. *gree't:* agreed. 64. *gie:* give. 65. *mony a gate:* many a road.
("An epidemical fever was then raging in that country."—Burns.) 69. *nick:*
cut. 71. *maun:* must. 73. *Sax:* six (alludes to commonly accepted date of
Creation: 4004 B.C.). 74. *butching:* butcher's trade. 76. *stap:* stop. *scar:*
scare. 78. *waur:* beat. 80. *king's-hood:* scrotum (of ox). *in:* into. *spleuchan:*
tobacco-pouch.

'He's grown sae weel acquaint wi' Buchan
      'And ither chaps,
'The weans haud out their fingers laughin,
      'An' pouk my hips.

'See, here's a scythe, an' there's a dart,   85
'They hae pierc'd mony a gallant heart;
'But Doctor Hornbook wi' his art
      'An' cursed skill,
'Has made them baith no worth a f—t,
      'D—n'd haet they'll kill!   90

' 'Twas but yestreen, nae farther gane,
'I threw a noble throw at ane—
'Wi' less, I'm sure, I've hundreds slain—
      'But deil may care!
'It just play'd dirl on the bane,   95
      'But did nae mair.

'Hornbook was by wi' ready art,
'And had sae fortified the part
'That, when I looked to my dart,
      'It was sae blunt,   100
'Fient haet o't wad hae pierc'd the heart
      'O' a kail-runt.

'I drew my scythe in sic a fury
'I near-hand cowpit wi' my hurry,
'But yet the bauld Apothecary   105
      'Withstood the shock;
'I might as weel hae tried a quarry
      'O' hard whin rock.

'E'en them he canna get attended,
'Altho' their face he ne'er had kenn'd it,   110
'Just sh— in a kail-blade, and send it,
      'As soon 's he smells 't,
'Baith their disease, and what will mend it,
      . 'At once he tells 't.

---

81. *Buchan:* (author of household book on medicine). 83. *weans:* children. *haud:* hold. 84. *pouk:* poke. 90. *D—n'd haet:* not a damned bit. 91. *yestreen:* last night. *nae . . . gane:* no longer ago. 92. *ane:* one (man). 95. *play'd dirl:* gave a bump. 101. *Fient . . . o't:* not a damned bit of it. 102. *kail-runt:* cabbage-stalk. 104. *near-hand:* nearly. *cowpit:* fell over. 105. *bauld:* bold. 108. *whin rock:* whinstone. 110. *kenn'd:* known. 111. *kail-blade:* cabbage-leaf. 113. *Baith:* both.

'And then a' doctor's saws and whittles,   115
'Of a' dimensions, shapes, an' mettles,
'A' kinds o' boxes, mugs, an' bottles,
                    'He's sure to hae;
'Their Latin names as fast he rattles
                    'As A B C.   120

'Calces o' fossils, earths, and trees;
'True *sal-marinum* o' the seas;
'The farina of beans and pease,
                    'He has 't in plenty;
'*Aqua-fortis,* what you please,   125
                    'He can content ye.

'Forbye some new, uncommon weapons,
'*Urinus spiritus* of capons;
'Or mite-horn shavings, filings, scrapings,
                    'Distill'd *per se;*   130
'*Sal-alkal;* o' midge-tail clippings,
                    'And mony mae.'

'Waes me for Johnie Ged's-Hole now,'
Quoth I, 'if that thae news be true!
'His braw calf-ward whare gowans grew,   135
                    'Sae white and bonie,
'Nae doubt they'll rive it wi' the plew;
                    'They'll ruin Johnie!'

The creature grain'd an eldritch laugh,
And says 'Ye needna yoke the pleugh;   140
'Kirkyards will soon be till'd eneugh,
                    'Tak ye nae fear:
'They'll a' be trench'd wi' mony a sheugh,
                    'In twa-three year.

'Whare I kill'd ane, a fair strae-death,   145
'By loss o' blood or want of breath,

---

115. *whittles:* scalpels. 118. *hae:* have. 121. *Calces:* powder. *fossils:* rocks.
125. *aqua-fortis:* strong water (nitric acid). 127. *Forbye:* not to mention.
130. *per se:* by itself. 132. *mae:* more. 133. *Waes me:* woe is me. *Johnie
Ged's-Hole:* the grave-digger. *Ged's-hole:* stomach of the pike (a voracious
fish), i.e., the grave. 134. *thae:* this. 135. *braw:* fine. *calf-ward:* churchyard.
gowans: daisies. 137. *rive . . . plew:* plough it up. 139. *grain'd:* groaned.
eldritch: ghastly. 143. *sheugh:* trench. 145. *strae-death:* death in bed.

'This night I'm free to tak my aith,
   'That Hornbook's skill
'Has clad a score i' their last claith,
    'By drap an' pill.   150

'An honest wabster to his trade,
'Whase wife's twa nieves were scarce weel-bred,
'Gat tippence-worth to mend her head,
   'When it was sair;
'The wife slade cannie to her bed,   155
    'But ne'er spak mair.

'A country laird had ta'en the batts,
'Or some curmurring in his guts,
'His only son for Hornbook sets,
    'An' pays him well: 16t
'The lad, for twa guid gimmer-pets,
    'Was laird himsel'.

'A bonnie lass, ye kenn'd her name,
'Some ill-brewn drink had hov'd her wame;
'She trusts hersel, to hide the shame,   165
    'In Hornbook's care;
'Horn sent her aff to her lang hame,
    'To hide it there.

'That's just a swatch o' Hornbook's way;
'Thus goes he on from day to day,   170
'Thus does he poison, kill, an' slay,
    'And 's weel pay'd for 't;
'Yet stops me o' my lawfu' prey
    'Wi' his damn'd dirt.

'But, hark! I'll tell you of a plot,   175
'Tho' dinna ye be speaking o't;
'I'll nail the self-conceited sot
    'As dead 's a herrin':
'Niest time we meet, I'll wad a groat,
    'He gets his fairin'!'   180

---

147. *aith:* oath. 149. *claith:* cloth. 151. *wabster:* weaver. 152. *nieves:* fists (she was a virago). 153. *tippence-worth:* two cents' worth (of medicine). 154. *sair:* sore. 155. *slade canny:* slid quietly. *mair:* more. 157. *batts:* botts (a horse-disease). 158. *curmurring:* disturbance. 161. *gimmer-pets:* two-year-old ewes (fee, or bribe, given Hornbook). 164. *hov'd:* swelled. *wame:* belly. 167. *lang hame:* (in the next world). 169. *swatch:* sample. 179. *Niest:* next. *wad:* wager. *groat:* small coin. *fairin':* reward.

But, just as he began to tell,
The auld kirk-hammer strak the bell
Some wee short hour ayont the twal,
    Which rais'd us baith:
I took the way that pleas'd mysel,   185
    And sae did Death.

      ◦◦

GREEN GROW THE RASHES

(1787)

Green grow the rashes O,
 Green grow the rashes O;
The sweetest hours that e'er I spend,
 Are spent amang the lasses O!

There's nought but care on ev'ry han',   5
 In ev'ry hour that passes O;
What signifies the life o' man,
 An' 'twere na for the lasses O.

The warly race may riches chase,
 An' riches still may fly them O;   10
An' tho' at last they catch them fast,
 Their hearts can ne'er enjoy them O.

But gie me a canny hour at e'en,
 My arms about my dearie O;
An' warly cares, an' warly men,   15
 May a' gae tapsalteerie O!

For you sae douce, ye sneer at this,
 Ye're nought but senseless asses O:
The wisest man the warl' saw,
 He dearly lov'd the lasses O.   20

Auld nature swears, the lovely dears
 Her noblest work she classes O;

---

183. *ayont:* beyond. *twal:* twelve.
 GREEN GROW THE RASHES: 1. *rashes:* rushes. 9. *warly:* worldly. 13. *canny.*
quiet. 16. *tapsalteerie:* topsy-turvy. 17. *douce:* solemn.

Her prentice han' she tried on man,
An' then she made the lasses O.

William Blake

From *Poetical Sketches*
(1783)

TO SPRING

O thou with dewy locks, who lookest down
Through the clear windows of the morning, turn
Thine angel eyes upon our western isle,
Which in full choir hails thy approach, O Spring!

The hills tell each other, and the listening   5
Valleys hear; all our longing eyes are turned
Up to thy bright pavillions: issue forth,
And let thy holy feet visit our clime.

Come o'er the eastern hills, and let our winds
Kiss thy perfumèd garments; let us taste   10
Thy morn and evening breath; scatter thy pearls
Upon our love-sick land that mourns for thee.

O deck her forth with thy fair fingers; pour
Thy soft kisses on her bosom; and put
Thy golden crown upon her languished head,   15
Whose modest tresses were bound up for thee!

HOW SWEET I ROAMED

How sweet I roamed from field to field,
    And tasted all the summer's pride,
Till I the prince of love beheld,
    Who in the sunny beams did glide!

He shewed me lilies for my hair, 5
   And blushing roses for my brow;
He led me through his gardens fair,
   Where all his golden pleasures grow.

With sweet May dews my wings were wet,
   And Phœbus fired my vocal rage; 10
He caught me in his silken net,
   And shut me in his golden cage.

He loves to sit and hear me sing,
   Then, laughing, sports and plays with me;
Then stretches out my golden wing, 15
   And mocks my loss of liberty.

❧

From *Songs of Innocence*

(1789)

INTRODUCTION

Piping down the valleys wild,
Piping songs of pleasant glee,
On a cloud I saw a child,
And he laughing said to me:

"Pipe a song about a Lamb!" 5
So I piped with merry cheer.
"Piper, pipe that song again;"
So I piped: he wept to hear.

"Drop thy pipe, thy happy pipe;
"Sing thy songs of happy cheer:" 10
So I sung the same again,
While he wept with joy to hear.

"Piper, sit thee down and write
"In a book, that all may read."
So he vanished from my sight, 15
And I plucked a hollow reed,

HOW SWEET I ROAMED: 10. *Phoebus:* God of sun, and of prophecy.

And I made a rural pen,
And I stained the water clear,
And I wrote my happy songs
Every child may joy to hear.   20

❧

THE ECCHOING GREEN

The Sun does arise,
And make happy the skies;
The merry bells ring
To welcome the Spring;
The skylark and thrush,   5
The birds of the bush,
Sing louder around
To the bells' cheerful sound,
While our sports shall be seen
On the Ecchoing Green.   10

Old John, with white hair,
Does laugh away care,
Sitting under the oak,
Among the old folk.
They laugh at our play,   15
And soon they all say:
"Such, such were the joys
"When we all, girls and boys,
"In our youth time were seen
"On the Ecchoing Green."   20

Till the little ones, weary,
No more can be merry;
The sun does descend,
And our sports have an end.
Round the laps of their mothers   25
Many sisters and brothers,
Like birds in their nest,
Are ready for rest,
And sport no more seen
On the darkening Green.   30

THE LAMB

Little lamb, who made thee?
Dost thou know who made thee?
Gave thee life, and bid thee feed,
By the stream and o'er the mead;
Gave thee clothing of delight,   5
Softest clothing, woolly, bright;
Gave thee such a tender voice,
Making all the vales rejoice?
    Little lamb, who made thee?
    Dost thou know who made thee?   10

Little lamb, I'll tell thee,
Little lamb, I'll tell thee:
He is called by thy name,
For he calls himself a Lamb.
He is meek, and he is mild;   15
He became a little child.
I a child, and thou a lamb,
We are called by his name.
    Little lamb, God bless thee!
    Little lamb, God bless thee!   20

THE DIVINE IMAGE

To Mercy, Pity, Peace, and Love
All pray in their distress;
And to these virtues of delight
Return their thankfulness.

For Mercy, Pity, Peace, and Love   5
Is God, our father dear,
And Mercy, Pity, Peace, and Love
Is Man, his child and care.

For Mercy has a human heart,
Pity a human face,   10

And Love, the human form divine,
And Peace, the human dress.

Then every man, of every clime,
That prays in his distress,
Prays to the human form divine,   15
Love, Mercy, Pity, Peace.

And all must love the human form,
In heathen, Turk, or Jew;
Where Mercy, Love, and Pity dwell
There God is dwelling too.   20

From *Songs of Experience*

(1794)

INTRODUCTION

Hear the voice of the Bard!
Who present, past, and future, sees;
Whose ears have heard
The Holy Word
That walked among the ancient trees,   5

Calling the lapsèd soul,
And weeping in the evening dew;
That might control
The starry pole,
And fallen, fallen light renew!   10

"O Earth, O Earth, return!
Arise from out the dewy grass;
Night is worn,
And the morn
Rises from the slumberous mass.   15

"Turn away no more;
Why wilt thou turn away?
The starry floor,
The watery shore,
Is given thee till the break of day."   20

THE CLOD AND THE PEBBLE

"Love seeketh not itself to please,
　　Nor for itself hath any care,
But for another gives its ease,
　　And builds a heaven in hell's despair."

So sung a little clod of clay,   5
　　Trodden with the cattle's feet,
But a pebble of the brook
　　Warbled out these metres meet:

"Love seeketh only self to please,
　　To bind another to its delight,   10
Joys in another's loss of ease,
　　And builds a hell in heaven's despite."

THE SICK ROSE

O Rose, thou art sick:
The invisible worm
That flies in the night
In the howling storm,

Has found out thy bed   5
Of crimson joy,
And his dark secret love
Does thy life destroy.

THE TIGER

Tiger, Tiger, burning bright
In the forests of the night,

What immortal hand or eye
Could frame thy fearful symmetry?

In what distant deeps or skies   5
Burnt the fire of thine eyes?
On what wings dare he aspire?
What the hand dare seize the fire?

And what shoulder, and what art,
Could twist the sinews of thy heart?   10
And when thy heart began to beat,
What dread hand and what dread feet?

What the hammer? What the chain?
In what furnace was thy brain?
What the anvil? What dread grasp   15
Dare its deadly terrors clasp?

When the stars threw down their spears,
And watered heaven with their tears,
Did He smile His work to see?
Did He who made the lamb make thee?   20

Tiger, Tiger, burning bright
In the forests of the night,
What immortal hand or eye
Dare frame thy fearful symmetry?

AH, SUNFLOWER

Ah, Sunflower! weary of time,
Who countest the steps of the sun;
Seeking after that sweet golden clime
Where the traveller's journey is done:

Where the Youth pined away with desire,   5
And the pale Virgin shrouded in snow
Arise from their graves, and aspire
Where my Sunflower wishes to go.

LONDON

I wander through each chartered street,
Near where the chartered Thames does flow,
And mark in every face I meet
Marks of weakness, marks of woe.

In every cry of every Man,   5
In every Infant's cry of fear,
In every voice, in every ban,
The mind-forged manacles I hear.

How the Chimney-sweeper's cry
Every blackening Church appalls;   10
And the hapless Soldier's sigh
Runs in blood down Palace walls.

But most through midnight streets I hear
How the youthful Harlot's curse
Blasts the new born Infant's tear,   15
And blights with plagues the Marriage hearse.

THE HUMAN ABSTRACT

Pity would be no more
If we did not make somebody poor;
And mercy no more could be
If all were as happy as we.

And mutual fear brings peace,   5
Till the selfish loves increase:
Then cruelty knits a snare,
And spreads his baits with care.

He sits down with holy fears,
And waters the ground with tears;   10
Then humility takes its root
Underneath his foot.

Soon spreads the dismal shade
Of mystery over his head;

And the catterpillar and fly   15
Feed on the mystery.

And it bears the fruit of deceit,
Ruddy and sweet to eat;
And the raven his nest has made
In its thickest shade.   20

The Gods of the earth and sea
Sought through nature to find this tree;
But their search was all in vain:
There grows one in the human brain.

❦

From *The Gates of Paradise*
(1820)

TO THE ACCUSER WHO IS THE GOD
OF THIS WORLD

Truly my Satan thou art but a dunce
And dost not know the garment from the man
Every harlot was a virgin once
Nor canst thou ever change Kate into Nan.

Though thou art worshiped by the names divine   5
Of Jesus and Jehovah, thou art still
The son of morn in weary night's decline
The lost traveller's dream under the hill.

❦

From *Milton*
(ca. 1806)

AND DID THOSE FEET . . .

And did those feet in ancient time
Walk upon England's mountains green?
And was the holy Lamb of God
On England's pleasant pastures seen?

And did the Countenance Divine   5
Shine forth upon our clouded hills?
And was Jerusalem builded here
Among these dark Satanic Mills?

Bring me my Bow of burning gold:
Bring me my Arrows of desire: 10
Bring me my Spear: O clouds unfold!
Bring me my Chariot of fire.

I will not cease from Mental Fight,
Nor shall my Sword sleep in my hand
Till we have built Jerusalem   15
In England's green and pleasant Land.

MOCK ON, MOCK ON, VOLTAIRE, ROUSSEAU

(ca. 1800)

Mock on, mock on, Voltaire, Rousseau:
Mock on, mock on; 'tis all in vain!
You throw the sand against the wind,
And the wind blows it back again.

And every sand becomes a gem   5
Reflected in the beams divine;
Blown back they blind the mocking eye,
But still in Israel's paths they shine.

The atoms of Democritus
And Newton's particles of light   10
Are sands upon the Red Sea shore,
Where Israel's tents do shine so bright.

AUGURIES OF INNOCENCE

(1863; written 1801-3)

To see a world in a grain of sand,
And a heaven in a wild flower;

MOCK ON, MOCK ON: 9. *Democritus:* early Greek philosopher, credited
with elaborating an atomic theory of matter.

Hold infinity in the palm of your hand,
 And eternity in an hour.
A robin redbreast in a cage   5
Puts all heaven in a rage;
A dove-house filled with doves and pigeons
Shudders hell through all its regions.
A dog starved at his master's gate
Predicts the ruin of the state.   10
A game-cock clipped and armed for fight
Doth the rising sun affright;
A horse misused upon the road
Calls to heaven for human blood.
Every wolf's and lion's howl   15
Raises from hell a human soul;
Each outcry of the hunted hare
A fibre from the brain does tear;
A skylark wounded on the wing
Doth make a cherub cease to sing.   20
He who shall hurt the little wren
Shall never be beloved by men;
He who the ox to wrath has moved
Shall never be by woman loved;
He who shall train the horse to war   25
Shall never pass the polar bar.
The wanton boy that kills the fly
Shall feel the spider's enmity;
He who torments the chafer's sprite
Weaves a bower in endless night.   30
The caterpillar on the leaf
Repeats to thee thy mother's grief;
The wild deer wandering here and there
Keep the human soul from care;
The lamb misused breeds public strife,   35
And yet forgives the butcher's knife.
Kill not the moth nor butterfly,
For the last judgment draweth nigh;
The beggar's dog and widow's cat,
Feed them and thou shalt grow fat.   40
Every tear from every eye
Becomes a babe in eternity;
The bleat, the bark, bellow, and roar,
Are waves that beat on heaven's shore.

---

29. *chafer:* a beetle.

The bat, that flits at close of eve,   45
Has left the brain that won't believe;
The owl, that calls upon the night,
Speaks the unbeliever's fright;
The gnat, that sings his summer's song,
Poison gets from Slander's tongue;   50
The poison of the snake and newt
Is the sweat of Envy's foot;
The poison of the honey-bee
Is the artist's jealousy;
The strongest poison ever known   55
Came from Caesar's laurel crown.
Nought can deform the human race
Like to the armorer's iron brace;
The soldier armed with sword and gun
Palsied strikes the summer's sun.   60
When gold and gems adorn the plough,
To peaceful arts shall Envy bow.
The beggar's rags fluttering in air
Do to rags the heavens tear;
The prince's robes and beggar's rags   65
Are toadstools on the miser's bags.
One mite wrung from the laborer's hands
Shall buy and sell the miser's lands,
Or, if protected from on high,
Shall that whole nation sell and buy;   70
The poor man's farthing is worth more
Than all the gold on Afric's shore.
The whore and gambler, by the state
Licensed, build that nation's fate;
The harlot's cry from street to street   75
Shall weave Old England's winding sheet;
The winner's shout, the loser's curse,
Shall dance before dead England's hearse.
He who mocks the infant's faith
Shall be mocked in age and death;   80
He who shall teach the child to doubt
The rotting grave shall ne'er get out;
He who respects the infant's faith
Triumphs over hell and death.
The babe is more than swaddling-bands   85
Throughout all these human lands;
Tools were made, and born were hands,

Every farmer understands.
The questioner who sits so sly
Shall never know how to reply;   90
He who replies to words of doubt
Doth put the light of knowledge out;
A riddle, or the cricket's cry,
Is to doubt a fit reply
The child's toys and the old man's reasons   95
Are the fruits of the two seasons.
The emmet's inch and eagle's mile
Make lame philosophy to smile.
A truth that's told with bad intent
Beats all the lies you can invent.   100
He who doubts from what he sees
Will ne'er believe, do what you please;
If the sun and moon should doubt,
They'd immediately go out.
Every night and every morn   105
Some to misery are born;
Every morn and every night
Some are born to sweet delight;
Some are born to sweet delight,
Some are born to endless night.   110
Joy and woe are woven fine,
A clothing for the soul divine;
Under every grief and pine
Runs a joy with silken twine.
It is right it should be so;   115
Man was made for joy and woe;
And, when this we rightly know,
Safely through the world we go.
We are led to believe a lie
When we see *with* not *through* the eye,   120
Which was born in a night to perish in a night
When the soul slept in beams of light.
God appears, and God is light
To those poor souls who dwell in night,
But doth a human form display   125
To those who dwell in realms of day.

---

17. *emmet:* ant.

The Romantics

The Romantics

William Wordsworth

LINES

Composed a Few Miles Above Tintern Abbey, on Revisiting the Banks of the Wye During a Tour, July 13, 1798

Five years have past; five summers, with the length
Of five long winters! and again I hear
These waters, rolling from their mountain-springs
With a soft inland murmur.—Once again
Do I behold these steep and lofty cliffs,   5
That on a wild secluded scene impress
Thoughts of more deep seclusion; and connect
The landscape with the quiet of the sky.
The day is come when I again repose
Here, under this dark sycamore, and view   10
These plots of cottage-ground, these orchard-tufts,
Which at this season, with their unripe fruits,
Are clad in one green hue, and lose themselves
'Mid groves and copses. Once again I see
These hedge-rows, hardly hedge-rows, little lines   15
Of sportive wood run wild: these pastoral farms,
Green to the very door; and wreaths of smoke
Sent up, in silence, from among the trees!
With some uncertain notice, as might seem
Of vagrant dwellers in the houseless woods,   20
Or of some Hermit's cave, where by his fire
The Hermit sits alone.

                              These beauteous forms,
Through a long absence, have not been to me
As is a landscape to a blind man's eye:
But oft, in lonely rooms, and 'mid the din   25
Of towns and cities, I have owed to them,
In hours of weariness, sensations sweet,
Felt in the blood, and felt along the heart;
And passing even into my purer mind,
With tranquil restoration:—feelings too   30
Of unremembered pleasure: such, perhaps,
As have no slight or trivial influence
On that best portion of a good man's life,
His little, nameless, unremembered acts
Of kindness and of love. Nor less, I trust,   35
To them I may have owed another gift,
Of aspect more sublime; that blessed mood,
In which the burthen of the mystery,
In which the heavy and the weary weight
Of all this unintelligible world,   40
Is lightened:—that serene and blessed mood,
In which the affections gently lead us on,—
Until, the breath of this corporeal frame
And even the motion of our human blood
Almost suspended, we are laid asleep   45
In body, and become a living soul:
While with an eye made quiet by the power
Of harmony, and the deep power of joy,
We see into the life of things.

                                    If this
Be but a vain belief, yet, oh! how oft—   50
In darkness and amid the many shapes
Of joyless daylight; when the fretful stir
Unprofitable, and the fever of the world,
Have hung upon the beatings of my heart—
How oft, in spirit, have I turned to thee,   55
O sylvan Wye! thou wanderer thro' the woods,
How often has my spirit turned to thee!

    And now, with gleams of half-extinguished thought
With many recognitions dim and faint,
And somewhat of a sad perplexity,   60
The picture of the mind revives again:
While here I stand, not only with the sense

Of present pleasure, but with pleasing thoughts
That in this moment there is life and food
For future years. And so I dare to hope,   65
Though changed, no doubt, from what I was when first
I came among these hills; when like a roe
I bounded o'er the mountains, by the sides
Of the deep rivers, and the lonely streams,
Wherever nature led: more like a man   70
Flying from something that he dreads than one
Who sought the thing he loved. For nature then
(The coarser pleasures of my boyish days,
And their glad animal movements all gone by)
To me was all in all.—I cannot paint   75
What then I was. The sounding cataract
Haunted me like a passion: the tall rock,
The mountain, and the deep and gloomy wood,
Their colours and their forms, were then to me
An appetite; a feeling and a love,   80
That had no need for a remoter charm,
By thought supplied, nor any interest
Unborrowed from the eye.—That time is past,
And all its aching joys are now no more,
And all its dizzy raptures. Not for this   85
Faint I, nor mourn nor murmur; other gifts
Have followed; for such loss, I would believe,
Abundant recompense. For I have learned
To look on nature, not as in the hour
Of thoughtless youth; but hearing oftentimes   90
The still, sad music of humanity,
Nor harsh nor grating, though of ample power
To chasten and subdue. And I have felt
A presence that disturbs me with the joy
Of elevated thoughts; a sense sublime   95
Of something far more deeply interfused,
Whose dwelling is the light of setting suns,
And the round ocean and the living air,
And the blue sky, and in the mind of man:
A motion and a spirit, that impels   100
All thinking things, all objects of all thought,
And rolls through all things. Therefore am I still
A lover of the meadows and the woods,
And mountains; and of all that we behold
From this green earth; of all the mighty world   105

Of eye, and ear,—both what they half create,
And what perceive; well pleased to recognise
In nature and the language of the sense
The anchor of my purest thoughts, the nurse,
The guide, the guardian of my heart, and soul   110
Of all my moral being.

                    Nor perchance,
If I were not thus taught, should I the more
Suffer my genial spirits to decay:
For thou art with me here upon the banks
Of this fair river; thou my dearest Friend,   115
My dear, dear Friend; and in thy voice I catch
The language of my former heart, and read
My former pleasures in the shooting lights
Of thy wild eyes. Oh! yet a little while
May I behold in thee what I was once,   120
My dear, dear Sister! and this prayer I make,
Knowing that Nature never did betray
The heart that loved her; 'tis her privilege,
Through all the years of this our life, to lead
From joy to joy: for she can so inform   125
The mind that is within us, so impress
With quietness and beauty, and so feed
With lofty thoughts, that neither evil tongues,
Rash judgments, nor the sneers of selfish men,
Nor greetings where no kindness is, nor all   130
The dreary intercourse of daily life,
Shall e'er prevail against us, or disturb
Our cheerful faith, that all which we behold
Is full of blessings. Therefore let the moon
Shine on thee in thy solitary walk;   135
And let the misty mountain-winds be free
To blow against thee: and, in after years,
When these wild ecstasies shall be matured
Into a sober pleasure; when thy mind
Shall be a mansion for all lovely forms,   140
Thy memory be as a dwelling-place
For all sweet sounds and harmonies; oh! then,
If solitude, or fear, or pain, or grief
Should be thy portion, with what healing thoughts
Of tender joy wilt thou remember me,   145
And these my exhortations! Nor, perchance—

If I should be where I no more can hear
Thy voice, nor catch from thy wild eyes these gleams
Of past existence—wilt thou then forget
That on the banks of this delightful stream   150
We stood together; and that I, so long
A worshipper of Nature, hither came
Unwearied in that service: rather say
With warmer love—oh! with far deeper zeal
Of holier love. Nor wilt thou then forget   155
That after many wanderings, many years
Of absence, these steep woods and lofty cliffs,
And this green pastoral landscape, were to me
More dear, both for themselves and for thy sake!

THE LUCY POEMS

(1800-1807)

I

Strange fits of passion have I known:
And I will dare to tell,
But in the Lover's ear alone,
What once to me befell.

When she I loved looked every day   5
Fresh as a rose in June,
I to her cottage bent my way,
Beneath an evening-moon.

Upon the moon I fixed my eye,
All over the wide lea;   10
With quickening pace my horse drew nigh
Those paths so dear to me.

And now we reached the orchard-plot;
And, as we climbed the hill,
The sinking moon to Lucy's cot   15
Came near, and nearer still.

In one of those sweet dreams I slept,
Kind Nature's gentlest boon!
And all the while my eyes I kept
On the descending moon.   20

My horse moved on; hoof after hoof
He raised, and never stopped:
When down behind the cottage roof,
At once, the bright moon dropped.

What fond and wayward thoughts will slide   25
Into a Lover's head!
"O mercy!" to myself I cried,
"If Lucy should be dead!"

II

She dwelt among the untrodden ways
 Beside the springs of Dove,
A Maid whom there were none to praise
 And very few to love:

A violet by a mossy stone   5
 Half hidden from the eye!
—Fair as a star, when only one
 Is shining in the sky.

She lived unknown, and few could know
 When Lucy ceased to be;   10
But she is in her grave, and, oh,
 The difference to me!

III

Three years she grew in sun and shower,
Then Nature said, "A lovelier flower
On earth was never sown;
This Child I to myself will take;
She shall be mine, and I will make   5
A Lady of my own.

"Myself will to my darling be
Both law and impulse: and with me
The Girl, in rock and plain,
In earth and heaven, in glade and bower,   10
Shall feel an overseeing power
To kindle or restrain.

"She shall be sportive as the fawn
That wild with glee across the lawn
Or up the mountain springs;   15
And hers shall be the breathing balm,

And hers the silence and the calm
Of mute insensate things.

"The floating clouds their state shall lend
To her; for her the willow bend;   20
Nor shall she fail to see
Even in the motions of the Storm
Grace that shall mould the Maiden's form
By silent sympathy.

"The stars of midnight shall be dear   25
To her; and she shall lean her ear
In many a secret place
Where rivulets dance their wayward round,
And beauty born of murmuring sound
Shall pass into her face.   30

"And vital feelings of delight
Shall rear her form to stately height,
Her virgin bosom swell;
Such thoughts to Lucy I will give
While she and I together live   35
Here in this happy dell."

Thus Nature spake— The work was done—
How soon my Lucy's race was run!
She died, and left to me
This heath, this calm, and quiet scene;   40
The memory of what has been,
And never more will be.

IV

A slumber did my spirit seal;
  I had no human fears:
She seemed a thing that could not feel
  The touch of earthly years.

No motion has she now, no force;   5
  She neither hears nor sees;
Rolled round in earth's diurnal course,
  With rocks, and stones, and trees.

V

I travelled among unknown men,
  In lands beyond the sea;

Nor, England! did I know till then
What love I bore to thee.

'Tis past, that melancholy dream!   5
Nor will I quit thy shore
A second time; for still I seem
To love thee more and more.

Among thy mountains did I feel
The joy of my desire;   10
And she I cherished turned her wheel
Beside an English fire.

Thy mornings showed, thy nights concealed,
The bowers where Lucy played;
And thine too is the last green field   15
That Lucy's eyes surveyed.

MICHAEL

A Pastoral Poem

(1800)

If from the public way you turn your steps
Up the tumultuous brook of Green-head Ghyll,
You will suppose that with an upright path
Your feet must struggle; in such bold ascent
The pastoral mountains front you, face to face.   5
But, courage! for around that boisterous brook
The mountains have all opened out themselves,
And made a hidden valley of their own.
No habitation can be seen; but they
Who journey thither find themselves alone   10
With a few sheep, with rocks and stones, and kites
That overhead are sailing in the sky.
It is in truth an utter solitude;
Nor should I have made mention of this Dell
But for one object which you might pass by,   15
Might see and notice not. Beside the brook

MICHAEL: 2. *Ghyll:* steep valley.

Appears a straggling heap of unhewn stones!
And to that simple object appertains
A story—unenriched with strange events,
Yet not unfit, I deem, for the fireside,   20
Or for the summer shade. It was the first
Of those domestic tales that spake to me
Of Shepherds, dwellers in the valleys, men
Whom I already loved;—not verily
For their own sakes, but for the fields and hills   25
Where was their occupation and abode.
And hence this Tale, while I was yet a Boy
Careless of books, yet having felt the power
Of Nature, by the gentle agency
Of natural objects, led me on to feel   30
For passions that were not my own, and think
(At random and imperfectly indeed)
On man, the heart of man, and human life.
Therefore although it be a history
Homely and rude, I will relate the same   35
For the delight of a few natural hearts;
And, with yet fonder feeling, for the sake
Of youthful Poets, who among these hills
Will be my second self when I am gone.

  Upon the forest-side in Grasmere Vale   40
There dwelt a Shepherd, Michael was his name;
An old man, stout of heart, and strong of limb.
His bodily frame had been from youth to age
Of an unusual strength: his mind was keen,
Intense, and frugal, apt for all affairs,   45
And in his shepherd's calling he was prompt
And watchful more than ordinary men.
Hence had he learned the meaning of all winds,
Of blasts of every tone; and oftentimes,
When others heeded not, he heard the South   50
Make subterraneous music, like the noise
Of bagpipers on distant Highland hills.
The Shepherd, at such warning, of his flock
Bethought him, and he to himself would say,
"The winds are now devising work for me!"   55
And, truly, at all times, the storm, that drives
The traveller to a shelter, summoned him
Up to the mountains: he had been alone

Amid the heart of many thousand mists,
That came to him, and left him, on the heights.   60
So lived he till his eightieth year was past.
And grossly that man errs, who should suppose
That the green valleys, and the streams and rocks,
Were things indifferent to the Shepherd's thoughts.
Fields, where with cheerful spirits he had breathed   65
The common air; hills, which with vigorous step
He had so often climbed; which had impressed
So many incidents upon his mind
Of hardship, skill or courage, joy or fear;
Which, like a book, preserved the memory   70
Of the dumb animals, whom he had saved,
Had fed or sheltered, linking to such acts
The certainty of honourable gain;
Those fields, those hills—what could they less? had laid
Strong hold on his affections, were to him   75
A pleasurable feeling of blind love,
The pleasure which there is in life itself.

   His days had not been passed in singleness.
His Helpmate was a comely matron, old—
Though younger than himself full twenty years.   80
She was a woman of a stirring life,
Whose heart was in her house: two wheels she had
Of antique form, this large, for spinning wool;
That small, for flax; and, if one wheel had rest,
It was because the other was at work.   85
The Pair had but one inmate in their house,
An only Child, who had been born to them
When Michael, telling o'er his years, began
To deem that he was old,—in shepherd's phrase,
With one foot in the grave. This only Son,   90
With two brave sheep-dogs tried in many a storm,
The one of an inestimable worth,
Made all their household. I may truly say,
That they were as a proverb in the vale
For endless industry. When day was gone,   95
And from their occupations out of doors
The Son and Father were come home, even then,
Their labour did not cease; unless when all
Turned to the cleanly supper-board, and there,
Each with a mess of pottage and skimmed milk,   100

Sat round the basket piled with oaten cakes,
And their plain home-made cheese. Yet when the meal
Was ended, Luke (for so the Son was named)
And his old Father both betook themselves
To such convenient work as might employ   105
Their hands by the fire-side; perhaps to card
Wool for the Housewife's spindle, or repair
Some injury done to sickle, flail, or scythe,
Or other implement of house or field.

   Down from the ceiling, by the chimney's edge,   110
That in our ancient uncouth country style
With huge and black projection overbrowed
Large space beneath, as duly as the light
Of day grew dim the Housewife hung a lamp;
An aged utensil, which had performed   115
Service beyond all others of its kind.
Early at evening did it burn—and late,
Surviving comrade of uncounted hours,
Which, going by from year to year, had found,
And left, the couple neither gay perhaps   120
Nor cheerful, yet with objects and with hopes,
Living a life of eager industry.
And now, when Luke had reached his eighteenth year,
There by the light of this old lamp they sate,
Father and Son, while far into the night   125
The Housewife plied her own peculiar work,
Making the cottage through the silent hours
Murmur as with the sound of summer flies.
This light was famous in its neighbourhood,
And was a public symbol of the life   130
That thrifty Pair had lived. For, as it chanced,
Their cottage on a plot of rising ground
Stood single, with large prospect, north and south,
High into Easedale, up to Dunmail-Raise,
And westward to the village near the lake;   135
And from this constant light, so regular,
And so far seen, the House itself, by all
Who dwelt within the limits of the vale,
Both old and young, was named THE EVENING STAR.

   Thus living on through such a length of years,   140
The Shepherd, if he loved himself, must needs
Have loved his Helpmate; but to Michael's heart

This son of his old age was yet more dear—
Less from instinctive tenderness, the same
Fond spirit that blindly works in the blood of all—   145
Than that a child, more than all other gifts
That earth can offer to declining man,
Brings hope with it, and forward-looking thoughts,
And stirrings of inquietude, when they
By tendency of nature needs must fail.   150
Exceeding was the love he bare to him,
His heart and his heart's joy! For oftentimes
Old Michael, while he was a babe in arms,
Had done him female service, not alone
For pastime and delight, as is the use   155
Of fathers, but with patient mind enforced
To acts of tenderness; and he had rocked
His cradle, as with a woman's gentle hand.

   And in a later time, ere yet the Boy
Had put on boy's attire, did Michael love,   160
Albeit of a stern unbending mind,
To have the Young-one in his sight, when he
Wrought in the field, or on his shepherd's stool
Sate with a fettered sheep before him stretched
Under the large old oak, that near his door   165
Stood single, and, from matchless depth of shade,
Chosen for the Shearer's covert from the sun,
Thence in our rustic dialect was called
The CLIPPING TREE, a name which yet it bears.
There, while they two were sitting in the shade,   170
With others round them, earnest all and blithe,
Would Michael exercise his heart with looks
Of fond correction and reproof bestowed
Upon the Child, if he disturbed the sheep
By catching at their legs, or with his shouts   175
Scared them, while they lay still beneath the shears.

   And when by Heaven's good grace the boy grew up
A healthy Lad, and carried in his cheek
Two steady roses that were five years old;
Then Michael from a winter coppice cut   180
With his own hand a sapling, which he hooped
With iron, making it throughout in all
Due requisites a perfect shepherd's staff,
And gave it to the Boy; wherewith equipt

He as a watchman oftentimes was placed   185
At gate or gap, to stem or turn the flock;
And, to his office prematurely called,
There stood the urchin, as you will divine,
Something between a hindrance and a help;
And for this cause not always, I believe,   190
Receiving from his Father hire of praise;
Though nought was left undone which staff, or voice,
Or looks, or threatening gestures, could perform.

But soon as Luke, full ten years old, could stand
Against the mountain blasts; and to the heights,   195
Not fearing toil, nor length of weary ways,
He with his Father daily went, and they
Were as companions, why should I relate
That objects which the Shepherd loved before
Were dearer now? that from the Boy there came   200
Feelings and emanations—things which were
Light to the sun and music to the wind;
And that the old Man's heart seemed born again?

Thus in his Father's sight the Boy grew up:
And now, when he had reached his eighteenth year,   205
He was his comfort and his daily hope.

While in this sort the simple household lived
From day to day, to Michael's ear there came
Distressful tidings. Long before the time
Of which I speak, the Shepherd had been bound   210
In surety for his brother's son, a man
Of an industrious life, and ample means;
But unforeseen misfortunes suddenly
Had prest upon him; and old Michael now
Was summoned to discharge the forfeiture,   215
A grievous penalty, but little less
Than half his substance. This unlooked-for claim,
At the first hearing, for a moment took
More hope out of his life than he supposed
That any old man ever could have lost.   220
As soon as he had armed himself with strength
To look his trouble in the face, it seemed
The Shepherd's sole resource to sell at once
A portion of his patrimonial fields.
Such was his first resolve; he thought again,   225

And his heart failed him. "Isabel," said he,
Two evenings after he had heard the news,
"I have been toiling more than seventy years,
And in the open sunshine of God's love
Have we all lived; yet, if these fields of ours   230
Should pass into a stranger's hand, I think
That I could not lie quiet in my grave.
Our lot is a hard lot; the sun himself
Has scarcely been more diligent than I;
And I have lived to be a fool at last   235
To my own family. An evil man
That was, and made an evil choice, if he
Were false to us; and, if he were not false,
There are ten thousand to whom loss like this
Had been no sorrow. I forgive him;—but   240
'Twere better to be dumb than to talk thus.
    When I began, my purpose was to speak
Of remedies and of a cheerful hope.
Our Luke shall leave us, Isabel; the land
Shall not go from us, and it shall be free;   245
He shall possess it, free as is the wind
That passes over it. We have, thou know'st,
Another kinsman—he will be our friend
In this distress. He is a prosperous man,
Thriving in trade—and Luke to him shall go,   250
And with his kinsman's help and his own thrift
He quickly will repair this loss, and then
He may return to us. If here he stay,
What can be done? Where every one is poor,
What can be gained?"
                        At this the old Man paused,   255
And Isabel sat silent, for her mind
Was busy, looking back into past times.
There's Richard Bateman, thought she to herself,
He was a parish-boy—at the church-door
They made a gathering for him, shillings, pence,   260
And halfpennies, wherewith the neighbours bought
A basket, which they filled with pedlar's wares;
And, with this basket on his arm, the lad
Went up to London, found a master there,
Who, out of many, chose the trusty boy   265
To go and overlook his merchandise
Beyond the seas; where he grew wondrous rich,

And left estates and monies to the poor,
And, at his birth-place, built a chapel floored
With marble, which he sent from foreign lands.   270
These thoughts, and many others of like sort,
Passed quickly through the mind of Isabel,
And her face brightened. The old Man was glad,
And thus resumed:—"Well, Isabel! this scheme
These two days has been meat and drink to me.   275
Far more than we have lost is left us yet.
    We have enough—I wish indeed that I
Were younger;—but this hope is a good hope.
Make ready Luke's best garments, of the best
Buy for him more, and let us send him forth   280
To-morrow, or the next day, or to-night:
    If he *could* go, the Boy should go tonight."

    Here Michael ceased, and to the fields went forth
With a light heart. The Housewife for five days
Was restless morn and night, and all day long   285
Wrought on with her best fingers to prepare
Things needful for the journey of her son.
But Isabel was glad when Sunday came
To stop her in her work: for, when she lay
By Michael's side, she through the last two nights   290
Heard him, how he was troubled in his sleep:
And when they rose at morning she could see
That all his hopes were gone. That day at noon
She said to Luke, while they two by themselves
Were sitting at the door, "Thou must not go: 295
We have no other Child but thee to lose,
None to remember—do not go away,
For if thou leave thy Father he will die."
The Youth made answer with a jocund voice;
And Isabel, when she had told her fears,   300
Recovered heart. That evening her best fare
Did she bring forth, and all together sat
Like happy people round a Christmas fire.

    With daylight Isabel resumed her work;
And all the ensuing week the house appeared   305
As cheerful as a grove in Spring: at length
The expected letter from their kinsman came,
With kind assurances that he would do
His utmost for the welfare of the Boy;

To which, requests were added, that forthwith   310
He might be sent to him. Ten times or more
The letter was read over; Isabel
Went forth to show it to the neighbours round;
Nor was there at that time on English land
A prouder heart than Luke's. When Isabel   315
Had to her house returned, the old Man said,
"He shall depart to-morrow." To this word
The Housewife answered, talking much of things
Which, if at such short notice he should go,
Would surely be forgotten. But at length   320
She gave consent, and Michael was at ease.

    Near the tumultuous brook of Green-head Ghyll,
In that deep valley, Michael had designed
To build a Sheep-fold; and, before he heard
The tidings of his melancholy loss,   325
For this same purpose he had gathered up
A heap of stones, which by the streamlet's edge
Lay thrown together, ready for the work.
With Luke that evening thitherward he walked;
And soon as they had reached the place he stopped,   330
And thus the old Man spake to him:—"My son,
Tomorrow thou wilt leave me: with full heart
I look upon thee, for thou art the same
That wert a promise to me ere thy birth,
And all thy life hast been my daily joy.   335
I will relate to thee some little part
Of our two histories; 'twill do thee good
When thou art from me, even if I should touch
On things thou canst not know of.—After thou
First cam'st into the world—as oft befalls   340
To new-born infants—thou didst sleep away
Two days, and blessings from thy Father's tongue
Then fell upon thee. Day by day passed on,
And still I loved thee with increasing love.
Never to living ear came sweeter sounds   345
Than when I heard thee by our own fireside
First uttering, without words, a natural tune;
While thou, a feeding babe, didst in thy joy
Sing at thy Mother's breast. Month followed month,
And in the open fields my life was passed   350
And on the mountains; else I think that thou

Hadst been brought up upon thy Father's knees.
But we were playmates, Luke: among these hills,
As well thou knowest, in us the old and young
Have played together, nor with me didst thou   355
Lack any pleasure which a boy can know."
Luke had a manly heart; but at these words
He sobbed aloud. The old Man grasped his hand,
And said, "Nay, do not take it so—I see
That these are things of which I need not speak.   360
—Even to the utmost I have been to thee
A kind and a good Father: and herein
I but repay a gift which I myself
Received at others' hands; for, though now old
Beyond the common life of man, I still   365
Remember them who loved me in my youth.
Both of them sleep together: here they lived,
As all their Forefathers had done; and, when
At length their time was come, they were not loth
To give their bodies to the family mould.   370
I wished that thou shouldst live the life they lived,
But 'tis a long time to look back, my Son,
And see so little gain from threescore years.
These fields were burthened when they came to me;
Till I was forty years of age, not more   375
Than half of my inheritance was mine.
I toiled and toiled; God blessed me in my work,
And till these three weeks past the land was free.
—It looks as if it never could endure
Another Master. Heaven forgive me, Luke,   380
If I judge ill for thee, but it seems good
That thou shouldst go."
                        At this the old Man paused;
Then, pointing to the stones near which they stood,
Thus, after a short silence, he resumed:
"This was a work for us; and now, my Son,   385
It is a work for me. But, lay one stone—
Here, lay it for me, Luke, with thine own hands.
Nay, Boy, be of good hope;—we both may live
To see a better day. At eighty-four
I still am strong and hale;—do thou thy part;   390
I will do mine.—I will begin again
With many tasks that were resigned to thee:
Up to the heights, and in among the storms,

Will I without thee go again, and do
All works which I was wont to do alone,   395
Before I knew thy face.—Heaven bless thee, Boy!
Thy heart these two weeks has been beating fast
With many hopes; it should be so—yes—yes—
I knew that thou couldst never have a wish
To leave me, Luke: thou hast been bound to me   400
Only by links of love: when thou art gone,
What will be left to us!—But I forget
My purposes. Lay now the corner-stone,
As I requested; and hereafter, Luke,
When thou art gone away, should evil men   405
Be thy companions, think of me, my Son,
And of this moment; hither turn thy thoughts,
And God will strengthen thee: amid all fear
And all temptation, Luke, I pray that thou
May'st bear in mind the life thy Fathers lived,   410
Who, being innocent, did for that cause
Bestir them in good deeds. Now, fare thee well—
When thou return'st, thou in this place wilt see
A work which is not here: a covenant
'Twill be between us; but, whatever fate   415
Befall thee, I shall love thee to the last,
And bear thy memory with me to the grave."

    The Shepherd ended here; and Luke stooped down,
And, as his Father had requested, laid
The first stone of the Sheep-fold. At the sight   420
The old Man's grief broke from him; to his heart
He pressed his Son, he kissèd him and wept;
And to the house together they returned.
—Hushed was that House in peace, or seeming peace
Ere the night fell:—with morrow's dawn the Boy   425
Began his journey, and, when he had reached
The public way, he put on a bold face;
And all the neighbours, as he passed their doors,
Came forth with wishes and with farewell prayers,
That followed him till he was out of sight.   430

    A good report did from their Kinsman come,
Of Luke and his well-doing: and the Boy
Wrote loving letters, full of wondrous news,
Which, as the Housewife phrased it, were throughout
"The prettiest letters that were ever seen."   435

Both parents read them with rejoicing hearts.
So, many months passed on: and once again
The Shepherd went about his daily work
With confident and cheerful thoughts; and now
Sometimes when he could find a leisure hour   440
He to that valley took his way, and there
Wrought at the Sheep-fold. Meantime Luke began
To slacken in his duty; and, at length,
He in the dissolute city gave himself
To evil courses: ignominy and shame   445
Fell on him, so that he was driven at last
To seek a hiding-place beyond the seas.

There is a comfort in the strength of love;
'Twill make a thing endurable, which else
Would overset the brain, or break the heart: 450
I have conversed with more than one who well
Remember the old Man, and what he was
Years after he had heard this heavy news.
His bodily frame had been from youth to age
Of an unusual strength. Among the rocks   455
He went, and still looked up to sun and cloud,
And listened to the wind; and, as before,
Performed all kinds of labour for his sheep,
And for the land, his small inheritance.
And to that hollow dell from time to time   460
Did he repair, to build the Fold of which
His flock had need. 'Tis not forgotten yet
The pity which was then in every heart
For the old Man—and 'tis believed by all
That many and many a day he thither went,   465
And never lifted up a single stone.
There, by the Sheep-fold, sometimes was he seen
Sitting alone, or with his faithful Dog,
Then old, beside him, lying at his feet.
The length of full seven years, from time to time,   470
He at the building of this Sheep-fold wrought,
And left the work unfinished when he died.
Three years, or little more, did Isabel
Survive her Husband: at her death the estate
Was sold, and went into a stranger's hand.   475
The Cottage which was named the EVENING STAR
Is gone—the ploughshare has been through the ground

On which it stood; great changes have been wrought
In all the neighbourhood:—yet the oak is left
That grew beside their door; and the remains   480
Of the unfinished Sheep-fold may be seen
Beside the boisterous brook of Green-head Ghyll.

RESOLUTION AND INDEPENDENCE

(1807)

There was a roaring in the wind all night;
The rain came heavily and fell in floods;
But now the sun is rising calm and bright;
The birds are singing in the distant woods;
Over his own sweet voice the Stock-dove broods;   5
The Jay makes answer as the Magpie chatters;
And all the air is filled with pleasant noise of waters.

All things that love the sun are out of doors;
The sky rejoices in the morning's birth;
The grass is bright with rain-drops;—on the moors   10
The hare is running races in her mirth;
And with her feet she from the plashy earth
Raises a mist; that, glittering in the sun,
Runs with her all the way, wherever she doth run.

I was a Traveller then upon the moor;   15
I saw the hare that raced about with joy;
I heard the woods and distant waters roar;
Or heard them not, as happy as a boy:
The pleasant season did my heart employ:
My old remembrances went from me wholly;   20
And all the ways of men, so vain and melancholy.

But, as it sometimes chanceth, from the might
Of joy in minds that can no further go,
As high as we have mounted in delight
In our dejection do we sink as low;   25
To me that morning did it happen so;
And fears and fancies thick upon me came;
Dim sadness—and blind thoughts, I knew not, nor could name.

I heard the sky-lark warbling in the sky;
And I bethought me of the playful hare: 30
Even such a happy Child of earth am I;
Even as these blissful creatures do I fare;
Far from the world I walk, and from all care;
But there may come another day to me—
Solitude, pain of heart, distress, and poverty.   35

My whole life I have lived in pleasant thought,
As if life's business were a summer mood;
As if all needful things would come unsought
To genial faith, still rich in genial good;
But how can He expect that others should   40
Build for him, sow for him, and at his call
Love him, who for himself will take no heed at all?

I thought of Chatterton, the marvellous Boy,
The sleepless Soul that perished in his pride;
Of him who walked in glory and in joy   45
Following his plough, along the mountain-side:
By our own spirits are we deified:
We Poets in our youth begin in gladness;
But thereof come in the end despondency and madness.

Now, whether it were by peculiar grace,   50
A leading from above, a something given,
Yet it befell that, in this lonely place,
When I with these untoward thoughts had striven,
Beside a pool bare to the eye of heaven
I saw a Man before me unawares: 55
The oldest man he seemed that ever wore grey hairs.

As a huge stone is sometimes seen to lie
Couched on the bald top of an eminence;
Wonder to all who do the same espy,
By what means it could thither come, and whence;   60
So that it seems a thing endued with sense:
Like a sea-beast crawled forth, that on a shelf
Of rock or sand reposeth, there to sun itself;

Such seemed this Man, not all alive nor dead,
Nor all asleep—in his extreme old age: 65

RESOLUTION AND INDEPENDENCE: 43. *Chatterton:* d. 1770, eighteen years old,
after publishing poems alleged to be from medieval mss. 45. *him:* Burns.

His body was bent double, feet and head
Coming together in life's pilgrimage;
As if some dire constraint of pain, or rage
Of sickness felt by him in times long past,
A more than human weight upon his frame had cast.   70

Himself he propped, limbs, body, and pale face,
Upon a long grey staff of shaven wood:
And, still as I drew near with gentle pace,
Upon the margin of that moorish flood
Motionless as a cloud the old Man stood,   75
That heareth not the loud winds when they call;
And moveth all together, if it move at all.

At length, himself unsettling, he the pond
Stirred with his staff, and fixedly did look
Upon the muddy water, which he conned,   80
As if he had been reading in a book:
And now a stranger's privilege I took;
And, drawing to his side, to him did say,
"This morning gives us promise of a glorious day."

A gentle answer did the old Man make,   85
In courteous speech which forth he slowly drew:
And him with further words I thus bespake,
"What occupation do you there pursue?
This is a lonesome place for one like you."
Ere he replied, a flash of mild surprise   90
Broke from the sable orbs of his yet-vivid eyes.

His words came feebly, from a feeble chest,
But each in solemn order followed each,
With something of a lofty utterance drest—
Choice word and measured phrase, above the reach   95
Of ordinary men; a stately speech;
Such as grave Livers do in Scotland use,
Religious men, who give to God and man their dues.

He told, that to these waters he had come
To gather leeches, being old and poor: 100
Employment hazardous and wearisome!
And he had many hardships to endure:
From pond to pond he roamed, from moor to moor;
Housing, with God's good help, by choice or chance;
And in this way he gained an honest maintenance.   105

The old Man still stood talking by my side;
But now his voice to me was like a stream
Scarce heard; nor word from word could I divide;
And the whole body of the Man did seem
Like one whom I had met with in a dream;   110
Or like a man from some far region sent,
To give me human strength, by apt admonishment.

My former thoughts returned: the fear that kills;
And hope that is unwilling to be fed;
Cold, pain, and labour, and all fleshly ills;   115
And mighty Poets in their misery dead.
—Perplexed, and longing to be comforted,
My question eagerly did I renew,
"How is it that you live, and what is it you do?"

He with a smile did then his words repeat;   120
And said that, gathering leeches, far and wide
He travelled; stirring thus about his feet
The waters of the pools where they abide.
"Once I could meet with them on every side;
But they have dwindled long by slow decay;   125
Yet still I persevere, and find them where I may."

While he was talking thus, the lonely place,
The old Man's shape, and speech—all troubled me:
In my mind's eye I seemed to see him pace
About the weary moors continually,   130
Wandering about alone and silently.
While I these thoughts within myself pursued,
He, having made a pause, the same discourse renewed.

And soon with this he other matter blended,
Cheerfully uttered, with demeanour kind,   135
But stately in the main; and, when he ended,
I could have laughed myself to scorn to find
In that decrepit Man so firm a mind.
"God," said I, "be my help and stay secure;
I'll think of the Leech-gatherer on the lonely moor!"   140

THE SOLITARY REAPER
(1807)

Behold her, single in the field,
Yon solitary Highland Lass!
Reaping and singing by herself;
Stop here, or gently pass!
Alone she cuts and binds the grain,   5
And sings a melancholy strain;
O listen! for the Vale profound
Is overflowing with the sound.

No Nightingale did ever chaunt
More welcome notes to weary bands   10
Of travellers in some shady haunt,
Among Arabian sands:
A voice so thrilling ne'er was heard
In spring-time from the Cuckoo-bird,
Breaking the silence of the seas   15
Among the farthest Hebrides.

Will no one tell me what she sings?—
Perhaps the plaintive numbers flow
For old, unhappy, far-off things,
And battles long ago: 20
Or is it some more humble lay,
Familiar matter of to-day?
Some natural sorrow, loss, or pain,
That has been, and may be again?

Whate'er the theme, the Maiden sang   25
As if her song could have no ending;
I saw her singing at her work,
And o'er the sickle bending:—
I listened, motionless and still;
And, as I mounted up the hill,   30
The music in my heart I bore,
Long after it was heard no more.

"I WANDERED LONELY AS A CLOUD . . ."
(1807)

I WANDERED lonely as a cloud
That floats on high o'er vales and hills,
When all at once I saw a crowd,
A host, of golden daffodils;
Beside the lake, beneath the trees,   5
Fluttering and dancing in the breeze.

Continuous as the stars that shine
And twinkle on the milky way,
They stretched in never-ending line
Along the margin of a bay: 10
Ten thousand saw I at a glance,
Tossing their heads in sprightly dance.

The waves beside them danced; but they
Out-did the sparkling waves in glee:
A poet could not but be gay,   15
In such a jocund company:
I gazed—and gazed—but little thought
What wealth the show to me had brought:

For oft, when on my couch I lie
In vacant or in pensive mood,   20
They flash upon that inward eye
Which is the bliss of solitude;
And then my heart with pleasure fills,
And dances with the daffodils.

THE WORLD IS TOO MUCH WITH US
(1807)

The world is too much with us; late and soon,
Getting and spending, we lay waste our powers:
Little we see in Nature that is ours;
We have given our hearts away, a sordid boon!
This Sea that bares her bosom to the moon;   5
The winds that will be howling at all hours,
And are up-gathered now like sleeping flowers;
For this, for everything, we are out of tune;
It moves us not.—Great God! I'd rather be
A Pagan suckled in a creed outworn;   10
So might I, standing on this pleasant lea,
Have glimpses that would make me less forlorn;
Have sight of Proteus rising from the sea;
Or hear old Triton blow his wreathèd horn.

ODE TO DUTY
(1805)

Stern Daughter of the Voice of God!
O Duty! if that name thou love
Who art a light to guide, a rod
To check the erring, and reprove;
Thou, who art victory and law   5
When empty terrors overawe;
From vain temptations dost set free;
And calm'st the weary strife of frail humanity!

There are who ask not if thine eye
Be on them; who, in love and truth,   10
Where no misgiving is, rely
Upon the genial sense of youth:
Glad Hearts! without reproach or blot
Who do thy work, and know it not:
Oh! if through confidence misplaced   15
They fail, thy saving arms, dread Power! around them cast.

Serene will be our days and bright,
And happy will our nature be,
When love is an unerring light,
And joy its own security.   20
And they a blissful course may hold
Even now, who, not unwisely bold,
Live in the spirit of this creed;
Yet seek thy firm support, according to their need.

I, loving freedom, and untried;   25
No sport of every random gust,
Yet being to myself a guide,
Too blindly have reposed my trust:
And oft, when in my heart was heard
Thy timely mandate, I deferred   30
The task, in smoother walks to stray;
But thee I now would serve more strictly, if I may.

Through no disturbance of my soul,
Or strong compunction in me wrought,
I supplicate for thy control;   35
But in the quietness of thought:
Me this unchartered freedom tires;
I feel the weight of chance-desires:
My hopes no more must change their name,
I long for a repose that ever is the same.   40

Stern Lawgiver! yet thou dost wear
The Godhead's most benignant grace;
Nor know we anything so fair
As is the smile upon thy face:
Flowers laugh before thee on their beds   45
And fragrance in thy footing treads;
Thou dost preserve the stars from wrong;
And the most ancient heavens, through Thee, are fresh and
     strong.

To humbler functions, awful Power!
I call thee: I myself commend   50
Unto thy guidance from this hour;
Oh, let my weakness have an end!
Give unto me, made lowly wise,
The spirit of self-sacrifice;
The confidence of reason give;   55
And in the light of truth thy Bondman let me live!

ELEGIAC STANZAS

Suggested by a Picture of Peele Castle, in a Storm, Painted by Sir George Beaumont

(1805)

I was thy neighbour once, thou rugged Pile!
Four summer weeks I dwelt in sight of thee:
I saw thee every day; and all the while
Thy Form was sleeping on a glassy sea.

So pure the sky, so quiet was the air!   5
So like, so very like, was day to day!
Whene'er I looked, thy Image still was there;
It trembled, but it never passed away.

How perfect was the calm! it seemed no sleep;
No mood, which season takes away, or brings: 10
I could have fancied that the mighty Deep
Was even the gentlest of all gentle Things.

Ah! THEN, if mine had been the Painter's hand,
To express what then I saw; and add the gleam,
The light that never was, on sea or land,   15
The consecration, and the Poet's dream;

I would have planted thee, thou hoary Pile
Amid a world how different from this!
Beside a sea that could not cease to smile;
On tranquil land, beneath a sky of bliss.   20

Thou shouldst have seemed a treasure-house divine
Of peaceful years; a chronicle of heaven;—
Of all the sunbeams that did ever shine
The very sweetest had to thee been given.

A Picture had it been of lasting ease,   25
Elysian quiet, without toil or strife;
No motion but the moving tide, a breeze,
Or merely silent Nature's breathing life.

Such, in the fond illusion of my heart,
Such Picture would I at that time have made: 30
And seen the soul of truth in every part,
A steadfast peace that might not be betrayed.

So once it would have been,—'tis so no more;
I have submitted to a new control:
A power is gone, which nothing can restore;   35
A deep distress hath humanized my Soul.

Not for a moment could I now behold
A smiling sea, and be what I have been:
The feeling of my loss will ne'er be old;
This, which I know, I speak with mind serene.   40

Then, Beaumont, Friend! who would have been the Friend,
If he had lived, of Him whom I deplore,
This work of thine I blame not, but commend;
This sea in anger, and that dismal shore.

O 'tis a passionate Work!—yet wise and well,   45
Well chosen is the spirit that is here;
That Hulk which labours in the deadly swell,
This rueful sky, this pageantry of fear!

And this huge Castle, standing here sublime,
I love to see the look with which it braves,   50
Cased in the unfeeling armour of old time,
The lightning, the fierce wind, and trampling waves.

Farewell, farewell the heart that lives alone,
Housed in a dream, at distance from the Kind!
Such happiness, wherever it be known,   55
Is to be pitied; for 'tis surely blind.

But welcome fortitude, and patient cheer,
And frequent sights of what is to be borne!
Such sights, or worse, as are before me here.—
Not without hope we suffer and we mourn.   60

~∙∙

MY HEART LEAPS UP WHEN I BEHOLD
(1807)

My heart leaps up when I behold
A rainbow in the sky:
So was it when my life began;
So is it now I am a man;

So be it when I shall grow old,   5
      Or let me die!
The child is father of the man;
And I could wish my days to be
Bound each to each by natural piety.

❧

ODE

Intimations of Immortality from Recollections of Early Childhood

(1807)

I

There was a time when meadow, grove, and stream,
The earth, and every common sight,
      To me did seem
      Apparelled in celestial light,
The glory and the freshness of a dream.   5
It is not now as it hath been of yore;—
      Turn whereso'er I may,
      By night or day,
The things which I have seen I now can see no more.

II

      The Rainbow comes and goes,   10
      And lovely is the Rose,
      The Moon doth with delight
Look round her when the heavens are bare,
      Waters on a starry night
      Are beautiful and fair;   15
   The sunshine is a glorious birth;
   But yet I know, where'er I go,
That there hath past away a glory from the earth.

III

Now, while the birds thus sing a joyous song,
   And while the young lambs bound   20
      As to the tabor's sound,
To me alone there came a thought of grief:

A timely utterance gave that thought relief,
    And I again am strong:
The cataracts blow their trumpets from the steep;   25
No more shall grief of mine the season wrong;
I hear the Echoes through the mountains throng,
The Winds come to me from the fields of sleep,
    And all the earth is gay;
        Land and sea   30
   Give themselves up to jollity,
    And with the heart of May
   Doth every Beast keep holiday;—
    Thou Child of Joy,
Shout round me, let me hear thy shouts, thou happy Shepherd- 35
   boy!

IV

Ye blessèd Creatures, I have heard the call
   Ye to each other make; I see
The heavens laugh with you in your jubilee;
   My heart is at your festival,
    My head hath its coronal,   40
The fulness of your bliss, I feel—I feel it all.
      Oh evil day! if I were sullen
     While Earth herself is adorning,
      This sweet May-morning,
     And the Children are culling   45
      On every side,
    In a thousand valleys far and wide,
    Fresh flowers; while the sun shines warm,
And the Babe leaps up on his Mother's arm:—
    I hear, I hear, with joy I hear!   50
   —But there's a Tree, of many, one,
A single Field which I have looked upon,
Both of them speak of something that is gone:
    The Pansy at my feet
    Doth the same tale repeat: 55
Whither is fled the visionary gleam?
Where is it now, the glory and the dream?

V

Our birth is but a sleep and a forgetting:
The Soul that rises with us, our life's Star,
    Hath had elsewhere its setting,   60

And cometh from afar:
Not in entire forgetfulness,
And not in utter nakedness,
But trailing clouds of glory do we come
    From God, who is our home: 65
Heaven lies about us in our infancy!
Shades of the prison-house begin to close
    Upon the growing Boy,
But He beholds the light, and whence it flows,
    He sees it in his joy; 70
The Youth, who daily farther from the east
    Must travel, still is Nature's Priest,
    And by the vision splendid
    Is on his way attended;
At length the Man perceives it die away, 75
And fade into the light of common day.

VI

Earth fills her lap with pleasures of her own;
Yearnings she hath in her own natural kind,
And, even with something of a Mother's mind,
    And no unworthy aim, 80
    The homely Nurse doth all she can
To make her Foster-child, her Inmate Man,
    Forget the glories he hath known,
And that imperial palace whence he came.

VII

Behold the Child among his new-born blisses, 85
A six years' Darling of a pigmy size!
See, where 'mid work of his own hand he lies,
Fretted by sallies of his mother's kisses,
With light upon him from his father's eyes!
See, at his feet, some little plan or chart, 90
Some fragment from his dream of human life,
Shaped by himself with newly-learnèd art;
    A wedding or a festival,
    A mourning or a funeral;
    And this hath now his heart, 95
    And unto this he frames his song:
    Then will he fit his tongue
To dialogues of business, love, or strife;

But it will not be long
    Ere this be thrown aside,   100
    And with new joy and pride
The little Actor cons another part;
Filling from time to time his "humorous stage"
With all the Persons, down to palsied Age,
That Life brings with her in her equipage;   105
    As if his whole vocation
    Were endless imitation.

VIII

Thou, whose exterior semblance doth belie
    Thy Soul's immensity;
Thou best Philosopher, who yet dost keep   110
Thy heritage, thou Eye among the blind,
That, deaf and silent, read'st the eternal deep,
Haunted for ever by the eternal mind,—
    Mighty Prophet! Seer blest!
    On whom those truths do rest,   115
Which we are toiling all our lives to find,
In darkness lost, the darkness of the grave;
Thou, over whom thy Immortality
Broods like the Day, a Master o'er a Slave,
A Presence which is not to be put by;   120
Thou little Child, yet glorious in the might
Of heaven-born freedom on thy being's height,
Why with such earnest pains dost thou provoke
The years to bring the inevitable yoke,
Thus blindly with thy blessedness at strife?   125
Full soon thy Soul shall have her earthly freight,
And custom lie upon thee with a weight,
Heavy as frost, and deep almost as life!

IX

    O joy! that in our embers
    Is something that doth live,   130
    That nature yet remembers
    What was so fugitive!
The thought of our past years in me doth breed
Perpetual benediction: not indeed
For that which is most worthy to be blest;   135
Delight and liberty, the simple creed
Of Childhood, whether busy or at rest,

With new-fledged hope still fluttering in his breast:—
    Not for these I raise
    The song of thanks and praise;   140
  But for those obstinate questionings
  Of sense and outward things,
  Fallings from us, vanishings;
  Blank misgivings of a Creature
Moving about in worlds not realised,   145
High instincts before which our mortal Nature
Did tremble like a guilty Thing surprised:
    But for those first affections,
    Those shadowy recollections,
    Which, be they what they may,   150
Are yet the fountain-light of all our day,
Are yet a master-light of all our seeing;
  Uphold us, cherish, and have power to make
Our noisy years seem moments in the being
Of the eternal Silence: truths that wake,   155
    To perish never:
Which neither listlessness, nor mad endeavour,
    Nor Man nor Boy,
Nor all that is at enmity with joy,
Can utterly abolish or destroy!   160
  Hence in a season of calm weather
    Though inland far we be,
Our Souls have sight of that immortal sea
    Which brought us hither,
    Can in a moment travel thither,   165
And see the Children sport upon the shore,
And hear the mighty waters rolling evermore.

x

Then sing, ye Birds, sing, sing a joyous song!
    And let the young Lambs bound
    As to the tabor's sound!   170
We in thought will join your throng,
    Ye that pipe and ye that play,
    Ye that through your hearts today
    Feel the gladness of the May!
What though the radiance which was once so bright   175
Be now for ever taken from my sight,
    Though nothing can bring back the hour
Of splendour in the grass, of glory in the flower;

We will grieve not, rather find
Strength in what remains behind;   180
In the primal sympathy
Which having been must ever be;
In the soothing thoughts that spring
Out of human suffering;
In the faith that looks through death,   185
In years that bring the philosophic mind.

XI

And O, ye Fountains, Meadows, Hills, and Groves,
Forebode not any severing of our loves!
Yet in my heart of hearts I feel your might;
I only have relinquished one delight   190
To live beneath your more habitual sway.
I love the Brooks which down their channels fret,
Even more than when I tripped lightly as they;
The innocent brightness of a new-born Day
        Is lovely yet;   195
The Clouds that gather round the setting sun
Do take a sober colouring from an eye
That hath kept watch o'er man's mortality;
Another race hath been, and other palms are won.
Thanks to the human heart by which we live,   200
Thanks to its tenderness, its joys, and fears,
To me the meanest flower that blows can give
Thoughts that do often lie too deep for tears.

❧

LAODAMIA

(1814)

"With sacrifice before the rising morn
Vows have I made by fruitless hope inspired;
And from the infernal Gods, 'mid shades forlorn
Of night, my slaughtered Lord have I required:
Celestial pity I again implore;—   5
Restore him to my sight—great Jove, restore!"

_____

3. *infernal:* (of the underworld).

So speaking, and by fervent love endowed
With faith, the Suppliant heavenward lifts her hands;
While, like the sun emerging from a cloud,
Her countenance brightens—and her eye expands;   10
Her bosom heaves and spreads, her stature grows;
And she expects the issue in repose.

O terror! what hath she perceived?—O joy!
What doth she look on?—whom doth she behold?
Her Hero slain upon the beach of Troy?   15
His vital presence? his corporeal mould?
It is—if sense deceive her not—'tis He!
And a God leads him, wingèd Mercury!

Mild Hermes spake—and touched her with his wand
That calms all fear; "Such grace hath crowned thy prayer,   20
Laodamía! that at Jove's command
Thy Husband walks the paths of upper air:
He comes to tarry with thee three hours' space;
Accept the gift, behold him face to face!"

Forth sprang the impassioned Queen her Lord to clasp;   25
Again that consummation she essayed;
But unsubstantial Form eludes her grasp
As often as that eager grasp was made.
The Phantom parts—but parts to re-unite,
And re-assume his place before her sight.   30

"Protesiláus, lo! thy guide is gone!
Confirm, I pray, the vision with thy voice:
This is our palace,—yonder is thy throne;
Speak, and the floor thou tread'st on will rejoice.
Not to appal me have the gods bestowed   35
This precious boon; and blest a sad abode."

"Great Jove, Laodamia! doth not leave
His gifts imperfect:—Spectre though I be,
I am not sent to scare thee or deceive;
But in reward of thy fidelity.   40
And something also did my worth obtain;
For fearless virtue bringeth boundless gain.

---

19. *Hermes:* Mercury, messenger of the gods. 29. *parts:* (cf. "The Rape of
the Lock," III, 152; *Paradise Lost,* VI, 330-31). 31. *Protesiláus:* (Laodamia's
husband).

"Thou knowest, the Delphic oracle foretold
That the first Greek who touched the Trojan strand
Should die; but me the threat could not withhold: 45
A generous cause a victim did demand;
And forth I leapt upon the sandy plain;
A self-devoted chief—by Hector slain."

"Supreme of Heroes—bravest, noblest, best!
Thy matchless courage I bewail no more,   50
Which then, when tens of thousands were deprest
By doubt, propelled thee to the fatal shore;
Thou found'st—and I forgive thee—here thou art—
A nobler counsellor than my poor heart.

"But thou, though capable of sternest deed,   55
Wert kind as resolute, and good as brave;
And he, whose power restores thee, hath decreed
Thou should'st elude the malice of the grave:
Redundant are thy locks, thy lips as fair
As when their breath enriched Thessalian air.   60

"No Spectre greets me,—no vain Shadow this;
Come, blooming Hero, place thee by my side!
Give, on this well-known couch, one nuptial kiss
To me, this day, a second time thy bride!"
Jove frowned in heaven: the conscious Parcæ threw   65
Upon those roseate lips a Stygian hue.

"This visage tells thee that my doom is past:
Nor should the change be mourned, even if the joys
Of sense were able to return as fast
And surely as they vanish. Earth destroys   70
Those raptures duly—Erebus disdains:
Calm pleasures there abide—majestic pains.

"Be taught, O faithful Consort, to control
Rebellious passion: for the Gods approve
The depth, and not the tumult, of the soul;   75
A fervent, not ungovernable, love.

---

48. *Hector:* chief Trojan leader. 59. *Redundant:* very abundant, thick and long. 60. *Thessalian:* in N. Greece. 65. *Parcæ:* Fates. 66. *Stygian:* deathly. 71. *Erebus:* the dark underworld.

Thy transports moderate; and meekly mourn
When I depart, for brief is my sojourn—"

"Ah, wherefore?—Did not Hercules by force
Wrest from the guardian Monster of the tomb   80
Alcestis, a reanimated corse,
Given back to dwell on earth in vernal bloom?
Medea's spells dispersed the weight of years,
And Æson stood a youth 'mid youthful peers.

"The Gods to us are merciful—and they   85
Yet further may relent: for mightier far
Than strength of nerve and sinew, or the sway
Of magic potent over sun and star,
Is love, though oft to agony distrest,
And though his favourite seat be feeble woman's breast.   90

"But if thou goest, I follow—" "Peace!" he said,
She looked upon him and was calmed and cheered;
The ghastly colour from his lips had fled;
In his deportment, shape, and mien, appeared
Elysian beauty, melancholy grace,   95
Brought from a pensive though a happy place.

He spake of love, such love as Spirits feel
In worlds whose course is equable and pure;
No fears to beat away—no strife to heal—
The past unsighed for, and the future sure;   100
Spake of heroic arts in graver mood
Revived, with finer harmony pursued;

Of all that is most beauteous—imaged there
In happier beauty; more pellucid streams,
An ampler ether, a diviner air,   105
And fields invested with purpureal gleams;
Climes which the sun, who sheds the brightest day
Earth knows, is all unworthy to survey.

Yet there the Soul shall enter which hath earned
That privilege by virtue.—"Ill," said he,   110
"The end of man's existence I discerned,

---

80. *Monster:* Death. 81. *Alcestis:* deceased wife of Hercules' friend Admetus. 83. *Medea:* legendary sorceress of Near East. 84. *Aeson:* Jason, Medea's lover. 95. *Elysian:* heavenly. 104. *pellucid:* very clear. 110. *virtue:* manliness, courage, self-control.

Who from ignoble games and revelry
Could draw, when we had parted, vain delight,
While tears were thy best pastime, day and night;

"And while my youthful peers before my eyes   115
(Each hero following his peculiar bent)
Prepared themselves for glorious enterprise
By martial sports,—or, seated in the tent,
Chieftains and kings in council were detained;
What time the fleet at Aulis lay enchained.   120

"The wished-for wind was given:—I then revolved
The oracle, upon the silent sea;
And, if no worthier led the way, resolved
That, of a thousand vessels, mine should be
The foremost prow in pressing to the strand,—   125
Mine the first blood that tinged the Trojan sand.

"Yet bitter, oft-times bitter, was the pang
When of thy loss I thought, belovèd Wife!
On thee too fondly did my memory hang,
And on the joys we shared in mortal life,—   130
The paths which we had trod—these fountains, flowers,
My new-planned cities, and unfinished towers.

"But should suspense permit the Foe to cry,
'Behold they tremble!—haughty their array,
Yet of their number no one dares to die?'   135
In soul I swept the indignity away:
Old frailties then recurred:—but lofty thought,
In act embodied, my deliverance wrought.

"And Thou, though strong in love, art all too weak
In reason, in self-government too slow;   140
I counsel thee by fortitude to seek
Our blest re-union in the shades below.
The invisible world with thee hath sympathised;
Be thy affections raised and solemnised.

"Learn, by a mortal yearning, to ascend—   145
Seeking a higher object. Love was given,
Encouraged, sanctioned, chiefly for that end;

---

120. *Aulis:* Greek port from which the expeditionary force sailed against
Troy.

For this the passion to excess was driven—
That self might be annulled: her bondage prove
The fetters of a dream opposed to love."—　　　　　　150

Aloud she shrieked! for Hermes reappears!
Round the dear Shade she would have clung—'tis vain:
The hours are past—too brief had they been years;
And him no mortal effort can detain:
Swift, toward the realms that know not earthly day,　　155
He through the portal takes his silent way,
And on the palace-floor a lifeless corpse she lay.

Thus, all in vain exhorted and reproved,
She perished; and, as for a wilful crime,
By the just Gods whom no weak pity moved,　　　　160
Was doomed to wear out her appointed time,
Apart from happy Ghosts, that gather flowers
Of blissful quiet 'mid unfading bowers.

—Yet tears to human suffering are due;
And mortal hopes defeated and o'erthrown　　　　　165
Are mourned by man, and not by man alone,
As fondly he believes.—Upon the side
Of Hellespont (such faith was entertained)
A knot of spiry trees for ages grew
From out the tomb of him for whom she died;　　　170
And ever, when such stature they had gained
That Ilium's walls were subject to their view,
The trees' tall summits withered at the sight;
A constant interchange of growth and blight!

✺

From *The Prelude*

(1850; *written* ca.1800-05)

CHILDHOOD OF A POET

　　　　　　　　　Was it for this
That one, the fairest of all rivers, loved　　　　　　270
To blend his murmurs with my nurse's song,
And, from his alder shades and rocky falls,
And from his fords and shallows, sent a voice
That flowed along my dreams? For this, didst thou,

---

152. *Shade:* ghost. 172. *Ilium:* Troy.

O Derwent! winding among grassy holms 275
Where I was looking on, a babe in arms,
Make ceaseless music that composed my thoughts
To more than infant softness, giving me
Amid the fretful dwellings of mankind
A foretaste, a dim earnest, of the calm 280
That Nature breathes among the hills and groves.

When he had left the mountains and received
On his smooth breast the shadow of those towers
That yet survive, a shattered monument
Of feudal sway, the bright blue river passed 285
Along the margin of our terrace walk;
A tempting playmate whom we dearly loved.
Oh, many a time have I, a five years' child,
In a small mill-race severed from his stream,
Made one long bathing of a summer's day; 290
Basked in the sun, and plunged and basked again
Alternate, all a summer's day, or scoured
The sandy fields, leaping through flowery groves
Of yellow ragwort; or, when rock and hill,
The woods, and distant Skiddaw's lofty height, 295
Were bronzed with deepest radiance, stood alone
Beneath the sky, as if I had been born
On Indian plains, and from my mother's hut
Had run abroad in wantonness, to sport
A naked savage, in the thunder shower. 300

Fair seed-time had my soul, and I grew up
Fostered alike by beauty and by fear:
Much favoured in my birth-place, and no less
In that belovèd Vale to which erelong
We were transplanted; there were we let loose 305
For sports of wider range. Ere I had told
Ten birth-days, when among the mountain slopes
Frost, and the breath of frosty wind, had snapped
The last autumnal crocus, 'twas my joy
With store of springes o'er my shoulder hung 310
To range the open heights where woodcocks run
Along the smooth green turf. Through half the night,
Scudding away from snare to snare, I plied
That anxious visitation;—moon and stars

THE PRELUDE: 305. *transplanted:* (sent away to school).

Were shining o'er my head. I was alone,   315
And seemed to be a trouble to the peace
That dwelt among them. Sometimes it befell
In these night wanderings, that a strong desire
O'erpowered my better reason, and the bird
Which was the captive of another's toil   320
Became my prey; and when the deed was done
I heard among the solitary hills
Low breathings coming after me, and sounds
Of undistinguishable motion, steps
Almost as silent as the turf they trod.   325

   Nor less, when spring had warmed the cultured Vale,
Moved we as plunderers where the mother-bird
Had in high places built her lodge; though mean
Our object and inglorious, yet the end
Was not ignoble. Oh! when I have hung   330
Above the raven's nest, by knots of grass
And half-inch fissures in the slippery rock
But ill sustained, and almost (so it seemed)
Suspended by the blast that blew amain,
Shouldering the naked crag, oh, at that time   335
While on the perilous ridge I hung alone,
With what strange utterance did the loud dry wind
Blow through my ear! the sky seemed not a sky
Of earth—and with what motion moved the clouds!

   Dust as we are, the immortal spirit grows   340
Like harmony in music; there is a dark
Inscrutable workmanship that reconciles
Discordant elements, makes them cling together
In one society. How strange, that all
The terrors, pains, and early miseries,   345
Regrets, vexations, lassitudes interfused
Within my mind, should e'er have borne a part,
And that a needful part, in making up
The calm existence that is mine when I
Am worthy of myself! Praise to the end!   350
Thanks to the means which Nature deigned to employ;
Whether her fearless visitings, or those
That came with soft alarm, like hurtless light
Opening the peaceful clouds; or she would use
Severer interventions, ministry   355
More palpable, as best might suit her aim.

One summer evening (led by her) I found
A little boat tied to a willow tree
Within a rocky cove, its usual home.
Straight I unloosed her chain, and stepping in   360
Pushed from the shore. It was an act of stealth
And troubled pleasure, nor without the voice
Of mountain-echoes did my boat move on;
Leaving behind her still, on either side,
Small circles glittering idly in the moon,   365
Until they melted all into one track
Of sparkling light. But now, like one who rows,
Proud of his skill, to reach a chosen point
With an unswerving line, I fixed my view
Upon the summit of a craggy ridge,   370
The horizon's utmost boundary; far above
Was nothing but the stars and the grey sky.
She was an elfin pinnace; lustily
I dipped my oars into the silent lake,
And, as I rose upon the stroke, my boat   375
Went heaving through the water like a swan;
When, from behind that craggy steep till then
The horizon's bound, a huge peak, black and huge,
As if with voluntary power instinct,
Upreared its head. I struck and struck again,   380
And growing still in stature the grim shape
Towered up between me and the stars, and still,
For so it seemed, with purpose of its own
And measured motion like a living thing,
Strode after me. With trembling oars I turned,   385
And through the silent water stole my way
Back to the covert of the willow tree;
There in her mooring-place I left my bark,—
And through the meadows homeward went, in grave
And serious mood; but after I had seen   390
That spectacle, for many days, my brain
Worked with a dim and undetermined sense
Of unknown modes of being; o'er my thoughts
There hung a darkness, call it solitude
Or blank desertion. No familiar shapes   395
Remained, no pleasant images of trees,
Of sea or sky, no colours of green fields;
But huge and mighty forms, that do not live
Like living men, moved slowly through the mind
By day, and were a trouble to my dreams.   400

Wisdom and Spirit of the universe!
Thou Soul that art the eternity of thought
That givest to forms and images a breath
And everlasting motion, not in vain
By day or star-light thus from my first dawn   405
Of childhood didst thou intertwine for me
The passions that build up our human soul;
Not with the mean and vulgar works of man,
But with high objects, with enduring things—
With life and nature—purifying thus   410
The elements of feeling and of thought,
And sanctifying, by such discipline,
Both pain and fear, until we recognise
A grandeur in the beatings of the heart.
Nor was this fellowship vouchsafed to me   415
With stinted kindness. In November days,
When vapours rolling down the valley made
A lonely scene more lonesome, among woods,
At noon and 'mid the calm of summer nights,
When, by the margin of the trembling lake,   420
Beneath the gloomy hills homeward I went
In solitude, such intercourse was mine;
Mine was it in the fields both day and night,
And by the waters, all the summer long.

.   .   .   .

Ye Presences of Nature in the sky
And on the earth! Ye Visions of the hills!   465
And Souls of lonely places! can I think
A vulgar hope was yours when ye employed
Such ministry, when ye, through many a year
Haunting me thus among my boyish sports,
On caves and trees, upon the woods and hills,   470
Impressed, upon all forms, the characters
Of danger or desire; and thus did make
The surface of the universal earth,
With triumph and delight, with hope and fear,
Work like a sea?
                        Not uselessly employed,   475
Might I pursue this theme through every change
Of exercise and play, to which the year
Did summon us in his delightful round.

We were a noisy crew; the sun in heaven
Beheld not vales more beautiful than ours;   480

Nor saw a band in happiness and joy
Richer, or worthier of the ground they trod.
I could record with no reluctant voice
The woods of autumn, and their hazel bowers
With milk-white clusters hung; the rod and line,   485
True symbol of hope's foolishness, whose strong
And unreproved enchantment led us on
By rocks and pools shut out from every star,
All the green summer, to forlorn cascades
Among the windings hid of mountain brooks.   490
—Unfading recollections! at this hour
The heart is almost mine with which I felt,
From some hill-top on sunny afternoons,
The paper kite high among fleecy clouds
Pull at her rein like an impetuous courser;   495
Or, from the meadows sent on gusty days,
Beheld her breast the wind, then suddenly
Dashed headlong, and rejected by the storm.

.   .   .   .

Yes, I remember when the changeful earth,
And twice five summers on my mind had stamped   560
The faces of the moving year, even then
I held unconscious intercourse with beauty
Old as creation, drinking in a pure
Organic pleasure from the silver wreaths
Of curling mist, or from the level plain   565
Of waters coloured by impending clouds.

    The sands of Westmoreland, the creeks and bays
Of Cumbria's rocky limits, they can tell
How, when the Sea threw off his evening shade,
And to the shepherd's hut on distant hills   570
Sent welcome notice of the rising moon,
How I have stood, to fancies such as these
A stranger, linking with the spectacle
No conscious memory of a kindred sight,
And bringing with me no peculiar sense   575
Of quietness or peace; yet have I stood,
Even while mine eye hath moved o'er many a league
Of shining water, gathering as it seemed,
Through every hair-breadth in that field of light,
New pleasure like a bee among the flowers.   580

Thus oft amid those fits of vulgar joy
Which, through all seasons, on a child's pursuits
Are prompt attendants, 'mid that giddy bliss
Which, like a tempest, works along the blood
And is forgotten; even then I felt   585
Gleams like the flashing of a shield;—the earth
And common face of Nature spake to me
Rememberable things; sometimes, 'tis true,
By chance collisions and quaint accidents
(Like those ill-sorted unions, work supposed   590
Of evil-minded fairies), yet not vain
Nor profitless, if haply they impressed
Collateral objects and appearances,
Albeit lifeless then, and doomed to sleep
Until maturer seasons called them forth   595
To impregnate and to elevate the mind.
—And if the vulgar joy by its own weight
Wearied itself out of the memory,
The scenes which were a witness of that joy
Remained in their substantial lineaments   600
Depicted on the brain, and to the eye
Were visible, a daily sight; and thus
By the impressive discipline of fear,
By pleasure and repeated happiness,
So frequently repeated, and by force   605
Of obscure feelings representative
Of things forgotten, these same scenes so bright,
So beautiful, so majestic in themselves,
Though yet the day was distant, did become
Habitually dear, and all their forms   610
And changeful colours by invisible links
Were fastened to the affections.

                   — I, 269-424; 464-98; 559-612.

THE CALLING

                    Yes, that heartless chase
Of trivial pleasures was a poor exchange
For books and nature at that early age.

298. *pleasures:* (the social round of a summer vacation from college).

'Tis true, some casual knowledge might be gained   300
Of character or life; but at that time,
Of manners put to school I took small note,
And all my deeper passions lay elsewhere.
Far better had it been to exalt the mind
By solitary study, to uphold   305
Intense desire through meditative peace;
And yet, for chastisement of these regrets,
The memory of one particular hour
Doth here rise up against me. 'Mid a throng
Of maids and youths, old men, and matrons staid,   310
A medley of all tempers, I had passed
The night in dancing, gaiety, and mirth,
With din of instruments and shuffling feet,
And glancing forms, and tapers glittering,
And unaimed prattle flying up and down;   315
Spirits upon the stretch, and here and there
Slight shocks of young love-liking interspersed,
Whose transient pleasure mounted to the head,
And tingled through the veins. Ere we retired,
The cock had crowed, and now the eastern sky   320
Was kindling, not unseen, from humble copse
And open field, through which the pathway wound,
And homeward led my steps. Magnificent
The morning rose, in memorable pomp,
Glorious as e'er I had beheld—in front,   325
The sea lay laughing at a distance; near,
The solid mountains shone, bright as the clouds,
Grain-tinctured, drenched in empyrean light;
And in the meadows and the lower grounds
Was all the sweetness of a common dawn—   330
Dews, vapours, and the melody of birds,
And labourers going forth to till the fields.
Ah! need I say, dear Friend! that to the brim
My heart was full; I made no vows, but vows
Were then made for me; bond unknown to me   335
Was given, that I should be, else sinning greatly,
A dedicated Spirit. On I walked
In thankful blessedness, which yet survives.

                                        —IV, 297-338.

THE ENCOUNTER WITH THE VETERAN

          Once, when those summer months   370
Were flown, and autumn brought its annual show
Of oars with oars contending, sails with sails,
Upon Winander's spacious breast, it chanced
That—after I had left a flower-decked room
(Whose in-door pastime, lighted up, survived   375
To a late hour), and spirits overwrought
Were making night do penance for a day
Spent in a round of strenuous idleness—
My homeward course led up a long ascent,
Where the road's watery surface, to the top   380
Of that sharp rising, glittered to the moon
And bore the semblance of another stream
Stealing with silent lapse to join the brook
That murmured in the vale. All else was still;
No living thing appeared in earth or air,   385
And, save the flowing water's peaceful voice,
Sound there was none—but, lo! an uncouth shape,
Shown by a sudden turning of the road,
So near that, slipping back into the shade
Of a thick hawthorn, I could mark him well,   390
Myself unseen. He was of stature tall,
A span above man's common measure, tall,
Stiff, lank, and upright; a more meagre man
Was never seen before by night or day.
Long were his arms, pallid his hands; his mouth   395
Looked ghastly in the moonlight: from behind,
A mile-stone propped him; I could also ken
That he was clothed in military garb,
Though faded, yet entire. Companionless,
No dog attending, by no staff sustained,   400
He stood, and in his very dress appeared
A desolation, a simplicity,
To which the trappings of a gaudy world
Make a strange back-ground. From his lips, ere long,
Issued low muttered sounds, as if of pain   405
Or some uneasy thought; yet still his form
Kept the same awful steadiness—at his feet

His shadow lay, and moved not. From self-blame
Not wholly free, I watched him thus; at length
Subduing my heart's specious cowardice,   410
I left the shady nook where I had stood
And hailed him. Slowly from his resting-place
He rose, and with a lean and wasted arm
In measured gesture lifted to his head
Returned my salutation; then resumed   415
His station as before; and when I asked
His history, the veteran, in reply,
Was neither slow nor eager; but, unmoved,
And with a quiet uncomplaining voice,
A stately air of mild indifference,   420
He told in few plain words a soldier's tale—
That in the Tropic Islands he had served,
Whence he had landed scarcely three weeks past;
That on his landing he had been dismissed,
And now was travelling towards his native home.   425
This heard, I said, in pity, "Come with me."
He stooped, and straightway from the ground took up
An oaken staff by me yet unobserved—
A staff which must have dropped from his slack hand
And lay till now neglected in the grass.   430
Though weak his step and cautious, he appeared
To travel without pain, and I beheld,
With an astonishment but ill suppressed,
His ghostly figure moving at my side;
Nor could I, while we journeyed thus, forbear   435
To turn from present hardships to the past,
And speak of war, battle, and pestilence,
Sprinkling this talk with questions, better spared,
On what he might himself have seen or felt.
He all the while was in demeanour calm,   440
Concise in answer; solemn and sublime
He might have seemed, but that in all he said
There was a strange half-absence, as of one
Knowing too well the importance of his theme,
But feeling it no longer. Our discourse   445
Soon ended, and together on we passed
In silence through a wood gloomy and still.
Up-turning, then, along an open field,
We reached a cottage. At the door I knocked,
And earnestly to charitable care   450

Commended him as a poor friendless man,
Belated and by sickness overcome.
Assured that now the traveller would repose
In comfort, I entreated that henceforth
He would not linger in the public ways,   455
But ask for timely furtherance and help
Such as his state required. At this reproof,
With the same ghastly mildness in his look,
He said, "My trust is in the God of Heaven,
And in the eye of him who passes me!"   460

    The cottage door was speedily unbarred,
And now the soldier touched his hat once more
With his lean hand, and in a faltering voice,
Whose tone bespake reviving interests
Till then unfelt, he thanked me; I returned   465
The farewell blessing of the patient man,
And so we parted. Back I cast a look,
And lingered near the door a little space,
Then sought with quiet heart my distant home.

                                    — IV, 370-469.

                              ✄

CROSSING THE ALPS

    Yet still in me with those soft luxuries
Mixed something of stern mood, an underthirst
Of vigour seldom utterly allayed:
And from that source how different a sadness   560
Would issue, let one incident make known.
When from the Vallais we had turned, and clomb
Along the Simplon's steep and rugged road,
Following a band of muleteers, we reached
A halting-place, where all together took   565
Their noon-tide meal. Hastily rose our guide,
Leaving us at the board; awhile we lingered,
Then paced the beaten downward way that led
Right to a rough stream's edge, and there broke off;
The only track now visible was one   570

---

557. *those . . . luxuries:* (the poet has been speaking of sentimental day-
dreams).

That from the torrent's further brink held forth
Conspicuous invitation to ascend
A lofty mountain. After brief delay
Crossing the unbridged stream, that road we took,
And clomb with eagerness, till anxious fears   575
Intruded, for we failed to overtake
Our comrades gone before. By fortunate chance,
While every moment added doubt to doubt,
A peasant met us, from whose mouth we learned
That to the spot which had perplexed us first   580
We must descend, and there should find the road,
Which in the stony channel of the stream
Lay a few steps, and then along its banks;
And, that our future course, all plain to sight,
Was downwards, with the current of that stream.   585
Loth to believe what we so grieved to hear,
For still we had hopes that pointed to the clouds,
We questioned him again, and yet again;
But every word that from the peasant's lips
Came in reply, translated by our feelings,   590
Ended in this,—*that we had crossed the Alps.*

   Imagination—here the Power so called
Through sad incompetence of human speech,
That awful Power rose from the mind's abyss
Like an unfathered vapour that enwraps,   595
At once, some lonely traveller. I was lost;
Halted without an effort to break through;
But to my conscious soul I now can say—
"I recognise thy glory:" in such strength
Of usurpation, when the light of sense   600
Goes out, but with a flash that has revealed
The invisible world, doth greatness make abode,
There harbours; whether we be young or old,
Our destiny, our being's heart and home,
Is with infinitude, and only there;   605
With hope it is, hope that can never die,
Effort, and expectation, and desire,
And something evermore about to be.
Under such banners militant, the soul
Seeks for no trophies, struggles for no spoils   610
That may attest her prowess, blest in thoughts
That are their own perfection and reward,

Strong in herself and in beatitude
That hides her, like the mighty flood of Nile
Poured from his fount of Abyssinian clouds   615
To fertilise the whole Egyptian plain.

   The melancholy slackening that ensued
Upon those tidings by the peasant given
Was soon dislodged. Downwards we hurried fast,
And, with the half-shaped road which we had missed,   620
Entered a narrow chasm. The brook and road
Were fellow-travellers in this gloomy strait,
And with them did we journey several hours
At a slow pace. The immeasurable height
Of woods decaying, never to be decayed,   625
The stationary blasts of waterfalls,
And in the narrow rent at every turn
Winds thwarting winds, bewildered and forlorn,
The torrents shooting from the clear blue sky,
The rocks that muttered close upon our ears,   630
Black drizzling crags that spake by the wayside
As if a voice were in them, the sick sight
And giddy prospect of the raving stream,
The unfettered clouds and region of the Heavens,
Tumult and peace, the darkness and the light—   635
Were all like workings of one mind, the features
Of the same face, blossoms upon one tree;
Characters of the great Apocalypse,
The types and symbols of Eternity,
Of first, and last, and midst, and without end.   640
                                                              — VI, 557-640.

॰ॐ

ON SNOWDON

In one of those excursions (may they ne'er
Fade from remembrance!) through the Northern tracts
Of Cambria ranging with a youthful friend,
I left Bethgelert's huts at couching-time,
And westward took my way, to see the sun   5
Rise, from the top of Snowdon. To the door

---

3. *Cambria:* Wales.

Of a rude cottage at the mountain's base
We came, and roused the shepherd who attends
The adventurous stranger's steps, a trusty guide;
Then, cheered by short refreshment, sallied forth.   10

It was a close, warm, breezeless summer night,
Wan, dull, and glaring, with a dripping fog
Low-hung and thick that covered all the sky;
But, undiscouraged, we began to climb
The mountain-side. The mist soon girt us round,   15
And, after ordinary travellers' talk
With our conductor, pensively we sank
Each into commerce with his private thoughts:
Thus did we breast the ascent, and by myself
Was nothing either seen or heard that checked   20
Those musings or diverted, save that once
The shepherd's lurcher, who, among the crags,
Had to his joy unearthed a hedgehog, teased
His coiled-up prey with barkings turbulent.
This small adventure, for even such it seemed   25
In that wild place and at the dead of night,
Being over and forgotten, on we wound
In silence as before. With forehead bent
Earthward, as if in opposition set
Against an enemy, I panted up   30
With eager pace, and no less eager thoughts.
Thus might we wear a midnight hour away,
Ascending at loose distance each from each,
And I, as chanced, the foremost of the band;
When at my feet the ground appeared to brighten,   35
And with a step or two seemed brighter still;
Nor was time given to ask or learn the cause,
For instantly a light upon the turf
Fell like a flash, and lo! as I looked up
The Moon hung naked in a firmament   40
Of azure without cloud, and at my feet
Rested a silent sea of hoary mist.
A hundred hills their dusky backs upheaved
All over this still ocean; and beyond,
Far, far beyond, the solid vapours stretched,   45
In headlands, tongues, and promontory shapes,
Into the main Atlantic, that appeared
To dwindle, and give up his majesty,

Usurped upon far as the sight could reach.
Not so the ethereal vault; encroachment none   50
Was there, nor loss; only the inferior stars
Had disappeared, or shed a fainter light
In the clear presence of the full-orbed Moon,
Who, from her sovereign elevation, gazed
Upon the billowy ocean, as it lay   55
All meek and silent, save that through a rift—
Not distant from the shore whereon we stood,
A fixed abysmal, gloomy, breathing-place—
Mounted the roar of waters, torrents, streams
Innumerable, roaring with one voice!   60
Heard over earth and sea, and, in that hour,
For so it seemed, felt by the starry heavens.

      When into air had partially dissolved
That vision, given to spirits of the night
And three chance human wanderers, in calm thought   65
Reflected, it appeared to me the type
Of a majestic intellect, its acts
And its possessions, what it has and craves,
What in itself it is, and would become.
There I beheld the emblem of a mind   70
That feeds upon infinity, that broods
Over the dark abyss, intent to hear
Its voices issuing forth to silent light
In one continuous stream; a mind sustained
By recognitions of transcendent power,   75
In sense conducting to ideal form,
In soul of more than mortal privilege.
One function, above all, of such a mind
Had Nature shadowed there, by putting forth,
'Mid circumstances awful and sublime,   80
That mutual domination which she loves
To exert upon the face of outward things,
So moulded, joined, abstracted, so endowed
With interchangeable supremacy,
That men, least sensitive, see, hear, perceive,   85
And cannot choose but feel. The power, which all
Acknowledge when thus moved, which Nature thus
To bodily sense exhibits, is the express
Resemblance of that glorious faculty
That higher minds bear with them as their own.   90

This is the very spirit in which they deal
With the whole compass of the universe:
They from their native selves can send abroad
Kindred mutations; for themselves create
A like existence; and, whene'er it dawns   95
Created for them, catch it, or are caught
By its inevitable mastery,
Like angels stopped upon the wing by sound
Of harmony from Heaven's remotest spheres.
Them the enduring and the transient both   100
Serve to exalt; they build up greatest things
From least suggestions; ever on the watch,
Willing to work and to be wrought upon,
They need not extraordinary calls
To rouse them; in a world of life they live,   105
By sensible impressions not enthralled,
But by their quickening impulse made more prompt
To hold fit converse with the spiritual world,
And with the generations of mankind
Spread over time, past, present, and to come,   110
Age after age, till Time shall be no more.
Such minds are truly from the Deity,
For they are Powers; and hence the highest bliss
That flesh can know is theirs—the consciousness
Of Whom they are, habitually infused   115
Through every image and through every thought,
And all affections by communion raised
From earth to heaven, from human to divine;
Hence endless occupation for the Soul,
Whether discursive or intuitive;   120
Hence cheerfulness for acts of daily life,
Emotions which best foresight need not fear,
Most worthy then of trust when most intense.
Hence, amid ills that vex and wrongs that crush
Our hearts—if here the words of Holy Writ   125
May with fit reverence be applied—that peace
Which passeth understanding, that repose
In moral judgments which from this pure source
Must come, or will by man be sought in vain.
                                        —XIV, 1-129.

Samuel Taylor Coleridge

THE RIME OF THE ANCIENT MARINER
(1798)
In Seven Parts

PART I

An ancient Mari-
ner meeteth three
Gallants bidden to
a wedding-feast,
and detaineth one.

It is an ancient Mariner,
And he stoppeth one of three.
"By thy long gray beard and glittering eye,
Now wherefore stopp'st thou me?

"The Bridegroom's doors are opened wide,   5
And I am next of kin;
The guests are met, the feast is set:
May'st hear the merry din."

He holds him with his skinny hand,
"There was a ship," quoth he.   10
"Hold off! unhand me, graybeard loon!"
Eftsoons his hand dropt he.

The Wedding-
Guest is spell-
bound by the eye
of the old seafar-
ing man, and con-
strained to hear
his tale.

He holds him with his glittering eye—
The Wedding-Guest stood still,
And listens like a three years' child: 15
The Mariner hath his will.

The Wedding-Guest sat on a stone:
He cannot choose but hear;
And thus spake on that ancient man,
The bright-eyed Mariner.   20

"The ship was cheered, the harbour cleared,
Merrily did we drop
Below the kirk, below the hill,
Below the light-house top.

The Mariner tells
how the ship
sailed southward
with a good wind
and fair weather,
till it reached the
line.

"The sun came up upon the left,   25
Out of the sea came he!
And he shone bright, and on the right
Went down into the sea.

"Higher and higher every day,
Till over the mast at noon—"   30
The Wedding-Guest here beat his breast,
For he heard the loud bassoon.

The bride hath paced into the hall,
Red as a rose is she;
Nodding their heads before her goes   35
The merry minstrelsy.

The Wedding-Guest he beat his breast,
Yet he cannot choose but hear;
And thus spake on that ancient man
The bright-eyed Mariner.   40

"And now the storm-blast came, and he
Was tyrannous and strong:
He struck with his o'ertaking wings,
And chased us south along.

"With sloping masts and dipping prow,   45
As who pursued with yell and blow

Still treads the shadow of his foe,
And forward bends his head,
The ship drove fast, loud roared the blast,
And southward aye we fled.   50

"And now there came both mist and snow,
And it grew wondrous cold:
And ice, mast-high, came floating by,
As green as emerald.

"And through the drifts the snowy clifts   55
Did send a dismal sheen:
Nor shapes of men nor beasts we ken—
The ice was all between.

"The ice was here, the ice was there,
The ice was all around: 60
It cracked and growled, and roared and howled,
Like noises in a swound!

"At length did cross an Albatross:
Through the fog it came:
As if it had been a Christian soul,   65
We hailed it in God's name.

"It ate the food it ne'er had eat,
And round and round it flew.
The ice did split with a thunder-fit;
The helmsman steered us through!   70

"And a good south wind sprung up behind;
The Albatross did follow,
And every day, for food or play,
Came to the mariners' hollo!

"In mist or cloud, on mast or shroud,   75
It perched for vespers nine;
Whiles all the night, through fog-smoke white,
Glimmered the white moon-shine."

"God save thee, ancient Mariner!
From the fiends, that plague thee thus!—   80
Why look'st thou so?"—"With my cross-bow
I shot the Albatross!"

PART II

"The sun now rose upon the right:
Out of the sea came he,
Still hid in mist, and on the left   85
Went down into the sea.

"And the good south wind still blew behind,
But no sweet bird did follow,
Nor any day, for food or play,
Came to the mariners' hollo!   90

"And I had done a hellish thing,
And it would work 'em woe;
For all averred, I had killed the bird
That made the breeze to blow.
Ah wretch! said they, the bird to slay   95
That made the breeze to blow!

"Nor dim nor red, like God's own head,
The glorious sun uprist:
Then all averred, I had killed the bird
That brought the fog and mist.   100
'Twas right, said they, such birds to slay,
That bring the fog and mist.

ceived with great joy and hospitality.

And lo! the Albatross proveth a bird of good omen, and followeth the ship as it returned northward through fog and floating ice.

The ancient Mariner inhospitably killeth the pious bird of good omen.

His shipmates cry out against the ancient Mariner for killing the bird of good luck.

But when the fog cleared off, they justify the same, and thus make themselves accomplices in the crime.

The fair breeze continues; the ship enters the Pacific Ocean, and sails northward, even till it reaches the line.

"The fair breeze blew, the white foam flew,
The furrow followed free;
We were the first that ever burst   105
Into that silent sea.

"Down dropt the breeze, the sails dropt down,
'Twas sad as sad could be;
And we did speak only to break
The silence of the sea!   110

The ship hath been suddenly becalmed.

"All in a hot and copper sky,
The bloody sun, at noon,
Right up above the mast did stand,
No bigger than the moon.

"Day after day, day after day,   115
We stuck, nor breath nor motion;
As idle as a painted ship
Upon a painted ocean.

And the Albatross begins to be avenged.

"Water, water, every where,
And all the boards did shrink;   120
Water, water, every where,
Nor any drop to drink.

"The very deep did rot: O Christ!
That ever this should be!
Yea, slimy things did crawl with legs   125
Upon the slimy sea.

"About, about, in reel and rout
The death-fires danced at night;
The water, like a witch's oils,
Burnt green, and blue and white.   130

A Spirit had followed them; one of the invisible inhabitants of this planet, neither departed souls nor angels; concerning whom the learned Jew, Josephus, and the Platonic Constantinopolitan, Michael Psellus, may be consulted.

"And some in dreams assurèd were
Of the spirit that plagued us so:
Nine fathom deep he had followed us,
From the land of mist and snow.

"And every tongue, through utter drought,   135
Was withered at the root;
We could not speak, no more than if
We had been choked with soot.

"Ah! well-a-day! what evil looks
Had I from old and young!   140

They are very nu-
merous, and there
is no climate or
Instead of the cross, the Albatross
About my neck was hung.

element without one or more. The shipmates, in their sore distress, would fain
throw the whole guilt on the ancient Mariner: in sign whereof they hang the
dead seabird round his neck.

PART III

The ancient Mari-
ner beholdeth a
sign in the ele-
ment afar off.
"There passed a weary time. Each throat
Was parched, and glazed each eye.
A weary time! A weary time!   145
How glazed each weary eye!
When looking westward I beheld
A something in the sky.

"At first it seemed a little speck,
And then it seemed a mist: 150
It moved and moved, and took at last
A certain shape, I wist.

"A speck, a mist, a shape, I wist!
And still it neared and neared:
As if it dodged a water-sprite,   155
It plunged and tacked and veered.

At its nearer ap-
proach, it seemeth
him to be a ship;
and at a dear ran-
som he freeth his
speech from the
bonds of thirst.
A flash of joy;
"With throats unslacked, with black lips baked,
We could nor laugh nor wail;
Through utter drought all dumb we stood!
I bit my arm, I sucked the blood,   160
And cried, 'A sail! a sail!'

"With throats unslaked, with black lips baked,
Agape they heard me call:
Gramercy! they for joy did grin,
And all at once their breath drew in,   165
As they were drinking all.

And horror fol-
lows. For can it
be a ship that
comes onward
without wind or
tide?
" 'See! see (I cried) she tacks no more!
Hither to work us weal;
Without a breeze, without a tide,
She steadies with upright keel!'   170

"The western wave was all a-flame
The day was well nigh done!
Almost upon the western wave
Rested the broad bright sun;

When that strange shape drove suddenly   175
Betwixt us and the sun.

It seemeth him but the skeleton of a ship.

"And straight the sun was flecked with bars,
(Heaven's Mother send us grace!)
As if through a dungeon-grate he peered
With broad and burning face.   180

"Alas! (thought I, and my heart beat loud)
How fast she nears and nears!
Are those her sails that glance in the sun,
Like restless gossameres?

And its ribs are seen as bars on the face of the setting sun.

"Are those her ribs through which the sun   185
Did peer, as through a grate?
And is that Woman all her crew?
Is that a Death? and are there two?
Is Death that woman's mate?

The Spectre-Woman and her Death-mate, and no other on board the skeleton-ship. Like vessel, like crew!

"Her lips were red, her looks were free,   190
Her locks were yellow as gold:
Her skin was as white as leprosy,
The Nightmare Life-in-Death was she,
Who thicks man's blood with cold.

Death and Life-in-Death have diced for the ship's crew, and she (the latter) winneth the ancient Mariner.

"The naked hulk alongside came,   195
And the twain were casting dice;
'The game is done! I've won! I've won!'
Quoth she, and whistles thrice.

"The sun's rim dips; the stars rush out:
At one stride comes the dark;   200
With far-heard whisper, o'er the sea,
Off shot the spectre-bark.

"We listened and looked sideways up!
Fear at my heart, as at a cup,
My life-blood seemed to sip!   205

No twilight within the courts of the sun.

The stars were dim, and thick the night,
The steersman's face by his lamp gleamed white;
From the sails the dew did drip—

At the rising of the moon

Till clomb above the eastern bar
The hornèd moon, with one bright star   210
Within the nether tip.

One after another,
His shipmates
drop down dead.

"One after one, by the star-dogged moon,
Too quick for groan or sigh,
Each turned his face with a ghastly pang,
And cursed me with his eye.   215

"Four times fifty living men,
(And I heard nor sigh nor groan)
With heavy thump, a lifeless lump,
They dropped down one by one.

But Life-in-Death
begins her work
on the ancient
Mariner.

"The souls did from their bodies fly,—   220
They fled to bliss or woe!
And every soul, it passed me by,
Like the whizz of my cross-bow!"

PART IV

The Wedding-
Guest feareth that
a spirit is talking
to him;

"I fear thee, ancient Mariner!
I fear thy skinny hand!   225
And thou art long, and lank, and brown,
As is the ribbed sea-sand.

But the ancient
Mariner assureth
him of his bodily
life, and proceed-
eth to relate his
horrible penance.

"I fear thee and thy glittering eye,
And thy skinny hand, so brown."—
"Fear not, fear not, thou Wedding-Guest!   230
This body dropt not down.

"Alone, alone, all, all alone,
Alone on a wide, wide sea!
And never a saint took pity on
My soul in agony.   235

He despiseth the
creatures of the
calm,

"The many men, so beautiful!
And they all dead did lie:
And a thousand thousand slimy things
Lived on; and so did I.

And envieth that
they should live,
and so many be
dead.

"I looked upon the rotting sea,   240
And drew my eyes away;
I looked upon the rotting deck,
And there the dead men lay.

"I looked to heaven, and tried to pray;
But or ever a prayer had gusht,   245

A wicked whisper came, and made
My heart as dry as dust.

"I closed my lids, and kept them close,
And the balls like pulses beat;
For the sky and the sea, and the sea and the
    sky,   250
Lay like a load on my weary eye,
And the dead were at my feet.

But the curse liv-
eth for him in the
eye of the dead
men.

"The cold sweat melted from their limbs,
Nor rot nor reek did they:
The look with which they looked on me   255
Had never passed away.

"An orphan's curse would drag to hell
A spirit from on high;
But oh! more horrible than that
Is the curse in a dead man's eye!   260
Seven days, seven nights, I saw that curse.
And yet I could not die.

In his loneliness
and fixedness he
yearneth towards
the journeying
moon, and the
stars that still so-
journ, yet still
move onward;
and every where
the blue sky be-
longs to them,
and is their ap-
pointed rest, and their native country and their own natural homes, which they
enter unannounced, as lords that are certainly expected and yet there is a silent
joy at their arrival.

"The moving moon went up the sky,
And no where did abide:
Softly she was going up,   265
And a star or two beside—

"Her beams bemocked the sultry main,
Like April hoar-frost spread;
But where the ship's huge shadow lay,
The charmed water burned away   270
A still and awful red.

By the light of the
moon he behold-
eth God's crea-
tures of the great
calm.

"Beyond the shadow of the ship,
I watched the water-snakes:
They moved in tracks of shining white,
And when they reared, the elfish light   275
Fell off in hoary flakes.

"Within the shadow of the ship
I watched their rich attire:
Blue, glossy green, and velvet black,

They coiled and swam; and every track   280
Was a flash of golden fire.

Their beauty and
their happiness.

"O happy living things! no tongue
Their beauty might declare:
A spring of love gushed from my heart,

He blesseth them
in his heart.

And I blessed them unaware: 285
Sure my kind saint took pity on me,
And I blessed them unaware.

The spell begins
to break.

"The selfsame moment I could pray;
And from my neck so free
The Albatross fell off, and sank   290
Like lead into the sea.

PART V

"O sleep! it is a gentle thing,
Beloved from pole to pole!
To Mary queen the praise be given!
She sent the gentle sleep from Heaven,   295
That slid into my soul.

By grace of the
holy Mother, the
ancient Mariner is
refreshed with
rain.

"The silly buckets on the deck,
That had so long remained,
I dreamt that they were filled with dew;
And when I awoke, it rained.   300

"My lips were wet, my throat was cold,
My garments all were dank;
Sure I had drunken in my dreams,
And still my body drank.

"I moved, and could not feel my limbs: 305
I was so light—almost
I thought that I had died in sleep,
And was a blessèd ghost.

He heareth sounds
and seeth strange
sights and com-
motions in the
sky and the ele-
ment.

"And soon I heard a roaring wind:
It did not come anear;   310
But with its sound it shook the sails,
That were so thin and sere.

"The upper air burst into life!
And a hundred fire-flags sheen,
To and fro they were hurried about!   315

And to and fro, and in and out,
The wan stars danced between.

"And the coming wind did roar more loud,
And the sails did sigh like sedge;
And the rain poured down from one black
    cloud;   320
The moon was at its edge.

"The thick black cloud was cleft, and still
The moon was at its side:
Like waters shot from some high crag,
The lightning fell with never a jag,   325
A river steep and wide.

The bodies of the   "The loud wind never reached the ship,
ship's crew are in-   Yet now the ship moved on!
spired, and the   Beneath the lightning and the moon
ship moves on.   The dead men gave a groan.   330

"They groaned, they stirred, they all uprose,
Nor spake, nor moved their eyes;
It had been strange, even in a dream,
To have seen those dead men rise.

"The helmsman steered, the ship moved on;   335
Yet never a breeze up-blew;
The mariners all 'gan work the ropes,
Where they were wont to do:
They raised their limbs like lifeless tools—
We were a ghastly crew.   340

"The body of my brother's son
Stood by me, knee to knee:
The body and I pulled at one rope,
But he said nought to me."

"I fear thee, ancient Mariner!"   345
"Be calm, thou Wedding-Guest!
But not by the   'Twas not those souls that fled in pain,
souls of the men,   Which to their corses came again,
nor by demons of   But a troop of spirits blest:
earth or middle
air, but by a   "For when it dawned—they dropped their
blessed troop of   arms,   350
angelic spirits,   And clustered round the mast:
sent down by the

invocation of the
guardian saint.

Sweet sounds rose slowly through their mouths,
And from their bodies passed.

"Around, around, flew each sweet sound,
Then darted to the sun;   355
Slowly the sounds came back again,
Now mixed, now one by one.

"Sometimes a-dropping from the sky
I heard the skylark sing;
Sometimes all little birds that are,   360
How they seemed to fill the sea and air
With their sweet jargoning!

"And now 'twas like all instruments,
Now like a lonely flute;
And now it is an angel's song,   365
That makes the heavens be mute.

"It ceased; yet still the sails made on
A pleasant noise till noon,
A noise like of a hidden brook
In the leafy month of June,   370
That to the sleeping woods all night
Singeth a quiet tune.

"Till noon we quietly sailed on,
Yet never a breeze did breathe:
Slowly and smoothly went the ship,   375
Moved onward from beneath.

The lonesome
Spirit from the
south pole carries
on the ship as far
as the line, in
obedience to the
angelic troop, but
still requireth
vengeance.

"Under the keel nine fathom deep,
From the land of mist and snow,
The spirit slid; and it was he
That made the ship to go.   380
The sails at noon left off their tune,
And the ship stood still also.

"The sun, right up above the mast,
Had fixed her to the ocean;
But in a minute she 'gan stir,   385
With a short uneasy motion—
Backwards and forwards half her length,
With a short uneasy motion.

"Then like a pawing horse let go,
She made a sudden bound: 390
It flung the blood into my head,
And I fell down in a swound.

The Polar Spirit's
fellow-demons,
the invisible inhab-
itants of the ele-
ment, take part in
his wrong, and
two of them re-
late, one to the
other, that pen-
ance long and
heavy for the an-
cient Mariner
hath been ac-
corded to the Po-
lar Spirit, who re-
turneth south-
ward.

"How long in that same fit I lay,
I have not to declare;
But ere my living life returned,   395
I heard, and in my soul discerned
Two voices in the air.

" 'Is it he?' quoth one, 'is this the man?
By Him who died on cross,
With his cruel bow he laid full low   400
The harmless Albatross.

" 'The spirit who bideth by himself
In the land of mist and snow,
He loved the bird that loved the man
Who shot him with his bow.'   405

"The other was a softer voice,
As soft as honey-dew:
Quoth he, 'The man hath penance done,
And penance more will do.'

PART VI

First Voice

" 'But tell me, tell me! speak again,   410
Thy soft response renewing—
What makes that ship drive on so fast?
What is the ocean doing?'

Second Voice

" 'Still as a slave before his lord,
The ocean hath no blast;   415
His great bright eye most silently
Up to the moon is cast—

" 'If he may know which way to go;
For she guides him smooth or grim.
See, brother, see! how graciously   420
She looketh down on him.'

First Voice

" 'But why drives on that ship so fast,
Without or wave or wind?'

Second Voice

" 'The air is cut away before,
And closes from behind.   425

" 'Fly, brother, fly! more high, more high!
Or we shall be belated:
For slow and slow that ship will go,
When the Mariner's trance is abated.'

"I woke, and we were sailing on   430
As in a gentle weather:
'Twas night, calm night, the moon was high;
The dead men stood together.

"All stood together on the deck,
For a charnel-dungeon fitter: 435
All fixed on me their stony eyes,
That in the moon did glitter.

"The pang, the curse, with which they died,
Had never passed away:
I could not draw my eyes from theirs,   440
Nor turn them up to pray.

"And now this spell was snapt: once more
I viewed the ocean green,
And looked far forth, yet little saw
Of what had else been seen—   445

"Like one, that on a lonesome road
Doth walk in fear and dread,
And having once turned round walks on,
And turns no more his head;
Because he knows, a frightful fiend   450
Doth close behind him tread.

"But soon there breathed a wind on me,
Nor sound nor motion made:
Its path was not upon the sea,
In ripple or in shade.   455

The Mariner hath been cast into a trance; for the angelic power causeth the vessel to drive northward faster than human life could endure.

The supernatural motion is retarded; the Mariner awakes and his penance begins anew.

The curse is finally expiated.

"It raised my hair, it fanned my cheek
Like a meadow-gale of spring—
It mingled strangely with my fears,
Yet it felt like a welcoming.

"Swiftly, swiftly flew the ship,   460
Yet she sailed softly too:
Sweetly, sweetly blew the breeze—
On me alone it blew.

And the ancient "Oh! dream of joy! is this indeed
Mariner beholdeth The light-house top I see?   465
his native country. Is this the hill? is this the kirk?
Is this mine own countree?

"We drifted o'er the harbour-bar,
And I with sobs did pray—
O let me be awake, my God!   470
Or let me sleep alway.

"The harbour-bay was clear as glass,
So smoothly it was strewn!
And on the bay the moonlight lay,
And the shadow of the moon.   475

"The rock shone bright, the kirk no less,
That stands above the rock:
The moonlight steeped in silentness
The steady weathercock.

The angelic spirits "And the bay was white with silent light   480
leave the dead Till rising from the same,
bodies. Full many shapes, that shadows were,
In crimson colours came.

And appear in "A little distance from the prow
their own forms Those crimson shadows were: 485
of light. I turned my eyes upon the deck—
Oh, Christ! what saw I there!

"Each corse lay flat, lifeless and flat,
And, by the holy rood!
A man all light, a seraph-man,   490
On every corse there stood.

"This seraph-band, each waved his hand:
It was a heavenly sight!
They stood as signals to the land,
Each one a lovely light: 495

"This seraph-band, each waved his hand,
No voice did they impart—
No voice; but oh! the silence sank
Like music on my heart.

"But soon I heard the dash of oars,   500
I heard the pilot's cheer;
My head was turned perforce away,
And I saw a boat appear.

"The pilot, and the pilot's boy,
I heard them coming fast: 505
Dear Lord in Heaven! it was a joy
The dead men could not blast.

"I saw a third—I heard his voice:
It is the Hermit good!
He singeth loud his godly hymns   510
That he makes in the wood.
He'll shrieve my soul, he'll wash away
The Albatross's blood.

PART VII

The Hermit of the
wood,

"This Hermit good lives in that wood
Which slopes down to the sea.   515
How loudly his sweet voice he rears!
He loves to talk with marineres
That come from a far countree.

"He kneels at morn, and noon, and eve—
He hath a cushion plump: 520
It is the moss that wholly hides
The rotted old oak-stump.

"The skiff-boat neared: I heard them talk,
'Why, this is strange, I trow!
Where are those lights so many and fair,   525
That signal made but now?'

Approacheth the
ship with wonder.

" 'Strange, by my faith!' the Hermit said—
'And they answered not our cheer!
The planks look warped! and see those sails,
How thin they are and sere!   530
I never saw aught like to them,
Unless perchance it were

" 'Brown skeletons of leaves that lag
My forest-brook along:
When the ivy-tod is heavy with snow,   535
And the owlet whoops to the wolf below,
That eats the she-wolf's young.'

" 'Dear Lord! it hath a fiendish look'—
(The pilot made reply)
'I am a-feared'—'Push on, push on!'   540
Said the Hermit cheerily.

"The boat came closer to the ship,
But I nor spake nor stirred;
The boat came close beneath the ship,
And straight a sound was heard.   545

The ship suddenly
sinketh.

"Under the water it rumbled on,
Still louder and more dread:
It reached the ship, it split the bay;
The ship went down like lead.

"Stunned by that loud and dreadful sound,   550
Which sky and ocean smote,

The ancient Mari-
ner is saved in the
pilot's boat.

Like one that hath been seven days drowned
My body lay afloat;
But swift as dreams, myself I found
Within the pilot's boat.   555

"Upon the whirl, where sank the ship
The boat spun round and round;
And all was still, save that the hill
Was telling of the sound.

"I moved my lips—the pilot shrieked   560
And fell down in a fit;
The holy Hermit raised his eyes
And prayed where he did sit.

"I took the oars: the pilot's boy,
Who now doth crazy go,   565
Laughing loud and long, and all the while
His eyes went to and fro.
'Ha! ha!' quoth he, 'full plain I see,
The Devil knows how to row.'

"And now, all in my own countree,   570
I stood on the firm land!
The Hermit stepped forth from the boat,
And scarcely he could stand.

The ancient Mariner earnestly entreateth the Hermit to shrieve him; and the penance of life falls on him.

"'O shrieve me, shrieve me, holy man!'
The Hermit crossed his brow.   575
'Say quick,' quoth he, 'I bid thee say—
What manner of man art thou?'

"Forthwith this frame of mine was wrenched
With a woeful agony,
Which forced me to begin my tale;   580
And then it left me free.

And ever and anon throughout his future life an agony constraineth him to travel from land to land,

"Since then at an uncertain hour,
That agony returns;
And till my ghastly tale is told,
This heart within me burns.   585

"I pass, like night, from land to land;
I have strange power of speech;
That moment that his face I see,
I know the man that must hear me:
To him my tale I teach.   590

"What loud uproar bursts from that door:
The wedding-guests are there;
But in the garden-bower the bride
And the bride-maids singing are;
And hark the little vesper bell,   595
Which biddeth me to prayer!

"O Wedding-Guest! this soul hath been
Alone on a wide, wide sea:
So lonely 'twas, that God himself
Scarce seemèd there to be.   600

"O sweeter than the marriage-feast,
'Tis sweeter far to me,
To walk together to the kirk
With a goodly company!—

"To walk together to the kirk,   605
And all together pray,
While each to his great Father bends,
Old men, and babes, and loving friends,
And youths and maidens gay!

And to teach, by
his own example,
love and reverence
to all things that
God made and
loveth.

"Farewell, farewell! but this I tell   610
To thee, thou Wedding-Guest!
He prayeth well, who loveth well
Both man and bird and beast.

"He prayeth best, who loveth best
All things both great and small;   615
For the dear God who loveth us,
He made and loveth all."

The Mariner, whose eye is bright,
Whose beard with age is hoar,
Is gone; and now the Wedding-Guest   620
Turned from the bridegroom's door.

He went like one that hath been stunned,
And is of sense forlorn:
A sadder and a wiser man,
He rose the morrow morn.   625

FROST AT MIDNIGHT

(1798)

The frost performs its secret ministry,
Unhelped by any wind. The owlet's cry
Came loud— and hark, again! loud as before.
The inmates of my cottage, all at rest,
Have left me to that solitude, which suits   5
Abstruser musings: save that at my side
My cradled infant slumbers peacefully.
'Tis calm indeed! so calm, that it disturbs

And vexes meditation with its strange
And extreme silentness. Sea, hill, and wood,   10
This populous village! Sea, and hill, and wood,
With all the numberless goings on of life
Inaudible as dreams! the thin blue flame
Lies on my low burnt fire, and quivers not;
Only that film, which fluttered on the grate,   15
Still flutters there, the sole unquiet thing.
Methinks, its motion in this hush of nature
Gives it dim sympathies with me who live,
Making it a companionable form,
Whose puny flaps and freaks the idling Spirit   20
By its own moods interprets, every where
Echo or mirror seeking of itself,
And makes a toy of Thought.

                           But O! how oft,
How oft, at school, with most believing mind,
Presageful, have I gazed upon the bars,   25
To watch that fluttering stranger! and as oft
With unclosed lids, already had I dreamt
Of my sweet birth-place, and the old church-tower,
Whose bells, the poor man's only music, rang
From morn to evening, all the hot Fair-day,   30
So sweetly, that they stirred and haunted me
With a wild pleasure, falling on mine ear
Most like articulate sounds of things to come!
So gazed I, till the soothing things I dreamt
Lulled me to sleep, and sleep prolonged my dreams!   35
And so I brooded all the following morn,
Awed by the stern preceptor's face, mine eye
Fixed with mock study on my swimming book:
Save if the door half opened, and I snatched
A hasty glance, and still my heart leaped up,   40
For still I hoped to see the stranger's face,
Townsman, or aunt, or sister more beloved,
My play-mate when we both were clothed alike!

    Dear babe, that sleepest cradled by my side,
Whose gentle breathings, heard in this deep calm,   45
Fill up the interspersed vacancies
And momentary pauses of the thought!
My babe so beautiful! it thrills my heart
With tender gladness, thus to look at thee,

And think that thou shalt learn far other lore   50
And in far other scenes! For I was reared
In the great city, pent 'mid cloisters dim,
And saw nought lovely but the sky and stars.
But thou, my babe! shalt wander like a breeze
By lakes and sandy shores, beneath the crags   55
Of ancient mountain, and beneath the clouds,
Which image in their bulk both lakes and shores
And mountain crags: so shalt thou see and hear
The lovely shapes and sounds intelligible
Of that eternal language, which thy God   60
Utters, who from eternity doth teach
Himself in all, and all things in himself.
Great universal Teacher! he shall mould
Thy spirit, and by giving make it ask.

   Therefore all seasons shall be sweet to thee,   65
Whether the summer clothe the general earth
With greenness, or the redbreast sit and sing
Betwixt the tufts of snow on the bare branch
Of mossy apple-tree, while the nigh thatch
Smokes in the sun-thaw; whether the eve-drops fall   70
Heard only in the trances of the blast,
Or if the secret ministry of frost
Shall hang them up in silent icicles,
Quietly shining to the quiet Moon.

KUBLA KHAN

(1816; *written* 1798)

In Xanadu did Kubla Khan
  A stately pleasure-dome decree;
Where Alph, the sacred river, ran
  Through caverns measureless to man
Down to a sunless sea.   5
So twice five miles of fertile ground
  With walls and towers were girdled round;
And here were gardens bright with sinuous rills
Where blossomed many an incense-bearing tree;

And here were forests ancient as the hills,   10
Enfolding sunny spots of greenery.

But O, that deep romantic chasm which slanted
Down the green hill athwart a cedarn cover!
A savage place! as holy and enchanted
As e'er beneath a waning moon was haunted   15
By woman wailing for her demon-lover!
And from this chasm, with ceaseless turmoil seething,
As if this earth in fast thick pants were breathing,
A mighty fountain momently was forced;
Amid whose swift, half-intermitted burst   20
Huge fragments vaulted like rebounding hail,
Or chaffy grain beneath the thresher's flail.
And 'mid these dancing rocks at once and ever
It flung up momently the sacred river.
Five miles meandering with a mazy motion   25
Through wood and dale the sacred river ran,
Then reached the caverns measureless to man,
And sank in tumult to a lifeless ocean;
And 'mid this tumult Kubla heard from far
Ancestral voices prophesying war!   30

    The shadow of the dome of pleasure
      Floated midway on the waves;
    Where was heard the mingled measure
      From the fountain and the caves.
It was a miracle of rare device,   35
A sunny pleasure-dome with caves of ice!

    A damsel with a dulcimer
      In a vision once I saw.
    It was an Abyssinian maid,
      And on her dulcimer she played,   40
    Singing of Mount Abora.
    Could I revive within me
      Her symphony and song,
To such a deep delight 'twould win me
That with music loud and long,   45
I would build that dome in air,
That sunny dome! those caves of ice!
And all who heard should see them there,
And all should cry, Beware! Beware!
His flashing eyes, his floating hair!   50

Weave a circle round him thrice,
  And close your eyes with holy dread,
  For he on honey-dew hath fed,
And drunk the milk of Paradise.

౬౼

DEJECTION: AN ODE

(1802)

Late, late yestreen I saw the new Moon,
With the old Moon in her arms;
And I fear, I fear, my Master dear!
We shall have a deadly storm.
                              BALLAD OF SIR PATRICK SPENCE

I

Well! If the bard was weather-wise, who made
  The grand old ballad of Sir Patrick Spence,
  This night, so tranquil now, will not go hence
Unroused by winds, that ply a busier trade
Than those which mould yon cloud in lazy flakes,   5
Or the dull sobbing draft, that moans and rakes
    Upon the strings of this Eolian lute,
    Which better far were mute.
  For lo! the new-moon winter-bright!
  And overspread with phantom light,   10
  (With swimming phantom light o'erspread
  But rimmed and circled by a silver thread)
I see the old Moon in her lap, foretelling
  The coming on of rain and squally blast.
And oh! that even now the gust were swelling,   15
  And the slant night-shower driving loud and fast!
Those sounds which oft have raised me, whilst they awed,
    And sent my soul abroad,
Might now perhaps their wonted impulse give,
Might startle this dull pain, and make it move and live! 20

II

A grief without a pang, void, dark, and drear,
  A stifled, drowsy, unimpassioned grief,
  Which finds no natural outlet, no relief,
    In word, or sigh, or tear—

O Lady! in this wan and heartless mood,   25
To other thoughts by yonder throstle woo'd,
   All this long eve, so balmy and serene,
Have I been gazing on the western sky,
   And its peculiar tint of yellow green:
And still I gaze—and with how blank an eye!   30
And those thin clouds above, in flakes and bars,
That give away their motion to the stars;
Those stars, that glide behind them or between,
Now sparkling, now bedimmed, but always seen:
Yon crescent moon as fixed as if it grew   35
In its own cloudless, starless lake of blue;
I see them all so excellently fair,
I see, not feel how beautiful they are!

III

   My genial spirits fail;
   And what can these avail   40
To lift the smothering weight from off my breast?
    It were a vain endeavour,
    Though I should gaze for ever
On that green light that lingers in the west:
I may not hope from outward forms to win   45
The passion and the life, whose fountains are within.

IV

O Lady! we receive but what we give,
And in our life alone does nature live:
Ours is her wedding-garment, ours her shroud!
   And would we aught behold, of higher worth,   50
Than that inanimate cold world allowed
To the poor loveless ever-anxious crowd,
   Ah! from the soul itself must issue forth,
A light, a glory, a fair luminous cloud
    Enveloping the earth—   55
And from the soul itself must there be sent
   A sweet and potent voice, of its own birth,
Of all sweet sounds the life and element!

V

O pure of heart! thou need'st not ask of me
What this strong music in the soul may be!   60
What, and wherein it doth exist,

This light, this glory, this fair luminous mist,
This beautiful and beauty-making power.
     Joy, virtuous Lady! Joy that ne'er was given,
Save to the pure, and in their purest hour,   65
Life, and Life's effluence, cloud at once and shower
Joy, Lady! is the spirit and the power,
     Which wedding Nature to us gives in dower,
          A new earth and new heaven,
Undreamt of by the sensual and the proud—   70
Joy is the sweet voice, Joy the luminous cloud—
          We in ourselves rejoice!
And thence flows all that charms or ear or sight,
     All melodies the echoes of that voice,
All colours a suffusion from that light.   75

VI

There was a time when, though my path was rough,
     This joy within me dallied with distress,
And all misfortunes were but as the stuff
     Whence Fancy made me dreams of happiness:
For hope grew round me, like the twining vine,   80
And fruits, and foliage, not my own, seemed mine.
But now afflictions bow me down to earth:
Nor care I that they rob me of my mirth,
          But oh! each visitation
Suspends what nature gave me at my birth,   85
     My shaping spirit of Imagination.
For not to think of what I needs must feel,
     But to be still and patient, all I can;
And haply by abstruse research to steal
     From my own nature all the natural man—   90
     This was my sole resource, my only plan:
Till that which suits a part infects the whole,
And now is almost grown the habit of my soul.

VII

Hence, viper thoughts, that coil around my mind,
          Reality's dark dream!   95
I turn from you, and listen to the wind,
     Which long has raved unnoticed. What a scream
Of agony by torture lengthened out
That lute sent forth! Thou Wind, that ravest without,
     Bare crag, or mountain-tairn, or blasted tree,   100

Or pine-grove whither woodman never clomb,
Or lonely house, long held the witches' home,
  Methinks were fitter instruments for thee,
Mad lutanist! who in this month of showers,
Of dark brown gardens, and of peeping flowers,   105
Mak'st Devils' yule, with worse than wintry song,
The blossoms, buds, and timorous leaves among.
  Thou actor, perfect in all tragic sounds!
Thou mighty poet, e'en to frenzy bold!
    What tell'st thou now about?   110
    'Tis of the rushing of a host in rout,
With groans of trampled men, with smarting wounds—
At once they groan with pain, and shudder with the cold!
But hush! there is a pause of deepest silence!
  And all that noise, as of a rushing crowd,   115
With groans, and tremulous shudderings—all is over—
  It tells another tale, with sounds less deep and loud!
    A tale of less affright,
    And tempered with delight,
As Otway's self had framed the tender lay,   120
    'Tis of a little child
    Upon a lonesome wild,
Not far from home, but she hath lost her way:
And now moans low in bitter grief and fear,
And now screams loud, and hopes to make her mother hear. 125

VIII

'Tis midnight, but small thoughts have I of sleep:
Full seldom may my friend such vigils keep!
Visit her, gentle Sleep! with wings of healing,
  And may this storm be but a mountain-birth,
May all the stars hang bright above her dwelling,   130
  Silent as though they watched the sleeping earth!
    With light heart may she rise,
    Gay fancy, cheerful eyes,
Joy lift her spirit, joy attune her voice;
To her may all things live, from pole to pole,   135
Their life the eddying of her living soul!
  O simple spirit, guided from above,
Dear Lady! friend devoutest of my choice,
Thus mayest thou ever, evermore rejoice.

DEJECTION: 120. *Otway:* Restoration dramatist, author of the tragedy
Venice Preserved.

George Gordon, Lord Byron

SHE WALKS IN BEAUTY
(1815)

She walks in beauty, like the night
  Of cloudless climes and starry skies;
And all that's best of dark and bright
  Meet in her aspect and her eyes:
Thus mellowed to that tender light   5
  Which heaven to gaudy day denies.

One shade the more, one ray the less,
  Had half impaired the nameless grace,
Which waves in every raven tress,
  Or softly lightens o'er her face;   10
Where thoughts serenely sweet express
  How pure, how dear their dwelling-place.

And on that cheek, and o'er that brow,
  So soft, so calm, yet eloquent,
The smiles that win, the tints that glow,   15
  But tell of days in goodness spent,
A mind at peace with all below,
  A heart whose love is innocent!

SO WE'LL GO NO MORE A-ROVING
(1830; *written* 1817)

So we'll go no more a-roving
  So late into the night,
Though the heart be still as loving,
  And the moon be still as bright.

For the sword outwears its sheath,   5
  And the soul wears out the breast,

And the heart must pause to breathe,
    And love itself have rest.

Though the night was made for loving,
    And the day returns too soon,   10
Yet we'll go no more a-roving
    By the light of the moon.

MY BOAT IS ON THE SHORE

To Thomas Moore

(1821; written 1817)

My boat is on the shore,
    And my bark is on the sea;
But, before I go, Tom Moore,
    Here's a double health to thee!

Here's a sigh to those who love me,   5
    And a smile to those who hate;
And, whatever sky's above me,
    Here's a heart for every fate.

Though the ocean roar around me,
    Yet it still shall bear me on;   10
Though a desert should surround me,
    It hath springs that may be won.

Were't the last drop in the well,
    As I gasped upon the brink,
Ere my fainting spirit fell,   15
    'Tis to thee that I would drink.

With that water, as this wine,
    The libation I would pour
Should be,—peace with thine and mine,
    And a health to thee, Tom Moore.   20

THE ISLES OF GREECE
(1821)

1

The isles of Greece, the isles of Greece!
  Where burning Sappho loved and sung,
Where grew the arts of war and peace,
  Where Delos rose, and Phœbus sprung!
Eternal summer gilds them yet,   5
But all, except their sun, is set.

2

The Scian and the Teian muse,
  The hero's harp, the lover's lute,
Have found the fame your shores refuse;
  Their place of birth alone is mute   10
To sounds which echo further west
Than your sires' "Islands of the Blest."

3

The mountains look on Marathon—
  And Marathon looks on the sea;
And musing there an hour alone,   15
  I dreamed that Greece might still be free;
For standing on the Persians' grave,
I could not deem myself a slave.

4

A king sate on the rocky brow
  Which looks o'er sea-born Salamis;   20
And ships, by thousands, lay below,
  And men in nations;—all were his!
He counted them at break of day—
And when the sun set where were they?

THE ISLES OF GREECE: 2. *Sappho:* Greek lyric poetess of Lesbos. 4. *Delos:*
reek island. *Phoebus:* sun god. 7. *Scian . . . muse:* (Homer and Anac-
on). 12. *Islands . . . Blest:* Heaven, in Greek myth. 13. *Marathon:*
ene of Greek land victory over Persia. 20. *Salamis:* scene of Greek naval
ctory over Xerxes, the Persian king (19).

5

And where are they? and where art thou,   25
  My country? On thy voiceless shore
The heroic lay is tuneless now—
  The heroic bosom beats no more!
And must thy lyre, so long divine,
Degenerate into hands like mine?   30

6

'Tis something, in the dearth of fame,
  Though linked among a fettered race,
To feel at least a patriot's shame,
  Even as I sing, suffuse my face;
For what is left the poet here?   35
For Greeks a blush—for Greece a tear.

7

Must *we* but weep o'er days more blest?
  Must *we* but blush?—Our fathers bled.
Earth! render back from out thy breast
  A remnant of our Spartan dead!   40
Of the three hundred grant but three,
To make a new Thermopylæ!

8

What, silent still? and silent all?
  Ah! no;—the voices of the dead
Sound like a distant torrent's fall,   45
  And answer, "Let one living head,
But one arise,—we come, we come!"
'Tis but the living who are dumb.

9

In vain—in vain: strike other chords;
  Fill high the cup with Samian wine!   50
Leave battles to the Turkish hordes,
  And shed the blood of Scio's vine!
Hark! rising to the ignoble call—
How answers each bold Bacchanal!

---

42. *Thermopylae:* scene of valiant stand of Spartans against Persians.

10

You have the Pyrrhic dance as yet,   55
   Where is the Pyrrhic phalanx gone?
Of two such lessons, why forget
   The nobler and the manlier one?
You have the letters Cadmus gave—
Think ye he meant them for a slave?   60

11

Fill high the bowl with Samian wine!
   We will not think of themes like these!
It made Anacreon's song divine:
   He served—but served Polycrates—
A tyrant; but our masters then   65
Were still, at least, our countrymen.

12

The tyrant of the Chersonese
   Was freedom's best and bravest friend;
That tyrant was Miltiades!
   Oh! that the present hour would lend   70
Another despot of the kind!
Such chains as his were sure to bind.

13

Fill high the bowl with Samian wine!
   On Suli's rock, and Parga's shore,
Exists the remnant of a line   75
   Such as the Doric mothers bore;
And there, perhaps, some seed is sown,
The Heracleidan blood might own.

14

Trust not for freedom to the Franks—
   They have a king who buys and sells;   80
In native swords, and native ranks,
   The only hope of courage dwells:
But Turkish force, and Latin fraud,
Would break your shield, however broad.

---

55. *Pyrrhic dance:* ancient war dance. 56. *phalanx:* troop formation. 59.
Cadmus: legendary inventor of alphabet. 69. *Miltiades:* Athenian general.
74. *Suli:* (in Albania). *Parga:* (in Turkey). 76. *Doric:* ancient Greek. 78.
Heracleidan: going back to Hercules.

15

Fill high the bowl with Samian wine!   85
  Our virgins dance beneath the shade—
I see their glorious black eyes shine;
  But gazing on each glowing maid,
My own the burning tear-drop laves,
To think such breasts must suckle slaves.   90

16

Place me on Sunium's marbled steep,
  Where nothing, save the waves and I,
May hear our mutual murmurs sweep;
  There, swan-like, let me sing and die:
A land of slaves shall ne'er be mine—   95
Dash down yon cup of Samian wine!

From CHILDE HAROLD'S PILGRIMAGE

CANTO III

(1816)

Waterloo

There was a sound of revelry by night,
And Belgium's Capital had gathered then
Her Beauty and her Chivalry, and bright
The lamps shone o'er fair women and brave men;
A thousand hearts beat happily; and when   5
Music arose with its voluptuous swell,
Soft eyes looked love to eyes which spake again,
And all went merry as a marriage-bell;—
But hush, hark! a deep sound strikes like a rising knell!

Did ye not hear it?—No; 'twas but the wind,   10
Or the car rattling o'er the stony street;
On with the dance! let joy be unconfined;
No sleep till morn, when Youth and Pleasure meet
To chase the glowing Hours with flying feet—
But hark!—that heavy sound breaks in once more,   15

---

91. *Sunium:* cliff near Athens.
    CHILDE HAROLD'S PILGRIMAGE. I. *revelry:* a ball given in Brussels by the
Duchess of Richmond on June 15, 1815.

As if the clouds its echo would repeat;
And nearer, clearer, deadlier than before!
Arm! Arm! it is—it is—the cannon's opening roar!

Within a windowed niche of that high hall
Sate Brunswick's fated chieftain; he did hear   20
That sound the first amidst the festival,
And caught its tone with Death's prophetic ear;
And when they smiled because he deemed it near,
His heart more truly knew that peal too well
Which stretched his father on a bloody bier,   25
And roused the vengeance blood alone could quell:
He rushed into the field, and, foremost fighting, fell.

Ah! then and there was hurrying to and fro,
And gathering tears, and tremblings of distress,
And cheeks all pale, which but an hour ago   30
Blushed at the praise of their own loveliness;
And there were sudden partings, such as press
The life from out young hearts, and choking sighs
Which ne'er might be repeated; who could guess
If ever more should meet those mutual eyes,   35
Since upon night so sweet such awful morn could rise!

And there was mounting in hot haste: the steed,
The mustering squadron, and the clattering car,
Went pouring forward with impetuous speed,
And swiftly forming in the ranks of war;   40
And the deep thunder peal on peal afar;
And near, the beat of the alarming drum
Roused up the soldier ere the morning star;
While thronged the citizens with terror dumb,
Or whispering, with white lips—"The foe! They come! they   45
    come!"

And wild and high the "Cameron's gathering" rose!
The war-note of Lochiel, which Albyn's hills
Have heard, and heard, too, have her Saxon foes:—
How in the noon of night that pibroch thrills,
Savage and shrill! But with the breath which fills   50

---

20. *Brunswick's . . . chieftain:* the Duke of Brunswick. 25. *his father:*
(killed at the battle of Auerbach, 1806). 46. *"Cameron's gathering":* the
clan-song of the Camerons. 47. *Lochiel:* title of Cameron chief. *Albyn:*
Scotland.

Their mountain-pipe, so fill the mountaineers
With the fierce native daring which instils
The stirring memory of a thousand years,
And Evan's, Donald's fame rings in each clansman's ears!

And Ardennes waves above them her green leaves,   55
Dewy with nature's tear-drops, as they pass,
Grieving, if aught inanimate e'er grieves,
Over the unreturning brave,—alas!
Ere evening to be trodden like the grass
Which now beneath them, but above shall grow   60
In its next verdure, when this fiery mass
Of living valour, rolling on the foe
And burning with high hope, shall moulder cold and low.

Last noon beheld them full of lusty life,
Last eve in Beauty's circle proudly gay,   65
The midnight brought the signal-sound of strife,
The morn the marshalling in arms,—the day
Battle's magnificently-stern array!
The thunder-clouds close o'er it, which when rent
The earth is covered thick with other clay,   70
Which her own clay shall cover, heaped and pent,
Rider and horse,—friend, foe,—in one red burial blent!

— Stas. 19-28.

Napoleon

The Psalmist numbered out the years of man:
They are enough, and if thy tale be *true,*
Thou, who didst grudge him even that fleeting span,
More than enough, thou fatal Waterloo!
Millions of tongues record thee, and anew   5
Their children's lips shall echo them, and say—
"Here, where the sword united nations drew,
Our contrymen were warring on that day!"
And this is much, and all which will not pass away.

There sunk the greatest, nor the worst of men,   10
Whose spirit antithetically mixt

54. *Evan, Donald:* former Cameron chiefs (died fighting the English).
55. *Ardennes:* (forest).
    1. *numbered:* "The days of our years are three-score years and ten."—
Psalms xc: 10.

One moment of the mightiest, and again
On little objects with like firmness fixt,
Extreme in all things! hadst thou been betwixt,
Thy throne had still been thine, or never been;   15
For daring made thy rise as fall: thou seek'st
Even now to re-assume the imperial mien,
And shake again the world, the Thunderer of the scene!

Conqueror and captive of the earth art thou!
She trembles at thee still, and thy wild name   20
Was ne'er more bruited in men's minds than now
That thou art nothing, save the jest of Fame,
Who wooed thee once, thy vassal, and became
The flatterer of thy fierceness, till thou wert
A god unto thyself; nor less the same   25
To the astounded kingdoms all inert,
Who deemed thee for a time whate'er thou didst assert.

Oh, more or less than man—in high or low,
Battling with nations, flying from the field;
Now making monarchs' necks thy footstool, now   30
More than thy meanest soldier taught to yield;
An empire thou couldst crush, command, rebuild,
But govern not thy pettiest passion, nor,
However deeply in men's spirits skilled,
Look through thine own, nor curb the lust of war,   35
Nor learn that tempted Fate will leave the loftiest star.

Yet well thy soul hath brooked the turning tide
With that untaught innate philosophy,
Which, be it wisdom, coldness, or deep pride,
Is gall and wormwood to an enemy.   40
When the whole host of hatred stood hard by,
To watch and mock thee shrinking, thou hast smiled
With a sedate and all-enduring eye;—
When Fortune fled her spoiled and favourite child,
He stood unbowed beneath the ills upon him piled.   45

Sager than in thy fortunes; for in them
Ambition steeled thee on too far to show
That just habitual scorn, which could contemn
Men and their thoughts; 'twas wise to feel, not so
To wear it ever on thy lip and brow,   50
And spurn the instruments thou wert to use

Till they were turned unto thine overthrow:
'Tis but a worthless world to win or lose;
So hath it proved to thee and all such lot who choose.

If, like a tower upon a headlong rock,   55
Thou hadst been made to stand or fall alone,
Such scorn of man had helped to brave the shock;
But men's thoughts were the steps which paved thy throne,
Their admiration thy best weapon shone;
The part of Philip's son was thine, not then   60
(Unless aside thy purple had been thrown)
Like stern Diogenes to mock at men;
For sceptred cynics earth were far too wide a den.

But quiet to quick bosoms is a hell,
And *there* hath been thy bane; there is a fire   65
And motion of the soul which will not dwell
In its own narrow being, but aspire
Beyond the fitting medium of desire;
And, but once kindled, quenchless evermore,
Preys upon high adventure, nor can tire   70
Of aught but rest; a fever at the core,
Fatal to him who bears, to all who ever bore.

This makes the madmen who have made men mad
By their contagion; Conquerors and Kings,
Founders of sects and systems, to whom add   75
Sophists, Bards, Statesmen, all unquiet things
Which stir too strongly the soul's secret springs,
And are themselves the fools to those they fool;
Envied, yet how unenviable! what stings
Are theirs! One breast laid open were a school   80
Which would unteach mankind the lust to shine or rule.

Their breath is agitation, and their life
A storm whereon they ride, to sink at last;
And yet so nursed and bigoted to strife,
That should their days, surviving perils past,   85
Melt to calm twilight, they feel overcast
With sorrow and supineness, and so die;
Even as a flame unfed which runs to waste

---

60. *part . . . son:* (the noble generosity of Alexander the Great). 62. *Diogenes:* Greek philosopher contemporary with Alexander.

With its own flickering, or a sword laid by,
Which eats into itself and rusts ingloriously.   90

He who ascends to mountain-tops, shall find
The loftiest peaks most wrapt in clouds and snow;
He who surpasses or subdues mankind,
Must look down on the hate of those below.
Though high *above* the sun of glory glow,   95
And far *beneath* the earth and ocean spread,
Round him are icy rocks, and loudly blow
Contending tempests on his naked head,
And thus reward the toils which to those summits led.

— stas. 35-45

Rousseau

Here the self-torturing sophist, wild Rousseau,
The apostle of affliction, he who threw
Enchantment over passion, and from woe
Wrung overwhelming eloquence, first drew
The breath which made him wretched; yet he knew   5
How to make madness beautiful, and cast
O'er erring deeds and thoughts a heavenly hue
Of words, like sunbeams, dazzling as they past
The eyes, which o'er them shed tears feelingly and fast.

His love was passion's essence—as a tree   10
On fire by lightning; with ethereal flame
Kindled he was, and blasted; for to be
Thus, and enamoured, were in him the same.
But his was not the love of living dame,
Nor of the dead who rise upon our dreams,   15
But of ideal beauty, which became
In him existence, and o'erflowing teems
Along his burning page, distempered though it seems.

This breathed itself to life in Julie, *this*
Invested her with all that's wild and sweet;   20
This hallowed, too, the memorable kiss
Which every morn his fevered lip would greet,
From hers who but with friendship his would meet;

---

1. *Here:* (in Switzerland). 19. *Julie:* a countess who inspired in Rousseau
emotions described in his *Confessions* [Book ix].

But to that gentle touch, through brain and breast
Flashed the thrilled spirit's love-devouring heat;   25
In that absorbing sigh perchance more blest
Than vulgar minds may be with all they seek possest.

His life was one long war with self-sought foes,
Or friends by him self-banished; for his mind
Had grown Suspicion's sanctuary, and chose,   30
For its own cruel sacrifice, the kind
'Gainst whom he raged with fury strange and blind.
But he was phrensied,—wherefore, who may know?
Since cause might be which skill could never find;
But he was phrensied by disease or woe   35
To that worst pitch of all, which wears a reasoning show.

For then he was inspired, and from him came,
As from the Pythian's mystic cave of yore,
Those oracles which set the world in flame,
Nor ceased to burn till kingdoms were no more: 40
Did he not this for France? which lay before
Bowed to the inborn tyranny of years?
Broken and trembling to the yoke she bore,
Till by the voice of him and his compeers
Roused up to too much wrath, which follows o'ergrown fears?   45

They made themselves a fearful monument!
The wreck of old opinions—things which grew,
Breathed from the birth of time: the veil they rent,
And what behind it lay, all earth shall view.
But good with ill they also overthrew,   50
Leaving but ruins, wherewith to rebuild
Upon the same foundation, and renew
Dungeons and thrones, which the same hour re-filled
As heretofore, because ambition was self-willed.

But this will not endure, nor be endured!   55
Mankind have felt their strength, and made it felt.
They might have used it better, but, allured
By their new vigour, sternly have they dealt
On one another; pity ceased to melt
With her once natural charities. But they,   60
Who in oppression's darkness caved had dwelt,
They were not eagles, nourished with the day;
What marvel then, at times, if they mistook their prey?

---

38. *Pythian:* priestess of Apollo at Delphi. 39. *oracles:* Rousseau's political
tracts, such as *Le Contrat Social* (1762).

What deep wounds ever closed without a scar?
The heart's bleed longest, and but heal to wear   65
That which disfigures it; and they who war
With their own hopes, and have been vanquished, bear
Silence, but not submission. In his lair
Fixed Passion holds his breath, until the hour
Which shall atone for years; none need despair: 70
It came, it cometh, and will come,—the power
To punish or forgive—in *one* we shall be slower.
                                        — Stanzas 77-84.

Voltaire and Gibbon

Lausanne! and Ferney! ye have been the abodes
Of names which unto you bequeathed a name;
Mortals, who sought and found, by dangerous roads
A path to perpetuity of fame:
They were gigantic minds, and their steep aim   5
Was, Titan-like, on daring doubts to pile
Thoughts which should call down thunder, and the flame
Of Heaven, again assailed, if Heaven the while
On man and man's research could deign do more than smile.

The one was fire and fickleness, a child,   10
Most mutable in wishes, but in mind
A wit as various,—gay, grave, sage, or wild,—
Historian, bard, philosopher, combined;
He multiplied himself among mankind,
The Proteus of their talents: but his own   15
Breathed most in ridicule,—which, as the wind,
Blew where it listed, laying all things prone,—
Now to o'erthrow a fool, and now to shake a throne.

The other, deep and slow, exhausting thought,
And hiving wisdom with each studious year,   20
In meditation dwelt, with learning wrought,
And shaped his weapon with an edge severe,
Sapping a solemn creed with solemn sneer;
The lord of irony,—that master-spell,
Which stung his foes to wrath which grew from fear,   25
And doomed him to the zealot's ready Hell,
Which answers to all doubts so eloquently well.

1. *Lausanne:* where Gibbon completed his *Decline and Fall of the Roman Empire. Ferney:* Swiss village founded by Voltaire. 10. *one:* Voltaire. 15. *Proteus:* multi-formed sea-god in Homer.

Yet, peace be with their ashes,—for by them,
If merited, the penalty is paid;
It is not ours to judge,—far less condemn;   30
The hour must come when such things shall be made
Known unto all,—or hope and dread allayed
By slumber, on one pillow,—in the dust,
Which, thus much we are sure, must lie decayed;
And when it shall revive, as is our trust,   35
'Twill be to be forgiven, or suffer what is just.

                                            — stas. 105-109.

CANTO IV
(1818)
Ocean

There is a pleasure in the pathless woods,
There is a rapture on the lonely shore,
There is a society where none intrudes,
By the deep Sea, and music in its roar:
I love not Man the less, but Nature more,   5
From these our interviews, in which I steal
From all I may be, or have been before,
To mingle with the Universe, and feel
What I can ne'er express, yet can not all conceal.

Roll on, thou deep and dark blue Ocean—roll!   10
Ten thousand fleets sweep over thee in vain;
Man marks the earth with ruin—his control
Stops with the shore;—upon the watery plain
The wrecks are all thy deed, nor doth remain
A shadow of man's ravage, save his own,   15
When, for a moment, like a drop of rain,
He sinks into thy depths with bubbling groan,
Without a grave, unknelled, uncoffined, and unknown.

His steps are not upon thy paths,—thy fields
Are not a spoil for him,—thou dost arise   20
And shake him from thee; the vile strength he wields
For earth's destruction thou dost all despise,

---

23. *Sapping . . . creed:* refers to Gibbon's treatment of Christianity in his
history.

Spurning him from thy bosom to the skies,
And send'st him, shivering in thy playful spray
And howling, to his Gods, where haply lies   25
His petty hope in some near port or bay,
And dashest him again to earth:—there let him lay.

The armaments which thunderstrike the walls
Of rock-built cities, bidding nations quake
And monarchs tremble in their capitals,   30
The oak leviathans, whose huge ribs make
Their clay creator the vain title take
Of lord of thee, and arbiter of war,—
These are thy toys, and, as the snowy flake,
They melt into thy yeast of waves, which mar   35
Alike the Armada's pride or spoils of Trafalgar.

Thy shores are empires, changed in all save thee—
Assyria, Greece, Rome, Carthage, what are they?
Thy waters washed them power while they were free,
And many a tyrant since; their shores obey   40
The stranger, slave, or savage; their decay
Has dried up realms to deserts:—not so thou,
Unchangeable save to thy wild waves' play;
Time writes no wrinkle on thine azure brow—
Such as creation's dawn beheld, thou rollest now.   45

Thou glorious mirror, where the Almighty's form
Glasses itself in tempests; in all time,
Calm or convulsed—in breeze, or gale, or storm,
Icing the pole, or in the torrid clime
Dark-heaving;—boundless, endless, and sublime—   50
The image of Eternity—the throne
Of the Invisible; even from out thy slime
The monsters of the deep are made; each zone
Obeys thee; thou goest forth, dread, fathomless, alone.

And I have loved thee, Ocean! and my joy   55
Of youthful sports was on thy breast to be
Borne, like thy bubbles, onward: from a boy
I wantoned with thy breakers—they to me
Were a delight; and if the freshening sea
Made them a terror—'twas a pleasing fear,   60
For I was as it were a child of thee,
And trusted to thy billows far and near,
And laid my hand upon thy mane—as I do here.
                                    —stas. 178-184.

DON JUAN
(1819)
FRAGMENT
On the back of the Poet's Ms. of Canto I

I would to heaven that I were so much clay,
    As I am blood, bone, marrow, passion, feeling—
Because at least the past were passed away—
    And for the future—(but I write this reeling,
Having got drunk exceedingly to-day,   5
    So that I seem to stand upon the ceiling)
I say—the future is a serious matter—
And so—for God's sake—hock and soda-water!

CANTO THE FIRST

I want a hero: an uncommon want,
    When every year and month sends forth a new one,
Till, after cloying the gazettes with cant,
    The age discovers he is not the true one;
Of such as these I should not care to vaunt,   5
    I'll therefore take our ancient friend Don Juan—
We all have seen him, in the pantomime,
Sent to the devil somewhat ere his time.

Vernon, the butcher Cumberland, Wolfe, Hawke,
    Prince Ferdinand, Granby, Burgoyne, Keppel, Howe,   10
Evil and good, have had their tithe of talk,
    And filled their sign-posts then, like Wellesley now;
Each in their turn like Banquo's monarchs stalk,
    Followers of fame, "nine farrow" of that sow:
France, too, had Buonaparté and Dumourier   15
Recorded in the Moniteur and Courier.

DON JUAN: 9-10. *Vernon . . . Howe:* British military and naval men;
except for Ferdinand, anti-Napoleonic Prince of Naples. 11. *Wellesley:* the
Duke of Wellington. 13. *Banquo:* (in *Macbeth*). 15. *Dumourier:* French
revolutionary general.

Barnave, Brissot, Condorcet, Mirabeau,
  Pétion, Clootz, Danton, Marat, La Fayette,
Were French, and famous people, as we know;
  And there were others, scarce forgotten yet,   20
Joubert, Hoche, Marceau, Lannes, Desaix, Moreau,
  With many of the military set,
Exceedingly remarkable at times,
But not at all adapted to my rhymes.

Nelson was once Britannia's god of war,   25
  And still should be so, but the tide is turned;
There's no more to be said of Trafalgar,
  'Tis with our hero quietly inurned;
Because the army's grown more popular,
  At which the naval people are concerned,   30
Besides, the prince is all for the land-service,
Forgetting Duncan, Nelson, Howe, and Jervis.

Brave men were living before Agamemnon
  And since, exceeding valorous and sage,
A good deal like him too, though quite the same none; 35
  But then they shone not on the poet's page,
And so have been forgotten:—I condemn none,
  But can't find any in the present age
Fit for my poem (that is, for my new one);
So, as I said, I'll take my friend Don Juan.   40

Most epic poets plunge "in medias res"
  (Horace makes this the heroic turnpike road),
And then your hero tells, whene'er you please,
  What went before—by way of episode,
While seated after dinner at his ease,   45
  Beside his mistress in some soft abode,
Palace, or garden, paradise, or cavern,
Which serves the happy couple for a tavern.

That is the usual method, but not mine—
  My way is to begin with the beginning;   50
The regularity of my design
  Forbids all wandering as the worst of sinning,

17-18. *Barnave . . . La Fayette:* orators and political leaders of the French Revolution. 21. *Joubert . . . Moreau:* generals of the revolutionary and Napoleonic era. 25. *Nelson:* beat French at naval battle of Trafalgar. 32. *Duncan . . . Jervis:* (admirals). 33. *Agamemnon:* commander of the Greek expedition against Troy. 41. *in medias res:* into the midst of the story.

And therefore I shall open with a line
  (Although it cost me half an hour in spinning)
Narrating somewhat of Don Juan's father,   55
And also of his mother, if you'd rather.

. . . .

Dying intestate, Juan was sole heir
  To a chancery suit, and messuages, and lands,   290
Which, with a long minority and care,
  Promised to turn out well in proper hands:
Inez became sole guardian, which was fair,
  And answered but to nature's just demands;
An only son left with an only mother   295
Is brought up much more wisely than another.

Sagest of women, even of widows, she
  Resolved that Juan should be quite a paragon,
And worthy of the noblest pedigree:
  (His sire was of Castile, his dam from Aragon).   300
Then for accomplishments of chivalry,
  In case our lord the king should go to war again,
He learned the arts of riding, fencing, gunnery,
And how to scale a fortress—or a nunnery.

But that which Donna Inez most desired,   305
  And saw into herself each day before all
The learned tutors whom for him she hired,
  Was, that his breeding should be strictly moral:
Much into all his studies she inquired,
  And so they were submitted first to her, all,   310
Arts, sciences, no branch was made a mystery
To Juan's eyes, excepting natural history.

The languages, especially the dead,
  The sciences, and most of all the abstruse,
The arts, at least all such as could be said   315
  To be the most remote from common use,
In all these he was much and deeply read;
  But not a page of anything that's loose,
Or hints continuation of the species,
Was ever suffered, lest he should grow vicious.   320

---

56. Lines 57-288, omitted here, give satiric character-sketches of Juan's parents, and conclude with an account of the death of his father, Don José. 293. *Inez:* Juan's mother.

His classic studies made a little puzzle,
  Because of filthy loves of gods and goddesses,
Who in the earlier ages raised a bustle,
  But never put on pantaloons or bodices;
His reverend tutors had at times a tussle,   325
  And for their Æneids, Iliads, and Odysseys,
Were forced to make an odd sort of apology,
For Donna Inez dreaded the Mythology.

Ovid's a rake, as half his verses show him,
  Anacreon's morals are a still worse sample,   330
Catullus scarcely has a decent poem,
  I don't think Sappho's Ode a good example,
Although Longinus tells us there is no hymn
  Where the sublime soars forth on wings more ample;
But Virgil's songs are pure, except that horrid one   335
Beginning with "Formosum Pastor Corydon."

Lucretius' irreligion is too strong
  For early stomachs, to prove wholesome food;
I can't help thinking Juvenal was wrong,
  Although no doubt his real intent was good,   340
For speaking out so plainly in his song,
  So much indeed as to be downright rude;
And then what proper person can be partial
To all those nauseous epigrams of Martial?

Juan was taught from out the best edition,   345
  Expurgated by learned men, who place,
Judiciously, from out the schoolboy's vision,
  The grosser parts; but, fearful to deface
Too much their modest bard by this omission,
  And pitying sore this mutilated case,   350
They only add them all in an appendix,
Which saves, in fact, the trouble of an index;

For there we have them all "at one fell swoop,"
  Instead of being scattered through the pages;
They stand forth marshalled in a handsome troop,   355
  To meet the ingenuous youth of future ages,
Till some less rigid editor shall stoop
  To call them back into their separate cages,
Instead of standing staring all together,
Like garden gods—and not so decent either.   360

---

335. *horrid:* (because homosexual).

The Missal too (it was the family Missal)
  Was ornamented in a sort of way
Which ancient mass-books often are, and this all
  Kinds of grotesques illumined; and how they,
Who saw those figures on the margin kiss all,   365
  Could turn their optics to the text and pray,
Is more than I know— But Don Juan's mother
Kept this herself, and gave her son another.

Sermons he read, and lectures he endured,
  And homilies, and lives of all the saints;   370
To Jerome and to Chrysostom inured,
  He did not take such studies for restraints;
But how faith is acquired, and then ensured,
  So well not one of the aforesaid paints
As Saint Augustine in his fine Confessions,   375
Which make the reader envy his transgressions.

This, too, was a sealed book to little Juan—
  I can't but say that his mamma was right,
If such an education was the true one.
  She scarcely trusted him from out her sight;   380
Her maids were old, and if she took a new one,
  You might be sure she was a perfect fright;
She did this during even her husband's life—
I recommend as much to every wife.

Young Juan waxed in godliness and grace;   385
  At six a charming child, and at eleven
With all the promise of as fine a face
  As e'er to man's maturer growth was given:
He studied steadily and grew apace,
  And seemed, at least, in the right road to heaven,   390
For half his days were passed at church, the other
Between his tutors, confessor, and mother.

At six, I said, he was a charming child,
  At twelve he was a fine, but quiet boy;
Although in infancy a little wild,   395
  They tamed him down amongst them: to destroy
His natural spirit not in vain they toiled.
  At least it seemed so; and his mother's joy

---

371. *Jerome, Chrysostom:* early (Latin, Greek) church fathers.

Was to declare how sage, and still, and steady,
Her young philosopher was grown already.   400

I had my doubts, perhaps I have them still
    But what I say is neither here nor there:
I knew his father well, and have some skill
    In character—but it would not be fair
From sire to son to augur good or ill: 405
    He and his wife were an ill sorted pair—
But scandal's my aversion—I protest
Against all evil speaking, even in jest.

For my part I say nothing—nothing—but
    This I will say—my reasons are my own—   410
That if I had an only son to put
    To school (as God be praised that I have none),
'Tis not with Donna Inez I would shut
    Him up to learn his catechism alone,
No—no—I'd send him out betimes to college,   415
For there it was I picked up my own knowledge.

For there one learns—'tis not for me to boast,
    Though I acquired—but I pass over *that,*
As well as all the Greek I since have lost:
    I say that there's the place—but *"Verbum sat,"*   420
I think I picked up too, as well as most,
    Knowledge of matters—but no matter *what*—
I never married—but, I think, I know
That sons should not be educated so.

Young Juan now was sixteen years of age,   425
    Tall, handsome, slender, but well knit: he seemed
Active, though not so sprightly, as a page;
    And everybody but his mother deemed
Him almost man; but she flew in a rage
    And bit her lips (for else she might have screamed)   430
If any said so, for to be precocious
Was in her eyes a thing the most atrocious.

Amongst her numerous acquaintance, all
    Selected for discretion and devotion,
There was the Donna Julia, whom to call   435
    Pretty were but to give a feeble notion
Of many charms in her as natural

---

420. *Verbum sat:* i.e., *verbum sat(is) sapienti:* a word to the wise is enough.

As sweetness to the flower, or salt to ocean,
Her zone to Venus, or his bow to Cupid,
(But this last simile is trite and stupid).   440

The darkness of her Oriental eye
    Accorded with her Moorish origin;
(Her blood was not all Spanish, by the by;
    In Spain, you know, this is a sort of sin).
When proud Granada fell, and, forced to fly,   445
    Boabdil wept, of Donna Julia's kin
Some went to Africa, some stayed in Spain,
Her great great grandmamma chose to remain.

She married (I forget the pedigree)
    With an Hidalgo, who transmitted down   450
His blood less noble than such blood should be;
    At such alliances his sires would frown,
In that point so precise in each degree
    That they bred *in and in,* as might be shown,
Marrying their cousins—nay, their aunts, and nieces,   455
Which always spoils the breed, if it increases.

This heathenish cross restored the breed again,
    Ruined its blood, but much improved its flesh;
For from a root the ugliest in old Spain
    Sprung up a branch as beautiful as fresh;   460
The sons no more were short, the daughters plain:
    But there's a rumour which I fain would hush,
'Tis said that Donna Julia's grandmamma
Produced her Don more heirs at love than law.

However this might be, the race went on   465
    Improving still through every generation,
Until it centred in an only son,
    Who left an only daughter: my narration
May have suggested that this single one
    Could be but Julia (whom on this occasion   470
I shall have much to speak about), and she
Was married, charming, chaste, and twenty-three.

Her eye (I'm very fond of handsome eyes)
    Was large and dark, suppressing half its fire
Until she spoke, then through its soft disguise   475

---

446. *Boabdil:* last Moorish king of Granada (ca. 1500). 450. *Hidalgo:* minor
nobleman.

Flashed an expression more of pride than ire,
And love than either; and there would arise
A something in them which was not desire,
But would have been, perhaps, but for the soul
Which struggled through and chastened down the whole.   480

Her glossy hair was clustered o'er a brow
    Bright with intelligence, and fair, and smooth;
Her eyebrow's shape was like the aërial bow,
    Her cheek all purple with the beam of youth,
Mounting, at times, to a transparent glow,   485
    As if her veins ran lightning; she, in sooth,
Possessed an air and grace by no means common:
Her stature tall—I hate a dumpy woman.

Wedded she was some years, and to a man
    Of fifty, and such husbands are in plenty;   490
And yet, I think, instead of such a ONE
    'Twere better to have TWO of five-and-twenty,
Especially in countries near the sun:
    And now I think on't, "mi vien in mente,"
Ladies even of the most uneasy virtue   495
Prefer a spouse whose age is short of thirty.

'Tis a sad thing, I cannot choose but say,
    And all the fault of that indecent sun,
Who cannot leave alone our helpless clay,
    But will keep baking, broiling, burning on,   500
That howsoever people fast and pray,
    The flesh is frail, and so the soul undone:
What men call gallantry, and gods adultery,
Is much more common where the climate's sultry.

Happy the nations of the moral North!   505
    Where all is virtue, and the winter season
Sends sin, without a rag on, shivering forth
    ('Twas snow that brought St. Anthony to reason);
Where juries cast up what a wife is worth,
    By laying whate'er sum, in mulct, they please on   510
The lover, who must pay a handsome price,
Because it is a marketable vice.

Alfonso was the name of Julia's lord,
    A man well looking for his years, and who

---

493. *mi . . . mente:* it occurs to me. 508. *St. Anthony:* fourth-century
Egyptian hermit, father of Christian monasticism.

Was neither much beloved nor yet abhorred: 515
　　They lived together as most people do,
Suffering each other's foibles by accord,
　　And not exactly either *one* or *two;*
Yet he was jealous, though he did not show it,
For jealousy dislikes the world to know it.   520

Julia was—yet I never could see why—
　　With Donna Inez quite a favourite friend;
Between their tastes there was small sympathy,
　　For not a line had Julia ever penned:
Some people whisper (but, no doubt, they lie,   525
　　For malice still imputes some private end)
That Inez had, ere Don Alfonso's marriage,
Forgot with him her very prudent carriage;

And that still keeping up the old connexion,
　　Which time had lately rendered much more chaste,   530
She took his lady also in affection,
　　And certainly this course was much the best:
She flattered Julia with her sage protection,
　　And complimented Don Alfonso's taste;
And if she could not (who can?) silence scandal,   535
At least she left it a more slender handle.

I can't tell whether Julia saw the affair
　　With other people's eyes, or if her own
Discoveries made, but none could be aware
　　Of this, at least no symptom e'er was shown;   540
Perhaps she did not know, or did not care,
　　Indifferent from the first, or callous grown:
I'm really puzzled what to think or say,
She kept her counsel in so close a way.

Juan she saw, and, as a pretty child,   545
　　Caressed him often—such a thing might be
Quite innocently done, and harmless styled,
　　When she had twenty years, and thirteen he;
But I am not so sure I should have smiled
　　When he was sixteen, Julia twenty-three;   550
These few short years make wondrous alterations,
Particularly amongst sun-burnt nations.

Whate'er the cause might be, they had become
　　Changed; for the dame grew distant, the youth shy,

Their looks cast down, their greetings almost dumb,   555
  And much embarrassment in either eye;
There surely will be little doubt with some
  That Donna Julia knew the reason why,
But as for Juan, he had no more notion
Than he who never saw the sea of ocean.   560

Yet Julia's very coldness still was kind,
  And tremulously gentle her small hand
Withdrew itself from his, but left behind
  A little pressure, thrilling, and so bland
And slight, so very slight, that to the mind   565
  'Twas but a doubt; but ne'er magician's wand
Wrought change with all Armida's fairy art
Like what this light touch left on Juan's heart.

And if she met him, though she smiled no more,
  She looked a sadness sweeter than her smile,   570
As if her heart had deeper thoughts in store
  She must not own, but cherished more the while
For that compression in its burning core;
  Even innocence itself has many a wile,
And will not dare to trust itself with truth,   575
And love is taught hypocrisy from youth.

But passion most dissembles, yet betrays
  Even by its darkness; as the blackest sky
Foretells the heaviest tempest, it displays
  Its workings through the vainly guarded eye,   580
And in whatever aspect it arrays
  Itself, 'tis still the same hypocrisy;
Coldness or anger, even disdain or hate,
Are masks it often wears, and still too late.

Then there were sighs, the deeper for suppression,   585
  And stolen glances, sweeter for the theft,
And burning blushes, though for no transgression,
  Tremblings when met, and restlessness when left;
All these are little preludes to possession,
  Of which young passion cannot be bereft,   590
And merely tend to show how greatly love is
Embarrassed at first starting with a novice.

------

567. *Armida*: Damascan sorceress in Tasso's epic *Jerusalem Delivered;* she
enchants the Christian hero Rinaldo.

Poor Julia's heart was in an awkward state;
  She felt it going, and resolved to make
The noblest efforts for herself and mate,   595
  For honour's, pride's, religion's, virtue's sake.
Her resolutions were most truly great,
  And almost might have made a Tarquin quake:
She prayed the Virgin Mary for her grace,
As being the best judge of a lady's case.   600

She vowed she never would see Juan more,
  And next day paid a visit to his mother,
And looked extremely at the opening door,
  Which, by the Virgin's grace, let in another;
Grateful she was, and yet a little sore—   605
  Again it opens, it can be no other,
'Tis surely Juan now— No! I'm afraid
That night the Virgin was no further prayed.

She now determined that a virtuous woman
  Should rather face and overcome temptation,   610
That flight was base and dastardly, and no man
  Should ever give her heart the least sensation;
That is to say, a thought beyond the common
  Preference, that we must feel upon occasion,
For people who are pleasanter than others,   615
But then they only seem so many brothers.

And even if by chance—and who can tell?
  The devil's so very sly—she should discover
That all within was not so very well,
  And, if still free, that such or such a lover   620
Might please perhaps, a virtuous wife can quell
  Such thoughts, and be the better when they're over;
And if the man should ask, 'tis but denial:
I recommend young ladies to make trial.

And then there are such things as love divine,   625
  Bright and immaculate, unmix'd and pure,
Such as the angels think so very fine,
  And matrons, who would be no less secure,
Platonic, perfect, "just such love as mine:"
  Thus Julia said—and thought so, to be sure;   630

---

598. *Tarquin:* Roman despot who raped the matron Lucretia.

And so I'd have her think, were I the man
On whom her reveries celestial ran.

Such love is innocent, and may exist
    Between young persons without any danger.
A hand may first, and then a lip be kist;   635
    For my part, to such doings I'm a stranger,
But *hear* these freedoms form the utmost list
    Of all o'er which such love may be a ranger:
If people go beyond, 'tis quite a crime,
But not my fault—I tell them all in time.   640

Love, then, but love within its proper limits,
    Was Julia's innocent determination
In young Don Juan's favour, and to him its
    Exertion might be useful on occasion;
And, lighted at too pure a shrine to dim its   645
    Ethereal lustre, with what sweet persuasion
He might be taught, by love and her together—
I really don't know what, nor Julia either.

Fraught with this fine intention, and well fenced
    In mail of proof—her purity of soul,   650
She, for the future of her strength convinced,
    And that her honour was a rock, or mole,
Exceeding sagely from that hour dispensed
    With any kind of troublesome control;
But whether Julia to the task was equal   655
Is that which must be mentioned in the sequel.

Her plan she deemed both innocent and feasible,
    And, surely, with a stripling of sixteen
Not scandal's fangs could fix on much that's seizable,
    Or if they did so, satisfied to mean   660
Nothing but what was good, her breast was peaceable:
    A quiet conscience makes one so serene!
Christians have burnt each other, quite persuaded
That all the Apostles would have done as they did.

And if in the mean time her husband died,   665
    But Heaven forbid that such a thought should cross
Her brain, though in a dream! (and then she sigh'd)
    Never could she survive that common loss;
But just suppose that moment should betide,

I only say suppose it—*inter nos*.   670
(This should be *entre nous*, for Julia thought
In French, but then the rhyme would go for nought.)

I only say, suppose this supposition:
    Juan being then grown up to man's estate
Would fully suit a widow of condition,   675
    Even seven years hence it would not be too late;
And in the interim (to pursue this vision)
    The mischief, after all, could not be great,
For he would learn the rudiments of love,
I mean the seraph way of those above.   680

So much for Julia. Now we'll turn to Juan.
    Poor little fellow! he had no idea
Of his own case, and never hit the true one;
    In feelings quick as Ovid's Miss Medea,
He puzzled over what he found a new one,   685
    But not as yet imagined it could be a
Thing quite in course, and not at all alarming,
Which, with a little patience, might grow charming.

Silent and pensive, idle, restless, slow,
    His home deserted for the lonely wood,   690
Tormented with a wound he could not know,
    His, like all deep grief, plunged in solitude:
I'm fond myself of solitude or so,
    But then, I beg it may be understood,
By solitude I mean a Sultan's, not   695
A hermit's, with a haram for a grot.

"Oh Love! in such a wilderness as this,
    Where transport and security entwine,
Here is the empire of thy perfect bliss,
    And here thou art a god indeed divine."   700
The bard I quote from does not sing amiss,
    With the exception of the second line,
For that same twining "transport and security"
Are twisted to a phrase of some obscurity.

The poet meant, no doubt, and thus appeals   705
    To the good sense and senses of mankind,

---

670. *inter nos:* among ourselves. 684. *Medea:* passionate mistress of Greek
legendary hero Jason.

The very thing which everybody feels,
　As all have found on trial, or may find,
That no one likes to be disturbed at meals
　Or love.—I won't say more about "entwined"　　　　710
Or "transport," as we knew all that before,
But beg "Security" will bolt the door.

Young Juan wandered by the glassy brooks,
　Thinking unutterable things; he threw
Himself at length within the leafy nooks　　　　715
　Where the wild branch of the cork forest grew;
There poets find materials for their books,
　And every now and then we read them through,
So that their plan and prosody are eligible,
Unless, like Wordsworth, they prove unintelligible.　　　　720

He, Juan (and not Wordsworth), so pursued
　His self-communion with his own high soul,
Until his mighty heart, in its great mood,
　Had mitigated part, though not the whole
Of its disease; he did the best he could　　　　725
　With things not very subject to control,
And turned, without perceiving his condition,
Like Coleridge, into a metaphysician.

He thought about himself, and the whole earth,
　Of man the wonderful, and of the stars,　　　　730
And how the deuce they ever could have birth;
　And then he thought of earthquakes, and of wars,
How many miles the moon might have in girth,
　Of air-balloons, and of the many bars
To perfect knowledge of the boundless skies;—　　　　735
And then he thought of Donna Julia's eyes.

In thoughts like these true wisdom may discern
　Longings sublime, and aspirations high,
Which some are born with, but the most part learn
　To plague themselves withal, they know not why:　　　　740
'Twas strange that one so young should thus concern
　His brain about the action of the sky;
If *you* think 'twas philosophy that this did,
I can't help thinking puberty assisted.

He pored upon the leaves, and on the flowers,　　　　745
　And heard a voice in all the winds; and then

He thought of wood-nymphs and immortal bowers,
  And how the goddesses came down to men:
He missed the pathway, he forgot the hours,
  And when he looked upon his watch again,   750
He found how much old Time had been a winner—
He also found that he had lost his dinner.

Sometimes he turned to gaze upon his book,
  Boscan, or Garcilasso;—by the wind
Even as the page is rustled while we look,   755
  So by the poesy of his own mind
Over the mystic leaf his soul was shook,
  As if 'twere one whereon magicians bind
Their spells, and give them to the passing gale
According to some good old woman's tale.   760

Thus would he while his lonely hours away
  Dissatisfied, nor knowing what he wanted;
Nor glowing reverie, nor poet's lay,
  Could yield his spirit that for which it panted,
A bosom whereon he his head might lay,   765
  And hear the heart beat with the love it granted,
With——several other things, which I forget,
Or which, at least, I need not mention yet.

Those lonely walks, and lengthening reveries,
  Could not escape the gentle Julia's eyes;   770
She saw that Juan was not at his ease;
  But that which chiefly may, and must surprise,
Is, that the Donna Inez did not tease
  Her only son with question or surmise;
Whether it was she did not see, or would not,   775
Or, like all very clever people, could not.

This may seem strange, but yet 'tis very common;
  For instance—gentlemen, whose ladies take
Leave to o'erstep the written rights of woman,
  And break the—— Which commandment is't they break?   780
(I have forgot the number, and think no man
  Should rashly quote, for fear of a mistake.)
I say, when these same gentlemen are jealous,
They make some blunder, which their ladies tell us.

754. *Boscan, Garcilasso:* Spanish Renaissance poets.

A real husband always is suspicious,   785
  But still no less suspects in the wrong place,
Jealous of some one who had no such wishes,
  Or pandering blindly to his own disgrace,
By harbouring some dear friend extremely vicious;
  The last indeed's infallibly the case: 790
And when the spouse and friend are gone off wholly,
He wonders at their vice, and not his folly.

Thus parents also are at times short-sighted;
  Though watchful as the lynx, they ne'er discover,
The while the wicked world beholds delighted,   795
  Young Hopeful's mistress, or Miss Fanny's lover,
Till some confounded escapade has blighted
  The plan of twenty years, and all is over;
And then the mother cries, the father swears,
And wonders why the devil he got heirs.   800

But Inez was so anxious, and so clear
  Of sight, that I must think, on this occasion,
She had some other motive much more near
  For leaving Juan to this new temptation;
But what that motive was, I shan't say here;   805
  Perhaps to finish Juan's education,
Perhaps to open Don Alfonso's eyes,
In case he thought his wife too great a prize.

It was upon a day, a summer's day;—
  Summer's indeed a very dangerous season,   810
And so is spring about the end of May;
  The sun, no doubt, is the prevailing reason;
But whatsoe'er the cause is, one may say,
  And stand convicted of more truth than treason,
That there are months which nature grows more merry in,—   815
March has its hares, and May must have its heroine.

'Twas on a summer's day—the sixth of June:—
  I like to be particular in dates,
Not only of the age, and year, but moon;
  They are a sort of post-house, where the Fates   820
Change horses, making history change its tune,
  Then spur away o'er empires and o'er states,
Leaving at last not much besides chronology,
Excepting the post-obits of theology.

---

824. *post-obits:* promises-to-pay.

'Twas on the sixth of June, about the hour   825
  Of half-past six—perhaps still nearer seven—
When Julia sate within as pretty a bower
  As e'er held houri in that heathenish heaven
Described by Mahomet, and Anacreon Moore,
  To whom the lyre and laurels have been given,   830
With all the trophies of triumphant song—
He won them well, and may he wear them long!

She sate, but not alone; I know not well
  How this same interview had taken place,
And even if I knew, I should not tell—   835
  People should hold their tongues in any case;
No matter how or why the thing befell,
  But there were she and Juan, face to face—
When two such faces are so, 'twould be wise,
But very difficult, to shut their eyes.   840

How beautiful she looked! her conscious heart
  Glowed in her cheek, and yet she felt no wrong.
Oh Love! how perfect is thy mystic art,
  Strengthening the weak, and trampling on the strong,
How self-deceitful is the sagest part   845
  Of mortals whom thy lure hath led along—
The precipice she stood on was immense,
So was her creed in her own innocence.

She thought of her own strength, and Juan's youth,
  And of the folly of all prudish fears,   850
Victorious virtue, and domestic truth,
  And then of Don Alfonso's fifty years:
I wish these last had not occurred, in sooth,
  Because that number rarely much endears,
And through all climes, the snowy and the sunny,   855
Sounds ill in love, whate'er it may in money.

When people say, "I've told you *fifty* times,"
  They mean to scold, and very often do;
When poets say, "I've written *fifty* rhymes,"
  They make you dread that they'll recite them too;   860
In gangs of *fifty*, thieves commit their crimes;
  At *fifty* love for love is rare, 'tis true,
But then, no doubt, it equally as true is,
A good deal may be bought for *fifty* Louis.

Julia had honour, virtue, truth, and love   865
    For Don Alfonso; and she inly swore,
By all the vows below to powers above,
    She never would disgrace the ring she wore,
Nor leave a wish which wisdom might reprove;
    And while she pondered this, besides much more,   870
One hand on Juan's carelessly was thrown,
Quite by mistake—she thought it was her own;

Unconsciously she leaned upon the other,
    Which played within the tangles of her hair;
And to contend with thoughts she could not smother   875
    She seemed, by the distraction of her air.
'Twas surely very wrong in Juan's mother
    To leave together this imprudent pair,
She who for many years had watched her son so—
I'm very certain *mine* would not have done so.   880

The hand which still held Juan's, by degrees
    Gently, but palpably confirmed its grasp,
As if it said, "Detain me, if you please;"
    Yet there's no doubt she only meant to clasp
His fingers with a pure Platonic squeeze;   885
    She would have shrunk as from a toad, or asp,
Had she imagined such a thing could rouse
A feeling dangerous to a prudent spouse.

I cannot know what Juan thought of this,
    But what he did, is much what you would do;   890
His young lip thanked it with a grateful kiss,
    And then, abashed at its own joy, withdrew
In deep despair, lest he had done amiss,—
    Love is so very timid when 'tis new:
She blushed, and frowned not, but she strove to speak,   895
And held her tongue, her voice was grown so weak.

The sun set, and up rose the yellow moon:
    The devil's in the moon for mischief; they
Who called her CHASTE, methinks, began too soon
    Their nomenclature; there is not a day,   900
The longest, not the twenty-first of June,
    Sees half the business in a wicked way
On which three single hours of moonshine smile—
And then she looks so modest all the while.

There is a dangerous silence in that hour,   905
  A stillness, which leaves room for the full soul
To open all itself, without the power
  Of calling wholly back its self-control;
The silver light which, hallowing tree and tower,
  Sheds beauty and deep softness o'er the whole,   910
Breathes also to the heart, and o'er it throws
A loving languor, which is not repose.

And Julia sate with Juan, half embraced
  And half retiring from the glowing arm,
Which trembled like the bosom where 'twas placed;   915
  Yet still she must have thought there was no harm,
Or else 'twere easy to withdraw her waist;
  But then the situation had its charm,
And then—— God knows what next—I can't go on;
I'm almost sorry that I e'er begun.   920

Oh Plato! Plato! you have paved the way,
  With your confounded fantasies, to more
Immoral conduct by the fancied sway
  Your system feigns o'er the controlless core
Of human hearts, than all the long array   925
  Of poets and romancers:— You're a bore,
A charlatan, a coxcomb—and have been,
At best, no better than a go-between.

And Julia's voice was lost, except in sighs,
  Until too late for useful conversation;   930
The tears were gushing from her gentle eyes,
  I wish, indeed, they had not had occasion,
But who, alas! can love, and then be wise?
  Not that remorse did not oppose temptation;
A little still she strove, and much repented,   935
And whispering "I will ne'er consent"—consented.

'Tis said that Xerxes offer'd a reward
  To those who could invent him a new pleasure:
Methinks the requisition's rather hard,
  And must have cost his majesty a treasure: 940
For my part, I'm a moderate-minded bard,
  Fond of a little love (which I call leisure);
I care not for new pleasures, as the old
Are quite enough for me, so they but hold.

---

937. *Xerxes:* Persian emperor.

Oh Pleasure! you're indeed a pleasant thing,   945
   Although one must be damned for you, no doubt:
I make a resolution every spring
   Of reformation, ere the year run out,
But somehow, this my vestal vow takes wing,
   Yet still, I trust, it may be kept throughout: 950
I'm very sorry, very much ashamed,
And mean, next winter, to be quite reclaimed.

Here my chaste Muse a liberty must take—
   Start not! still chaster reader—she'll be nice hence-
Forward, and there is no great cause to quake;   955
   This liberty is a poetic licence,
Which some irregularity may make
   In the design, and as I have a high sense
Of Aristotle and the Rules, 'tis fit
To beg his pardon when I err a bit.   960

This licence is to hope the reader will
   Suppose from June the sixth (the fatal day
Without whose epoch my poetic skill
   For want of facts would all be thrown away),
But keeping Julia and Don Juan still   965
   In sight, that several months have passed; we'll say
'Twas in November, but I'm not so sure
About the day—the era's more obscure.

We'll talk of that anon.—'Tis sweet to hear
   At midnight on the blue and moonlit deep   970
The song and oar of Adria's gondolier,
   By distance mellowed, o'er the waters sweep;
'Tis sweet to see the evening star appear;
   'Tis sweet to listen as the night-winds creep
From leaf to leaf; 'tis sweet to view on high   975
The rainbow, based on ocean, span the sky.

'Tis sweet to hear the watch-dog's honest bark
   Bay deep-mouthed welcome as we draw near home;
'Tis sweet to know there is an eye will mark
   Our coming, and look brighter when we come;   980
'Tis sweet to be awakened by the lark,
   Or lulled by falling waters; sweet the hum
Of bees, the voice of girls, the song of birds,
The lisp of children, and their earliest words.

---

959. *Rules*: i.e., of "epic" poetry, as laid down in Aristotle's *Poetics*.

Sweet is the vintage, when the showering grapes   985
  In Bacchanal profusion reel to earth,
Purple and gushing: sweet are our escapes
  From civic revelry to rural mirth;
Sweet to the miser are his glittering heaps,
  Sweet to the father is his first-born's birth,   990
Sweet is revenge—especially to women,
Pillage to soldiers, prize-money to seamen.

Sweet is a legacy, and passing sweet
  The unexpected death of some old lady
Or gentleman of seventy years complete,   995
  Who've made "us youth" wait too—too long already
For an estate, or cash, or country seat,
  Still breaking, but with stamina so steady
That all the Israelites are fit to mob its
Next owner for their double-damned post-obits.   1000

'Tis sweet to win, no matter how, one's laurels,
  By blood or ink! 'tis sweet to put an end
To strife; 'tis sometimes sweet to have our quarrels,
  Particularly with a tiresome friend:
Sweet is old wine in bottles, ale in barrels;   1005
  Dear is the helpless creature we defend
Against the world; and dear the schoolboy spot
We ne'er forget, though there we are forgot.

But sweeter still than this, than these, than all,
  Is first and passionate love—it stands alone,   1010
Like Adam's recollection of his fall;
  The tree of knowledge has been plucked—all's known—
And life yields nothing further to recall
  Worthy of this ambrosial sin, so shown,
No doubt in fable, as the unforgiven   1015
Fire which Prometheus filched for us from heaven.

Man's strange animal, and makes strange use
  Of his own nature, and the various arts,
And likes particularly to produce
  Some new experiment to show his parts;   1020
This is the age of oddities let loose,

1016. *Prometheus:* Greek demigod; brought fire to man against Zeus's orders.

Where different talents find their different marts;
You'd best begin with truth, and when you've lost your
Labour, there's a sure market for imposture.

What opposite discoveries we have seen!   1025
    (Signs of true genius, and of empty pockets.)
One makes new noses, one a guillotine,
    One breaks your bones, one sets them in their sockets;
But vaccination certainly has been
    A kind antithesis to Congreve's rockets,   1030
With which the Doctor paid off an old pox,
By borrowing a new one from an ox.

Bread has been made (indifferent) from potatoes;
    And galvanism has set some corpses grinning,
But has not answered like the apparatus   1035
    Of the Humane Society's beginning,
By which men are unsuffocated gratis:
    What wondrous new machines have late been spinning!
I said the small pox has gone out of late;
Perhaps it may be followed by the great.   1040

'Tis said the great came from America;
    Perhaps it may set out on its return,—
The population there so spreads, they say
    'Tis grown high time to thin it in its turn,
With war, or plague, or famine, any way,   1045
    So that civilisation they may learn;
And which in ravage the more loathsome evil is—
Their real lues, or our pseudo-syphilis?

This is the patent age of new inventions
    For killing bodies, and for saving souls,   1050
All propagated with the best intentions;
    Sir Humphry Davy's lantern, by which coals
Are safely mined for in the mode he mentions,
    Tombuctoo travels, voyages to the Poles,
Are ways to benefit mankind, as true,   1055
Perhaps, as shooting them at Waterloo.

Man's a phenomenon, one knows not what,
    And wonderful beyond all wondrous measure;

1030. *rockets:* (then the latest advance in military science). 1031. *the Doctor:* Dr. Edward Jenner, discoverer of vaccination. 1040. *the great* (*pox*): syphilis. 1048. *lues:* syphilis.

'Tis pity though, in this sublime world, that
   Pleasure's a sin, and sometimes sin's a pleasure;   1060
Few mortals know what end they would be at,
   But whether glory, power, or love, or treasure,
The path is through perplexing ways, and when
The goal is gained, we die, you know—and then——

What then?—I do not know, no more do you—   1065
   And so good night.—Return we to our story:
'Twas in November, when fine days are few,
   And the far mountains wax a little hoary,
And clap a white cape on their mantles blue;
   And the sea dashes round the promontory,   1070
And the loud breaker boils against the rock,
And sober suns must set at five o'clock.

'Twas, as the watchmen say, a cloudy night;
   No moon, no stars, the wind was low or loud
By gusts, and many a sparkling hearth was bright   1075
   With the piled wood, round which the family crowd;
There's something cheerful in that sort of light,
   Even as a summer sky's without a cloud:
I'm fond of fire, and crickets, and all that,
A lobster salad, and champagne, and chat.   1080

'Twas midnight—Donna Julia was in bed,
   Sleeping, most probably,—when at her door
Arose a clatter might awake the dead,
   If they had never been awoke before,
And that they have been so we all have read,   1085
   And are to be so, at the least, once more;—
The door was fastened, but with voice and fist
First knocks were heard, then "Madam—Madam—hist!

"For God's sake, Madam—Madam—here's my master,
   With more than half the city at his back—   1090
Was ever heard of such a curst disaster!
   'Tis not my fault—I kept good watch—— Alack!
Do pray undo the bolt a little faster—
   They're on the stair just now, and in a crack
Will all be here; perhaps he yet may fly—   1095
Surely the window's not so *very* high!"

By this time Don Alfonso was arrived,
   With torches, friends, and servants in great number;

The major part of them had long been wived,
   And therefore paused not to disturb the slumber   1100
Of any wicked woman, who contrived
   By stealth her husband's temples to encumber:
Examples of this kind are so contagious,
Were *one* not punish'd, *all* would be outrageous.

I can't tell how, or why, or what suspicion   1105
   Could enter into Don Alfonso's head;
But for a cavalier of his condition
   It surely was exceedingly ill-bred,
Without a word of previous admonition,
   To hold a levee round his lady's bed,   1110
And summon lackeys, armed with fire and sword,
To prove himself the thing he most abhorred.

Poor Donna Julia! starting as from sleep
   (Mind—that I do not say—she had not slept),
Began at once to scream, and yawn, and weep;   1115
   Her maid, Antonia, who was an adept,
Contrived to fling the bed-clothes in a heap,
   As if she had just now from out them crept:
I can't tell why she should take all this trouble
To prove her mistress had been sleeping double.   1120

But Julia mistress, and Antonia maid,
   Appeared like two poor harmless women, who
Of goblins, but still more of men afraid,
   Had thought one man might be deterred by two,
And therefore side by side were gently laid,   1125
   Until the hours of absence should run through,
And truant husband should return, and say,
"My dear, I was the first who came away."

Now Julia found at length a voice, and cried,
   "In heaven's name, Don Alfonso, what d'ye mean?   1130
Has madness seized you? would that I had died
   Ere such a monster's victim I had been!
What may this midnight violence betide,
   A sudden fit of drunkenness or spleen?
Dare you suspect me, whom the thought would kill?   1135
Search, then, the room!"—Alfonso said, "I will."

1102. *her . . . encumber:* (to commit adultery).

He searched, *they* searched, and rummaged everywhere,
  Closet and clothes-press, chest and window-seat,
And found much linen, lace, and several pair
  Of stockings, slippers, brushes, combs, complete,   1140
With other articles of ladies fair,
  To keep them beautiful, or leave them neat:
Arras they pricked and curtains with their swords,
And wounded several shutters, and some boards.

Under the bed they searched, and there they found—   1145
  No matter what—it was not that they sought;
They opened windows, gazing if the ground
  Had signs or footmarks, but the earth said nought;
And then they stared each other's faces round:
  'Tis odd, not one of all these seekers thought,   1150
And seems to me almost a sort of blunder,
Of looking *in* the bed as well as under.

During this inquisition Julia's tongue
  Was not asleep— "Yes, search and search," she cried,
"Insult on insult heap, and wrong on wrong!   1155
  It was for this that I became a bride!
For this in silence I have suffered long
  A husband like Alfonso at my side;
But now I'll bear no more, nor here remain,
If there be law or lawyers in all Spain.   1160

"Yes, Don Alfonso! husband now no more,
  If ever you indeed deserved the name,
Is't worthy of your years?—you have three-score—
  Fifty, or sixty, it is all the same—
Is't wise or fitting, causeless to explore   1165
  For facts against a virtuous woman's fame?
Ungrateful, perjured, barbarous Don Alfonso,
How dare you think your lady would go on so?

"Is it for this I have disdained to hold
  The common privileges of my sex?   1170
That I have chosen a confessor so old
  And deaf, that any other it would vex,
And never once he has had cause to scold,
  But found my very innocence perplex
So much, he always doubted I was married—   1175
How sorry you will be when I've miscarried!

"Was it for this that no Cortejo e'er
    I yet have chosen from out the youth of Seville?
Is it for this I scarce went anywhere,
    Except to bull-fights, mass, play, rout, and revel?   1180
Is it for this, whate'er my suitors were,
    I favoured none—nay, was almost uncivil?
Is it for this that General Count O'Reilly,
Who took Algiers, declares I used him vilely?

"Did not the Italian Musico Cazzani   1185
    Sing at my heart six months at least in vain?
Did not his countryman, Count Corniani,
    Call me the only virtuous wife in Spain?
Were there not also Russians, English, many?
    The Count Strongstroganoff I put in pain,   1190
And Lord Mount Coffeehouse, the Irish peer,
Who killed himself for love (with wine) last year.

"Have I not had two bishops at my feet?
    The Duke of Ichar, and Don Fernan Nunez?
And is it thus a faithful wife you treat?   1195
    I wonder in what quarter now the moon is:
I praise your vast forbearance not to beat
    Me also, since the time so opportune is—
Oh, valiant man! with sword drawn and cocked trigger,
Now, tell me, don't you cut a pretty figure?   1200

"Was it for this you took your sudden journey,
    Under pretence of business indispensable,
With that sublime of rascals your attorney,
    Whom I see standing there, and looking sensible
Of having played the fool? though both I spurn, he   1205
    Deserves the worst, his conduct's less defensible,
Because, no doubt, 'twas for his dirty fee,
And not from any love to you nor me.

"If he comes here to take a deposition,
    By all means let the gentleman proceed;   1210
You've made the apartment in a fit condition:—
    There's pen and ink for you, sir, when you need—
Let everything be noted with precision,
    I would not you for nothing should be fee'd—
But, as my maid's undressed, pray turn your spies out."   1215
"Oh!" sobbed Antonia, "I could tear their eyes out."

1177. *Cortejo:* lover.

"There is the closet, there the toilet, there
    The antechamber—search them under, over;
There is the sofa, there the great arm-chair,
    The chimney—which would really hold a lover.   1220
I wish to sleep, and beg you will take care
    And make no further noise, till you discover
The secret cavern of this lurking treasure—
And when 'tis found, let me, too, have that pleasure.

"And now, Hidalgo! now that you have thrown   1225
    Doubt upon me, confusion over all,
Pray have the courtesy to make it known
    Who is the man you search for? how d'ye call
Him? what's his lineage? let him but be shown—
    I hope he's young and handsome—is he tall?   1230
Tell me—and be assured, that since you stain
Mine honour thus, it shall not be in vain.

"At least, perhaps, he has not sixty years,
    At that age he would be too old for slaughter,
Or for so young a husband's jealous fears—   1235
    (Antonia! let me have a glass of water.)
I am ashamed of having shed these tears,
    They are unworthy of my father's daughter;
My mother dreamed not in my natal hour,
That I should fall into a monster's power.   1240

"Perhaps 'tis of Antonia you are jealous,
    You saw that she was sleeping by my side
When you broke in upon us with your fellows:
    Look where you please—we've nothing, sir, to hide;
Only another time, I trust, you'll tell us,   1245
    Or for the sake of decency abide
A moment at the door, that we may be
Drest to receive so much good company.

"And now, sir, I have done, and say no more;
    The little I have said may serve to show   1250
The guileless heart in silence may grieve o'er
    The wrongs to whose exposure it is slow:—
I leave you to your conscience as before,
    'Twill one day ask you *why* you used me so?
God grant you feel not then the bitterest grief!   1255
Antonia! where's my pocket-handkerchief?"

She ceased, and turned upon her pillow; pale
  She lay, her dark eyes flashing through their tears,
Like skies that rain and lighten; as a veil,
  Waved and o'ershading her wan cheek, appears   1260
Her streaming hair: the black curls strive, but fail,
  To hide the glossy shoulder, which uprears
Its snow through all;—her soft lips lie apart,
And louder than her breathing beats her heart.

The Senhor Don Alfonso stood confused;   1265
  Antonia bustled round the ransacked room,
And, turning up her nose, with looks abused
  Her master, and his myrmidons, of whom
Not one, except the attorney, was amused;
  He, like Achates, faithful to the tomb,   1270
So there were quarrels, cared not for the cause,
Knowing they must be settled by the laws.

With prying snub-nose, and small eyes, he stood,
  Following Antonia's motions here and there,
With much suspicion in his attitude;   1275
  For reputations he had little care;
So that a suit or action were made good,
  Small pity had he for the young and fair,
And ne'er believed in negatives, till these
Were proved by competent false witnesses.   1280

But Don Alfonso stood with downcast looks,
  And, truth to say, he made a foolish figure;
When, after searching in five hundred nooks,
  And treating a young wife with so much rigour,
He gained no point, except some self-rebukes,   1285
  Added to those his lady with such vigour
Had poured upon him for the last half-hour,
Quick, thick, and heavy—as a thunder-shower.

At first he tried to hammer an excuse,
  To which the sole reply was tears and sobs,   1290
And indications of hysterics, whose
  Prologue is always certain throes, and throbs,
Gasps, and whatever else the owners choose:
  Alfonso saw his wife, and thought of Job's;

1270. *Achates:* close friend of Aeneas, legendary founder of Rome. 1294.
Job's: (she told Job to curse God, and die).

He saw too, in perspective, her relations,   1295
And then he tried to muster all his patience.

He stood in act to speak, or rather stammer,
   But sage Antonia cut him short before
The anvil of his speech received the hammer,
   With "Pray, sir, leave the room, and say no more,   1300
Or madam dies."—Alfonso mutter'd, "D—n her."
   But nothing else, the time of words was o'er;
He cast a rueful look or two, and did,
He knew not wherefore, that which he was bid.

With him retired his *"posse comitatus,"*   1305
   The attorney last, who lingered near the door
Reluctantly, still tarrying there as late as
   Antonia let him—not a little sore
At this most strange and unexplained *"hiatus"*
   In Don Alfonso's facts, which just now wore   1310
An awkward look; as he revolved the case,
The door was fastened in his legal face.

No sooner was it bolted, than— Oh shame!
   Oh sin! Oh sorrow! and Oh womankind!
How can you do such things and keep your fame,   1315
   Unless this world, and t'other too, be blind?
Nothing so dear as an unfilched good name!
   But to proceed—for there is more behind:
With much heartfelt reluctance be it said,
Young Juan slipped, half-smothered, from the bed.   1320

He had been hid—I don't pretend to say
   How, nor can I indeed describe the where—
Young, slender, and packed easily, he lay,
   No doubt, in little compass, round or square;
But pity him I neither must nor may   1325
   His suffocation by that pretty pair;
'Twere better, sure, to die so, than be shut
With maudlin Clarence in his Malmsey butt.

And, secondly, I pity not, because
   He had no business to commit a sin,
Forbid by heavenly, fined by human laws,   1330
   At least 'twas rather early to begin;

1328. *Malmsey butt:* wine keg (the Duke of Clarence was drowned in one).

But at sixteen the conscience rarely gnaws
  So much as when we call our old debts in
At sixty years, and draw the accompts of evil,   1335
And find a deuced balance with the devil.

Of his position I can give no notion:
  'Tis written in the Hebrew Chronicle,
How the physicians, leaving pill and potion,
  Prescribed, by way of blister, a young belle,   1340
When old King David's blood grew dull in motion,
  And that the medicine answered very well;
Perhaps 'twas in a different way applied,
For David lived, but Juan nearly died.

What's to be done? Alfonso will be back   1345
  The moment he has sent his fools away.
Antonia's skill was put upon the rack,
  But no device could be brought into play—
And how to parry the renewed attack?
  Besides, it wanted but few hours of day: 1350
Antonia puzzled; Julia did not speak,
But pressed her bloodless lip to Juan's cheek.

He turned his lip to hers, and with his hand
  Called back the tangles of her wandering hair;
Even then their love they could not all command,   1355
  And half forgot their danger and despair:
Antonia's patience now was at a stand—
  "Come, come, 'tis no time now for fooling there,"
She whispered, in great wrath— "I must deposit
This pretty gentleman within the closet: 1360

"Pray, keep your nonsense for some luckier night—
  Who can have put my master in this mood?
What will become on't—I'm in such a fright,
  The devil's in the urchin, and no good—
Is this a time for giggling? this a plight?   1365
  Why, don't you know that it may end in blood?
You'll lose your life, and I shall lose my place,
My mistress all, for that half-girlish face.

"Had it but been for a stout cavalier
  Of twenty-five or thirty—(come, make haste)   1370
But for a child, what piece of work is here!

1338. *Chronicle:* See I Kings 1:1-4 for the episode.

I really, madam, wonder at your taste—
(Come, sir, get in)—my master must be near:
   There, for the present, at the least, he's fast,
And if we can but till the morning keep   1375
Our counsel—(Juan, mind, you must not sleep)."

Now, Don Alfonso entering, but alone,
   Closed the oration of the trusty maid:
She loitered, and he told her to be gone,
   An order somewhat sullenly obeyed;   1380
However, present remedy was none,
   And no great good seemed answered if she staid:
Regarding both with slow and sidelong view,
She snuffed the candle, curtsied, and withdrew.

Alfonso paused a minute—then begun   1385
   Some strange excuses for his late proceeding;
He would not justify what he had done,
   To say the best, it was extreme ill-breeding;
But there were ample reasons for it, none
   Of which he specified in this his pleading: 1390
His speech was a fine sample, on the whole,
Of rhetoric, which the learn'd call "rigmarole."

Julia said nought; though all the while there rose
   A ready answer, which at once enables
A matron, who her husband's foible knows,   1395
   By a few timely words to turn the tables,
Which, if it does not silence, still must pose,—
   Even if it should comprise a pack of fables;
'Tis to retort with firmness, and when he
Suspects with one, do you reproach with three.   1400

Julia, in fact, had tolerable grounds,—
   Alfonso's loves with Inez were well known;
But whether 'twas that one's own guilt confounds—
   But that can't be, as has been often shown,
A lady with apologies abounds;—   1405
   It might be that her silence sprang alone
From delicacy to Don Juan's ear,
To whom she knew his mother's fame was dear.

There might be one more motive, which makes two;
   Alfonso ne'er to Juan had alluded,—   1410
Mentioned his jealousy, but never who

Had been the happy lover, he concluded,
Concealed amongst his premises; 'tis true,
   His mind the more o'er this its mystery brooded;
To speak of Inez now were, one may say,   1415
Like throwing Juan in Alfonso's way.

A hint, in tender cases, is enough;
   Silence is best, besides there is a *tact*—
(That modern phrase appears to me sad stuff,
   But it will serve to keep my verse compact)—   1420
Which keeps, when pushed by questions rather rough,
   A lady always distant from the fact:
The charming creatures lie with such a grace,
There's nothing so becoming to the face.

They blush, and we believe them; at least I   1425
   Have always done so; 'tis of no great use,
In any case, attempting a reply,
   For then their eloquence grows quite profuse;
And when at length they're out of breath, they sigh,
   And cast their languid eyes down, and let loose   1430
A tear or two, and then we make it up;
And then—and then—and then—sit down and sup.

Alfonso closed his speech, and begged her pardon,
   Which Julia half withheld, and then half granted,
And laid conditions, he thought very hard on,   1435
   Denying several little things he wanted:
He stood like Adam lingering near his garden,
   With useless penitence perplexed and haunted,
Beseeching she no further would refuse,
When, lo! he stumbled o'er a pair of shoes.   1440

A pair of shoes!—what then? not much, if they
   Are such as fit with ladies' feet, but these
(No one can tell how much I grieve to say)
   Were masculine; to see them, and to seize,
Was but a moment's act.—Ah! well-a-day!   1445
   My teeth begin to chatter, my veins freeze—
Alfonso first examined well their fashion,
And then flew out into another passion.

He left the room for his relinquished sword,
   And Julia instant to the closet flew.   1450
"Fly, Juan, fly! for heaven's sake—not a word—

The door is open—you may yet slip through
The passage you so often have explored—
    Here is the garden-key— Fly—fly— Adieu!
Haste—haste! I hear Alfonso's hurrying feet—   1455
Day has not broke—there's no one in the street."

None can say that this was not good advice,
    The only mischief was, it came too late;
Of all experience 'tis the usual price,
    A sort of income-tax laid on by fate: 1460
Juan had reached the room-door in a trice,
    And might have done so by the garden-gate,
But met Alfonso in his dressing-gown,
Who threatened death—so Juan knocked him down.

Dire was the scuffle, and out went the light;   1465
    Antonia cried out "Rape!" and Julia "Fire!"
But not a servant stirred to aid the fight.
    Alfonso, pommelled to his heart's desire,
Swore lustily he'd be revenged this night;
    And Juan, too, blasphemed an octave higher;   1470
His blood was up: though young, he was a Tartar,
And not at all disposed to prove a martyr.

Alfonso's sword had dropped ere he could draw it,
    And they continued battling hand to hand,
For Juan very luckily ne'er saw it;   1475
    His temper not being under great command,
If at that moment he had chanced to claw it,
    Alfonso's days had not been in the land
Much longer.—Think of husbands', lovers' lives!
And how ye may be doubly widows—wives!   1480

Alfonso grappled to detain the foe,
    And Juan throttled him to get away,
And blood ('twas from the nose) began to flow;
    At last, as they more faintly wrestling lay,
Juan contrived to give an awkward blow,   1485
    And then his only garment quite gave way;
He fled, like Joseph, leaving it; but there,
I doubt, all likeness ends between the pair.

1487. *Joseph:* (who refused the advances of Potiphar's wife—Genesis
39:7 ff.)

Lights came at length, and men, and maids, who found
   An awkward spectacle their eyes before;   1490
Antonia in hysterics, Julia swooned,
   Alfonso leaning, breathless, by the door;
Some half-torn drapery scattered on the ground,
   Some blood, and several footsteps, but no more:
Juan the gate gained, turned the key about,   1495
And liking not the inside, locked the out.

Here ends this canto.—Need I sing, or say,
   How Juan, naked, favoured by the night,
Who favours what she should not, found his way,
   And reached his home in an unseemly plight?   1500
The pleasant scandal which arose next day,
   The nine days' wonder which was brought to light,
And how Alfonso sued for a divorce,
Were in the English newspapers, of course.

If you would like to see the whole proceedings,   1505
   The depositions, and the cause at full,
The names of all the witnesses, the pleadings
   Of counsel to nonsuit, or to annul,
There's more than one edition, and the readings
   Are various, but they none of them are dull;   1510
The best is that in short-hand ta'en by Gurney,
Who to Madrid on purpose made a journey.

But Donna Inez, to divert the train
   Of one of the most circulating scandals
That had for centuries been known in Spain,   1515
   At least since the retirement of the Vandals,
First vowed (and never had she vowed in vain)
   To Virgin Mary several pounds of candles;
And then, by the advice of some old ladies,
She sent her son to be shipped off from Cadiz.   1520

She had resolved that he should travel through
   All European climes, by land or sea,
To mend his former morals, and get new,
   Especially in France and Italy
(At least this is the thing most people do).   1525
   Julia was sent into a convent: she

1511. *Gurney:* William Brodie Gurney, well-known trial reporter of the
period.

Grieved, but, perhaps, her feelings may be better
Shown in the following copy of her Letter:—

"They tell me 'tis decided; you depart:
    'Tis wise—'tis well, but not the less a pain;   1530
I have no further claim on your young heart,
    Mine is the victim, and would be again;
To love too much has been the only art
    I used;—I write in haste, and if a stain
Be on this sheet, 'tis not what it appears;   1535
My eyeballs burn and throb, but have no tears.

"I loved, I love you, for this love have lost
    State, station, heaven, mankind's, my own esteem,
And yet can not regret what it hath cost,
    So dear is still the memory of that dream;   1540
Yet, if I name my guilt, 'tis not to boast,
    None can deem harshlier of me than I deem:
I trace this scrawl because I cannot rest—
I've nothing to reproach or to request.

"Man's love is of man's life a thing apart,   1545
    'Tis woman's whole existence; man may range
The court, camp, church, the vessel, and the mart;
    Sword, gown, gain, glory, offer in exchange
Pride, fame, ambition, to fill up his heart,
    And few there are whom these cannot estrange;   1550
Men have all these resources, we but one,
To love again, and be again undone.

"You will proceed in pleasure, and in pride,
    Beloved and loving many; all is o'er
For me on earth, except some years to hide   1555
    My shame and sorrow deep in my heart's core;
These I could bear, but cannot cast aside
    The passion which still rages as before,—
And so farewell—forgive me, love me— No,
That word is idle now—but let it go.   1560

"My breast has been all weakness, is so yet;
    But still I think I can collect my mind;
My blood still rushes where my spirit's set,
    As roll the waves before the settled wind;
My heart is feminine, nor can forget—   1565
    To all, except one image, madly blind;

So shakes the needle, and so stands the pole,
As vibrates my fond heart to my fixed soul.

"I have no more to say, but linger still,
    And dare not set my seal upon this sheet,   1570
And yet I may as well the task fulfil,
    My misery can scarce be more complete:
I had not lived till now, could sorrow kill;
    Death shuns the wretch who fain the blow would meet,
And I must even survive this last adieu,   1575
And bear with life, to love and pray for you!"

This note was written upon gilt-edged paper
    With a neat little crow-quill, slight and new;
Her small white hand could hardly reach the taper,
    It trembled as magnetic needles do,   1580
And yet she did not let one tear escape her;
    The seal a sun-flower; *"Elle vous suit partout,"*
The motto, cut upon a white cornelian;
The wax was superfine, its hue vermilion.

This was Don Juan's earliest scrape; but whether   1585
    I shall proceed with his adventures is
Dependent on the public altogether;
    We'll see, however, what they say to this,
Their favour in an author's cap's a feather,
    And no great mischief's done by their caprice;   1590
And if their approbation we experience,
Perhaps they'll have some more about a year hence.

My poem's epic, and is meant to be
    Divided in twelve books; each book containing,
With love, and war, a heavy gale at sea,   1595
    A list of ships, and captains, and kings reigning,
New characters; the episodes are three:
    A panoramic view of hell's in training,
After the style of Virgil and of Homer,
So that my name of Epic's no misnomer.   1600

All these things will be specified in time,
    With strict regard to Aristotle's rules,
The *Vade Mecum* of the true sublime,
    Which makes so many poets, and some fools:

1582. *Elle . . . partout:* It follows you everywhere. 1603. *Vade mecum:*
manual, handbook.

Prose poets like blank-verse, I'm fond of rhyme,   1605
  Good workmen never quarrel with their tools;
I've got new mythological machinery,
And very handsome supernatural scenery.

There's only one slight difference between
  Me and my epic brethren gone before,   1610
And here the advantage is my own, I ween
  (Not that I have not several merits more,
But this will more peculiarly be seen);
  They so embellish, that 'tis quite a bore
Their labyrinth of fables to thread through,   1615
Whereas this story's actually true.

If any person doubt it, I appeal
  To history, tradition, and to facts,
To newspapers, whose truth all know and feel,
  To plays in five, and operas in three acts;   1620
All these confirm my statement a good deal,
  But that which more completely faith exacts
Is, that myself, and several now in Seville,
Saw Juan's last elopement with the devil.

If ever I should condescend to prose,   1625
  I'll write poetical commandments, which
Shall supersede beyond all doubt all those
  That went before; in these I shall enrich
My text with many things that no one knows,
  And carry precept to the highest pitch: 1630
I'll call the work "Longinus o'er a Bottle,
Or, Every Poet his *own* Aristotle."

Thou shalt believe in Milton, Dryden, Pope;
  Thou shalt not set up Wordsworth, Coleridge, Southey;
Because the first is crazed beyond all hope,   1635
  The second drunk, the third so quaint and mouthy:
With Crabbe it may be difficult to cope,
  And Campbell's Hippocrene is somewhat drouthy:
Thou shalt not steal from Samuel Rogers, nor
Commit—flirtation with the muse of Moore.   1640

1631. *Longinus:* ancient literary critic. 1637-41. *Crabbe, Campbell, Rogers, Moore, Sotheby:* English poets contemporary with Byron. 1638. *Hippocrene:* see Keats, "Ode to a Nightingale," 16n.

Thou shalt not covet Mr. Sotheby's Muse,
   His Pegasus, nor anything that's his;
Thou shalt not bear false witness like "the Blues"—
   (There's one, at least, is very fond of this);
Thou shalt not write, in short, but what I choose: 1645
   This is true criticism, and you may kiss—
Exactly as you please, or not,—the rod;
But if you don't, I'll lay it on, by G—d!

If any person should presume to assert
   This story is not moral, first, I pray,   165(
That they will not cry out before they're hurt,
   Then that they'll read it o'er again, and say
(But, doubtless, nobody will be so pert),
   That this is not a moral tale, though gay;
Besides, in Canto Twelfth, I mean to show   1655
The very place where wicked people go.

If, after all, there should be some so blind
   To their own good this warning to despise,
Led by some tortuosity of mind,
   Not to believe my verse and their own eyes,   1660
And cry that they "the moral cannot find,"
   I tell him, if a clergyman, he lies;
Should captains the remark, or critics, make,
They also lie too—under a mistake.

The public approbation I expect,   1665
   And beg they'll take my word about the moral,
Which I with their amusement will connect
   (So children cutting teeth receive a coral);
Meantime they'll doubtless please to recollect
   My epical pretensions to the laurel: 1670
For fear some prudish readers should grow skittish,
I've bribed my grandmother's review—the British.

I sent it in a letter to the Editor,
   Who thank'd me duly by return of post—
I'm for a handsome article his creditor;   1675
   Yet, if my gentle Muse he please to roast,
And break a promise after having made it her,
   Denying the receipt of what it cost,

1643. *Blues:* i.e., Bluestockings (intellectual women).

And smear his page with gall instead of honey,
All I can say is—that he had the money.   1680

I think that with this holy new alliance
  I may ensure the public, and defy
All other magazines of art or science,
  Daily, or monthly, or three monthly; I
Have not essay'd to multiply their clients,   1685
  Because they tell me 'twere in vain to try,
And that the Edinburgh Review and Quarterly
Treat a dissenting author very martyrly.

"*Non ego hoc ferrem calida juventâ*
  Consule Planco," Horace said, and so   1690
Say I; by which quotation there is meant a
  Hint that some six or seven good years ago
(Long ere I dreamt of dating from the Brenta)
  I was most ready to return a blow,
And would not brook at all this sort of thing   1695
In my hot youth—when George the Third was King.

But now at thirty years my hair is gray—
  (I wonder what it will be like at forty?
I thought of a peruke the other day—)
  My heart is not much greener; and, in short, I   1700
Have squandered my whole summer while 'twas May,
  And feel no more the spirit to retort; I
Have spent my life, both interest and principal,
And deem not, what I deemed, my soul invincible.

No more—no more— Oh! never more on me   1705
  The freshness of the heart can fall like dew,
Which out of all the lovely things we see
  Extracts emotions beautiful and new,
Hived in our bosom like the bag o' the bee:
  Think'st thou the honey with those objects grew?   1710
Alas! 'twas not in them, but in thy power
To double even the sweetness of a flower.

1689-90. *Non . . . Planco:* I wouldn't have stood for this in my hot youth,
in the consulship of Plancus. (*Odes* III, xiv). 1693. *Brenta:* Italian river
(near which Byron then lived).

No more—no more— Oh! never more, my heart,
  Canst thou be my sole world, my universe!
Once all in all, but now a thing apart,   1715
  Thou canst not be my blessing or my curse:
The illusion's gone for ever, and thou art
  Insensible, I trust, but none the worse,
And in thy stead I've got a deal of judgment,
Though heaven knows how it ever found a lodgment.   1720

My days of love are over; me no more
  The charms of maid, wife, and still less of widow,
Can make the fool of which they made before,—
  In short, I must not lead the life I did do;
The credulous hope of mutual minds is o'er,   1725
  The copious use of claret is forbid too,
So for a good old-gentlemanly vice,
I think I must take up with avarice.

Ambition was my idol, which was broken
  Before the shrines of Sorrow, and of Pleasure;   1730
And the two last have left me many a token
  O'er which reflection may be made at leisure:
Now, like Friar Bacon's brazen head, I've spoken,
  "Time is, Time was, Time's past:"—a chymic treasure
Is glittering youth, which I have spent betimes—   1735
My heart in passion, and my head on rhymes.

What is the end of fame? 'tis but to fill
  A certain portion of uncertain paper:
Some liken it to climbing up a hill,
  Whose summit, like all hills, is lost in vapour;   1740
For this men write, speak, preach, and heroes kill,
  And bards burn what they call their "midnight taper,"
To have, when the original is dust,
A name, a wretched picture, and worse bust.

What are the hopes of man? Old Egypt's King   1745
  Cheops erected the first pyramid
And largest, thinking it was just the thing
  To keep his memory whole, and mummy hid:
But somebody or other rummaging,
  Burglariously broke his coffin's lid: 1750

1733. *Bacon:* medieval magician.

Let not a monument give you or me hopes,
Since not a pinch of dust remains of Cheops.

But I, being fond of true philosophy,
  Say very often to myself, "Alas!
All things that have been born were born to die,   1755
  And flesh (which Death mows down to hay) is grass;
You've passed your youth not so unpleasantly,
  And if you had it o'er again—'twould pass—
So thank your stars that matters are no worse,
And read your Bible, sir, and mind your purse."   1760

But for the present, gentle reader! and
  Still gentler purchaser! the bard—that's I—
Must, with permission, shake you by the hand,
  And so your humble servant, and good-bye!
We meet again, if we should understand   1765
  Each other; and if not, I shall not try
Your patience further than by this short sample—
'Twere well if others follow'd my example.

"Go, little book, from this my solitude!
  I cast thee on the waters—go thy ways!   1770
And if, as I believe, thy vein be good,
  The world will find thee after many days."
When Southey's read, and Wordsworth understood,
  I can't help putting in my claim to praise—
The four first rhymes are Southey's, every line: 1775
For God's sake, reader! take them not for mine!

Percy Bysshe Shelley

STANZAS

April, 1814

Away! the moor is dark beneath the moon,
  Rapid clouds have drank the last pale beam of even;
Away! the gathering winds will call the darkness soon,
  And profoundest midnight shroud the serene lights of heaven

Pause not! the time is past! Every voice cries, Away!   5
  Tempt not with one last tear thy friend's ungentle mood:
Thy lover's eye, so glazed and cold, dares not entreat thy stay:
  Duty and dereliction guide thee back to solitude.

Away, away! to thy sad and silent home;
  Pour bitter tears on its desolated hearth;   10
Watch the dim shades as like ghosts they go and come,
  And complicate strange webs of melancholy mirth.

The leaves of wasted autumn woods shall float around thine head:
  The blooms of dewy spring shall gleam beneath thy feet:
But thy soul or this world must fade in the frost that binds the dead,
  Ere midnight's frown and morning's smile, ere thou and peace may
    meet.

The cloud shadows of midnight possess their own repose,   17
  For the weary winds are silent, or the moon is in the deep:
Some respite to its turbulence unresting ocean knows;
  Whatever moves, or toils, or grieves, hath its appointed sleep.   20

Thou in the grave shalt rest—yet till the phantoms flee
  Which that house and heath and garden made dear to thee erewhile,
Thy remembrance, and repentance, and deep musings are not free
  From the music of two voices and the light of one sweet smile.

❧

OZYMANDIAS
(1818)

I met a traveller from an antique land
Who said: Two vast and trunkless legs of stone
Stand in the desert . . . Near them, on the sand,
Half sunk, a shattered visage lies, whose frown,
And wrinkled lip, and sneer of cold command,   5
Tell that its sculptor well those passions read
Which yet survive, stamped on these lifeless things,
The hand that mocked them, and the heart that fed:
And on the pedestal these words appear:
'My name is Ozymandias, king of kings: 10
Look on my works, ye Mighty, and despair!'
Nothing beside remains. Round the decay
Of that colossal wreck, boundless and bare
The lone and level sands stretch far away.

STANZAS

Written in Dejection, near Naples

(1824; *written* 1818)

The sun is warm, the sky is clear,
  The waves are dancing fast and bright,
Blue isles and snowy mountains wear
  The purple noon's transparent might,
  The breath of the moist earth is light,   5
Around its unexpanded buds;
  Like many a voice of one delight,
The winds, the birds, the ocean floods,
The City's voice itself, is soft like Solitude's.

I see the Deep's untrampled floor   10
  With green and purple seaweeds strown;
I see the waves upon the shore,
  Like light dissolved in star-showers, thrown:
  I sit upon the sands alone,—
The lightning of the noontide ocean   15
  Is flashing round me, and a tone
Arises from its measured motion,
How sweet! did any heart now share in my emotion.

Alas! I have nor hope nor health,
  Nor peace within nor calm around,   20
Nor that content surpassing wealth
  The sage in meditation found,
  And walked with inward glory crowned—
Nor fame, nor power, nor love, nor leisure.
  Others I see whom these surround—   25
Smiling they live, and call life pleasure;—
To me that cup has been dealt in another measure.

Yet now despair itself is mild,
  Even as the winds and waters are;
I could lie down like a tired child,   30
  And weep away the life of care
  Which I have borne and yet must bear,
Till death like sleep might steal on me,

And I might feel in the warm air
My cheek grow cold, and hear the sea   35
Breathe o'er my dying brain its last monotony.

Some might lament that I were cold,
  As I, when this sweet day is gone,
Which my lost heart, too soon grown old,
  Insults with this untimely moan;   40
  They might lament—for I am one
Whom men love not,—and yet regret,
  Unlike this day, which, when the sun
Shall on its stainless glory set,
Will linger, though enjoyed, like joy in memory yet.   45

ODE TO THE WEST WIND
(1820)

I

O wild West Wind, thou breath of Autumn's being,
Thou, from whose unseen presence the leaves dead
Are driven, like ghosts from an enchanter fleeing,

Yellow, and black, and pale, and hectic red,
Pestilence-stricken multitudes: O thou,   5
Who chariotest to their dark wintry bed

The wingèd seeds, where they lie cold and low,
Each like a corpse within its grave, until
Thine azure sister of the Spring shall blow

Her clarion o'er the dreaming earth, and fill   10
(Driving sweet buds like flocks to feed in air)
With living hues and odours plain and hill:

Wild Spirit, which art moving everywhere;
Destroyer and preserver; hear, oh, hear!

II

Thou on whose stream, mid the steep sky's commotion,   15
Loose clouds like earth's decaying leaves are shed,
Shook from the tangled boughs of Heaven and Ocean,

Angels of rain and lightning: there are spread
On the blue surface of thine aëry surge,
Like the bright hair uplifted from the head   20

Of some fierce Maenad, even from the dim verge
Of the horizon to the zenith's height,
The locks of the approaching storm. Thou dirge

Of the dying year, to which this closing night
Will be the dome of a vast sepulchre,   25
Vaulted with all thy congregated might

Of vapours, from whose solid atmosphere
Black rain, and fire, and hail will burst: oh, hear!

III

Thou who didst waken from his summer dreams
The blue Mediterranean, where he lay,   30
Lulled by the coil of his crystàlline streams,

Beside a pumice isle in Baiae's bay,
And saw in sleep old palaces and towers
Quivering within the wave's intenser day,

All overgrown with azure moss and flowers   35
So sweet, the sense faints picturing them! Thou
For whose path the Atlantic's level powers

Cleave themselves into chasms, while far below
The sea-blooms and the oozy woods which wear
The sapless foliage of the ocean, know   40

Thy voice, and suddenly grow gray with fear,
And tremble and despoil themselves: oh, hear!

IV

If I were a dead leaf thou mightest bear;
If I were a swift cloud to fly with thee;
A wave to pant beneath thy power, and share   45

The impulse of thy strength, only less free
Than thou, O uncontrollable! If even
I were as in my boyhood, and could be

The comrade of thy wanderings over Heaven,

ODE: 21. *Maenad:* devotee of Bacchus. 32. *Baiae:* Italian sea-port.

As then, when to outstrip thy skiey speed   50
Scarce seemed a vision; I would ne'er have striven

As thus with thee in prayer in my sore need.
Oh, lift me as a wave, a leaf, a cloud!
I fall upon the thorns of life! I bleed!

A heavy weight of hours has chained and bowed   55
One too like thee: tameless, and swift, and proud.

V

Make me thy lyre, even as the forest is:
What if my leaves are falling like its own!
The tumult of thy mighty harmonies

Will take from both a deep, autumnal tone,   60
Sweet though in sadness. Be thou, Spirit fierce,
My spirit! Be thou me, impetuous one!

Drive my dead thoughts over the universe
Like withered leaves to quicken a new birth!
And, by the incantation of this verse,   65

Scatter, as from an unextinguished hearth
Ashes and sparks, my words among mankind!
Be through my lips to unawakened earth

The trumpet of a prophecy! O, Wind,
If Winter comes, can Spring be far behind?   70

TO ————

(1824)

Music, when soft voices die,
Vibrates in the memory—
Odours, when sweet violets sicken,
Live within the sense they quicken.

Rose leaves, when the rose is dead,   5
Are heaped for the belovèd's bed;
And so thy thoughts, when thou art gone,
Love itself shall slumber on.

TO A SKYLARK

(1820)

HAIL to thee, blithe Spirit!
   Bird thou never wert,
That from Heaven, or near it,
   Pourest thy full heart
In profuse strains of unpremeditated art.   5

   Higher still and higher
   From the earth thou springest
Like a cloud of fire;
   The blue deep thou wingest,
And singing still dost soar, and soaring ever singest.   10

   In the golden lightning
   Of the sunken sun,
O'er which clouds are bright'ning,
   Thou dost float and run;
Like an unbodied joy whose race is just begun.   15

   The pale purple even
   Melts around thy flight;
Like a star of Heaven,
   In the broad daylight
Thou art unseen, but yet I hear thy shrill delight,   20

   Keen as are the arrows
   Of that silver sphere,
Whose intense lamp narrows
   In the white dawn clear
Until we hardly see—we feel that it is there.   25

   All the earth and air
   With thy voice is loud,
As, when night is bare,
   From one lonely cloud
The moon rains out her beams, and heaven is overflow'd.   30

   What thou art we know not;
   What is most like thee?
From rainbow clouds there flow not
   Drops so bright to see,
As from thy presence showers a rain of melody:—   35

Like a poet hidden
  In the light of thought,
Singing hymns unbidden,
  Till the world is wrought
To sympathy with hopes and fears it heeded not: 40

Like a high-born maiden
  In a palace tower,
Soothing her love-laden
  Soul in secret hour
With music sweet as love, which overflows her bower: 45

Like a glow-worm golden
  In a dell of dew,
Scattering unbeholden
  Its aërial hue
Among the flowers and grass which screen it from the view: 50

Like a rose embower'd
  In its own green leaves,
By warm winds deflower'd,
  Till the scent it gives
Makes faint with too much sweet those heavy-wingèd thieves. 57

Sound of vernal showers
  On the twinkling grass,
Rain-awaken'd flowers—
  All that ever was
Joyous and clear and fresh—thy music doth surpass.   60

Teach us, sprite or bird,
  What sweet thoughts are thine:
I have never heard
  Praise of love or wine
That panted forth a flood of rapture so divine.   65

Chorus hymeneal,
  Or triumphal chant,
Match'd with thine would be all
  But an empty vaunt—
A thing wherein we feel there is some hidden want.   70

What objects are the fountains
  Of thy happy strain?
What fields, or waves, or mountains?

What shapes of sky or plain?
What love of thine own kind? what ignorance of pain?   75

With thy clear keen joyance
    Languor cannot be:
Shadow of annoyance
    Never came near thee:
Thou lovest, but ne'er knew love's sad satiety.   80

Waking or asleep,
    Thou of death must deem
Things more true and deep
    Than we mortals dream,
Or how could thy notes flow in such a crystal stream?   85

We look before and after,
    And pine for what is not:
Our sincerest laughter
    With some pain is fraught;
Our sweetest songs are those that tell of saddest thought.   90

Yet, if we could scorn
    Hate and pride and fear,
If we were things born
    Not to shed a tear,
I know not how thy joy we ever should come near.   95

Better than all measures
    Of delightful sound,
Better than all treasures
    That in books are found,
Thy skill to poet were, thou scorner of the ground!   100

Teach me half the gladness
    That thy brain must know,
Such harmonious madness
    From my lips would flow
The world should listen then—as I am listening now.   105

From *Hellas*
CHORUS
(1822)

The world's great age begins anew,
  The golden years return,
The earth doth like a snake renew
  Her winter weeds outworn:
Heaven smiles, and faiths and empires gleam,   5
Like wrecks of a dissolving dream.

A brighter Hellas rears its mountains
  From waves serener far;
A new Peneus rolls his fountains
  Against the morning star.   10
Where fairer Tempes bloom, there sleep
Young Cyclads on a sunnier deep.

A loftier Argo cleaves the main,
  Fraught with a later prize;
Another Orpheus sings again,   15
  And loves, and weeps, and dies.
A new Ulysses leaves once more
Calypso for his native shore.

Oh, write no more the tale of Troy,
  If earth Death's scroll must be!   20
Nor mix with Laian rage the joy
  Which dawns upon the free;
Although a subtler Sphinx renew
Riddles of death Thebes never knew.

Another Athens shall arise,   25
  And to remoter time
Bequeath, like sunset to the skies,

CHORUS: 7. *Hellas:* Greece. 9. *Peneus:* river in Arcadia (Greece). 11.
Tempes: (valleys). 12. *Cyclads:* (islands). 13. *Argo:* (ship that sailed for
golden fleece). 14. *Orpheus:* legendary Greek poet and musician. 18.
Calypso: nymph who detained the hero Ulysses on his way home from
Troy. 21. *Laian:* (Laius was king of Thebes and father of Oedipus, who
killed him unwittingly). 23. *Sphinx:* monster whose riddle Oedipus solved

The splendour of its prime;
And leave, if nought so bright may live,
All earth can take or Heaven can give.   30

Saturn and Love their long repose
  Shall burst, more bright and good
Than all who fell, than One who rose,
  Than many unsubdued:
Not gold, not blood, their altar dowers,   35
But votive tears and symbol flowers.

Oh, cease! must hate and death return?
  Cease! must men kill and die?
Cease! drain not to its dregs the urn
  Of bitter prophecy.   40
The world is weary of the past,
Oh, might it die or rest at last!

LINES: 'WHEN THE LAMP IS SHATTERED'

(1824)

When the lamp is shattered
The light in the dust lies dead—
  When the cloud is scattered
The rainbow's glory is shed.
  When the lute is broken,   5
Sweet tones are remembered not;
  When the lips have spoken,
Loved accents are soon forgot.

  As music and splendour
Survive not the lamp and the lute,   10
  The heart's echoes render
No song when the spirit is mute:—
  No song but sad dirges,
Like the wind through a ruined cell,
  Or the mournful surges   15
That ring the dead seaman's knell.

31. *Saturn:* God who ruled in Golden Age.

When hearts have once mingled
Love first leaves the well-built nest;
　The weak one is singled
To endure what it once possessed.   20
　O Love! who bewailest
The frailty of all things here,
　Why choose you the frailest
For your cradle, your home, and your bier?

　Its passions will rock thee   25
As the storms rock the ravens on high;
　Bright reason will mock thee,
Like the sun from a wintry sky.
　From thy nest every rafter
Will rot, and thine eagle home   30
　Leave thee naked to laughter,
When leaves fall and cold winds come.

A DIRGE

(1824)

Rough wind, that moanest loud
　Grief too sad for song;
Wild wind, when sullen cloud
　Knells all the night long;
Sad storm, whose tears are vain,   5
Bare woods, whose branches strain,
Deep caves and dreary main,—
　Wail, for the world's wrong!

From *Prometheus Unbound*

(1820)

IN THE CAVE OF DEMOGORGON

PANTHEA. What veilèd form sits on that ebon throne?
ASIA. The veil has fallen.
PANTHEA.   I see a mighty darkness
Filling the seat of power, and rays of gloom
Dart round, as light from the meridian sun.
—Ungazed upon and shapeless; neither limb,   5
Nor form, nor outline; yet we feel it is
A living Spirit.
DEMOGORGON. Ask what thou wouldst know.
ASIA. What canst thou tell?
DEMOGORGON.   All things thou dar'st demand.
ASIA. Who made the living world?
DEMOGORGON.   God.
ASIA.   Who made all
That it contains? thought, passion, reason, will,   10
Imagination?
DEMOGORGON. God: Almighty God.
ASIA. Who made that sense which, when the winds of Spring
In rarest visitation, or the voice
Of one belovèd heard in youth alone,
Fills the faint eyes with falling tears which dim   15
The radiant looks of unbewailing flowers,
And leaves this peopled earth a solitude
When it returns no more?
DEMOGORGON.   Merciful God.
ASIA. And who made terror, madness, crime, remorse,
Which from the links of the great chain of things,   20
To every thought within the mind of man
Sway and drag heavily, and each one reels
Under the load towards the pit of death;

THE CAVE OF DEMOGORGON: 2. *Asia:* (she and her sister nymph Panthea
are on a visit to the mysterious divinity, or fate, Demogorgon, shortly be-
fore the overthrow of Jove).

Abandoned hope, and love that turns to hate;
And self-contempt, bitterer to drink than blood;   25
Pain, whose unheeded and familiar speech
Is howling, and keen shrieks, day after day;
And Hell, or the sharp fear of Hell?
    DEMOGORGON.   He reigns.
    ASIA. Utter his name: a world pining in pain
Asks but his name: curses shall drag him down.   30
    DEMOGORGON. He reigns.
    ASIA.   I feel, I know it: who?
    DEMOGORGON.   He reigns.
    ASIA. Who reigns? There was the Heaven and Earth at first,
And Light and Love; then Saturn, from whose throne
Time fell, an envious shadow: such the state
Of the earth's primal spirits beneath his sway,   35
As the calm joy of flowers and living leaves
Before the wind or sun has withered them
And semivital worms; but he refused
The birthright of their being, knowledge, power,
The skill which wields the elements, the thought   40
Which pierces this dim universe like light,
Self-empire, and the majesty of love;
For thirst of which they fainted. Then Prometheus
Gave wisdom, which is strength, to Jupiter,
And with this law alone, 'Let man be free,'   45
Clothed him with the dominion of wide Heaven.
To know nor faith, nor love, nor law; to be
Omnipotent but friendless is to reign;
And Jove now reigned; for on the race of man
First famine, and then toil, and then disease,   50
Strife, wounds, and ghastly death unseen before,
Fell; and the unseasonable seasons drove
With alternating shafts of frost and fire,
Their shelterless, pale tribes to mountain caves:
And in their desert hearts fierce wants he sent,   55
And mad disquietude, and shadows idle
Of unreal good, which levied mutual war,
So ruining the lair wherein they raged.
Prometheus saw, and waked the legioned hopes
Which sleep within folded Elysian flowers,   60
Nepenthe, Moly, Amaranth, fadeless blooms,
That they might hide with thin and rainbow wings
The shape of Death; and Love he sent to bind

The disunited tendrils of that vine
Which bears the wine of life, the human heart;   65
And he tamed fire which like some beast of prey,
Most terrible, but lovely, played beneath
The frown of man; and tortured to his will
Iron and gold, the slaves and signs of power,
And gems and poisons, and all subtlest forms   70
Hidden beneath the mountains and the waves.
He gave man speech, and speech created thought,
Which is the measure of the universe;
And Science struck the thrones of earth and heaven,
Which shook, but fell not; and the harmonious mind   75
Poured itself forth in all-prophetic song;
And music lifted up the listening spirit
Until it walked, exempt from mortal care,
Godlike, o'er the clear billows of sweet sound;
And human hands first mimicked and then mocked,   80
With moulded limbs more lovely than its own,
The human form, till marble grew divine;
And mothers, gazing, drank the love men see
Reflected in their race, behold, and perish.
He told the hidden power of herbs and springs,   85
And Disease drank and slept. Death grew like sleep.
He taught the implicated orbits woven
Of the wide-wandering stars; and how the sun
Changes his lair, and by what secret spell
The pale moon is transformed, when her broad eye   90
Gazes not on the interlunar sea:
He taught to rule, as life directs the limbs,
The tempest-wingèd chariots of the Ocean,
And the Celt knew the Indian. Cities then
Were built, and through their snow-like columns flowed   95
The warm winds, and the azure aether shone,
And the blue sea and shadowy hills were seen.
Such, the alleviations of his state,
Prometheus gave to man, for which he hangs
Withering in destined pain: but who rains down   100
Evil, the immedicable plague, which, while
Man looks on his creation like a God
And sees that it is glorious, drives him on,
The wreck of his own will, the scorn of earth,
The outcast, the abandoned, the alone?   105

Not Jove: while yet his frown shook Heaven, ay, when
His adversary from adamantine chains
Cursed him, he trembled like a slave. Declare
Who is his master? Is he too a slave?
  DEMOGORGON. All spirits are enslaved which serve things evil:
Thou knowest if Jupiter be such or no.   111
  ASIA. Whom calledst thou God?
  DEMOGORGON.   I spoke but as ye speak,
For Jove is the supreme of living things.
  ASIA. Who is the master of the slave?
  DEMOGORGON.   If the abysm
Could vomit forth its secrets. . . . But a voice   115
Is wanting, the deep truth is imageless;
For what would it avail to bid thee gaze
On the revolving world? What to bid speak
Fate, Time, Occasion, Chance, and Change? To these
All things are subject but eternal Love.   120
  ASIA. So much I asked before, and my heart gave
The response thou hast given; and of such truths
Each to itself must be the oracle. . . .
                    — Act II, Scene iv.

❧

THE FALL OF JOVE

[*The Mouth of a great River in the Island Atlantis.* OCEAN *is discovered reclining near the Shore;* APOLLO *stands beside him.*]

  OCEAN. He fell, thou sayest, beneath his conqueror's frown?
  APOLLO. Ay, when the strife was ended which made dim
The orb I rule, and shook the solid stars,
The terrors of his eye illumined heaven
With sanguine light, through the thick ragged skirts   5
Of the victorious darkness, as he fell:
Like the last glare of day's red agony,
Which, from a rent among the fiery clouds,
Burns far along the tempest-wrinkled deep.
  OCEAN. He sunk to the abyss? To the dark void?   10

THE FALL OF JOVE: I. *He:* (Jove).

APOLLO. An eagle so caught in some bursting cloud
On Caucasus, his thunder-baffled wings
Entangled in the whirlwind, and his eyes
Which gazed on the undazzling sun, now blinded
By the white lightning, while the ponderous hail   15
Beats on his struggling form, which sinks at length
Prone, and the aëreal ice clings over it.
   OCEAN. Henceforth the fields of heaven-reflecting sea
Which are my realm, will heave, unstained with blood,
Beneath the uplifting winds, like plains of corn   20
Swayed by the summer air; my streams will flow
Round many-peopled continents, and round
Fortunate isles; and from their glassy thrones
Blue Proteus and his humid nymphs shall mark
The shadow of fair ships, as mortals see   25
The floating bark of the light-laden moon
With that white star, its sightless pilot's crest,
Borne down the rapid sunset's ebbing sea;
Tracking their path no more by blood and groans,
And desolation, and the mingled voice   30
Of slavery and command; but by the light
Of wave-reflected flowers, and floating odours,
And music soft, and mild, free, gentle voices,
And sweetest music, such as spirits love.
   APOLLO. And I shall gaze not on the deeds which make   35
My mind obscure with sorrow, as eclipse
Darkens the sphere I guide; but list, I hear
The small, clear, silver lute of the young Spirit
That sits i' the morning star.
   OCEAN.   Thou must away;
Thy steeds will pause at even, till when farewell: 40
The loud deep calls me home even now to feed it
With azure calm out of the emerald urns
Which stand for ever full beside my throne.
Behold the Nereids under the green sea,
Their wavering limbs borne on the wind-like stream,   45
Their white arms lifted o'er their streaming hair
With garlands pied and starry sea-flower crowns,
Hastening to grace their mighty sister's joy.
                          [A sound of waves is heard.
It is the unpastured sea hungering for calm.

---

24. *Proteus:* sea-god of many forms. 44. *Nereids:* sea nymphs.

Peace, monster; I come now. Farewell.
APOLLO.   Farewell.   50
                                        — Act III, Scene ii.

〜

EARTH'S SONG

It interpenetrates my granite mass,
  Through tangled roots and trodden clay doth pass
Into the utmost leaves and delicatest flowers;
  Upon the winds, among the clouds 'tis spread,
  It wakes a life in the forgotten dead,   5
They breathe a spirit up from their obscurest bowers.

And like a storm bursting its cloudy prison
  With thunder, and with whirlwind, has arisen
Out of the lampless caves of unimagined being:
  With earthquake shock and swiftness making shiver   10
  Thought's stagnant chaos, unremoved for ever,
Till hate, and fear, and pain, light-vanquished shadows, fleeing,

Leave Man, who was a many-sided mirror,
  Which could distort to many a shape of error,
This true fair world of things, a sea reflecting love;   15
  Which over all his kind, as the sun's heaven
  Gliding o'er ocean, smooth, serene, and even,
Darting from starry depths radiance and life, doth move:

Leave Man, even as a leprous child is left,
  Who follows a sick beast to some warm cleft   20
Of rocks, through which the might of healing springs is poured;
  Then when it wanders home with rosy smile,
  Unconscious, and its mother fears awhile
It is a spirit, then, weeps on her child restored.

Man, oh, not men! a chain of linkèd thought,   25
  Of love and might to be divided not,
Compelling the elements with admantine stress;
  As the sun rules, even with a tyrant's gaze,
  The unquiet republic of the maze
Of planets, struggling fierce towards heaven's free wilderness.   30

Man, one harmonious soul of many a soul,
  Whose nature is its own divine control,
Where all things flow to all, as rivers to the sea;
  Familiar acts are beautiful through love;
  Labour, and pain, and grief, in life's green grove   35
Sport like tame beasts, none knew how gentle they could be!

His will, with all mean passions, bad delights,
  And selfish cares, its trembling satellites,
A spirit ill to guide, but mighty to obey,
  Is a tempest-wingèd ship, whose helm   40
  Love rules, through waves which dare not overwhelm,
Forcing life's wildest shores to own its sovereign sway.

All things confess his strength. Through the cold mass
  Of marble and of colour his dreams pass;
Bright threads whence mothers weave the robes their children
    wear;   45
  Language is a perpetual Orphic song,
  Which rules with Dædal harmony a throng
Of thoughts and forms, which else senseless and shapeless were.

The lightning is his slave; heaven's utmost deep
  Gives up her stars, and like a flock of sheep   50
They pass before his eye, are numbered, and roll on!
  The tempest is his steed, he strides the air;
  And the abyss shouts from her depth laid bare,
Heaven, hast thou secrets? Man unveils me; I have none.

                                    — *From* Act IV.

ADONAIS

(1821)

I weep for Adonais—he is dead!
  O, weep for Adonais! though our tears
Thaw not the frost which binds so dear a head!
  And thou, sad Hour, selected from all years
  To mourn our loss, rouse thy obscure compeers,   5
  And teach them thine own sorrow, say: 'With me
Died Adonais; till the Future dares

Forget the Past, his fate and fame shall be
An echo and a light unto eternity!'

Where wert thou, mighty Mother, when he lay,   10
When thy Son lay, pierced by the shaft which flies
In darkness? where was lorn Urania
When Adonais died? With veilèd eyes,
'Mid listening Echoes, in her Paradise
She sate, while one, with soft enamoured breath,   15
Rekindled all the fading melodies,
With which, like flowers that mock the corse beneath,
He had adorned and hid the coming bulk of Death.

Oh, weep for Adonais—he is dead!
Wake, melancholy Mother, wake and weep!   20
Yet wherefore? Quench within their burning bed
Thy fiery tears, and let thy loud heart keep
Like his, a mute and uncomplaining sleep;
For he is gone, where all things wise and fair
Descend;—oh, dream not that the amorous Deep   25
Will yet restore him to the vital air;
Death feeds on his mute voice, and laughs at our despair.

Most musical of mourners, weep again!
Lament anew, Urania!—He died,
Who was the Sire of an immortal strain,   30
Blind, old, and lonely, when his country's pride,
The priest, the slave, and the liberticide,
Trampled and mocked with many a loathèd rite
Of lust and blood; he went, unterrified,
Into the gulf of death; but his clear Sprite   35
Yet reigns o'er earth; the third among the sons of light.

Most musical of mourners, weep anew!
Not all to that bright station dared to climb;
And happier they their happiness who knew,
Whose tapers yet burn through that night of time   40
In which suns perished; others more sublime,
Struck by the envious wrath of man or god,
Have sunk, extinct in their refulgent prime;
And some yet live, treading the thorny road,
Which leads, through toil and hate, to Fame's serene abode.   45

ADONAIS: 12. *Urania:* Muse of astronomy and of heavenly wisdom (in-
voked by Milton in *Paradise Lost*). 29. *He:* Milton.

But now, thy youngest, dearest one, has perished—
The nursling of thy widowhood, who grew,
Like a pale flower by some sad maiden cherished,
And fed with true-love tears, instead of dew;
Most musical of mourners, weep anew!   50
Thy extreme hope, the loveliest and the last,
The bloom, whose petals nipped before they blew
Died on the promise of the fruit, is waste;
The broken lily lies—the storm is overpast.

To that high Capital, where kingly Death   55
Keeps his pale court in beauty and decay,
He came; and bought, with price of purest breath,
A grave among the eternal.—Come away!
Haste, while the vault of blue Italian day
Is yet his fitting charnel-roof! while still   60
He lies, as if in dewy sleep he lay;
Awake him not! surely he takes his fill
Of deep and liquid rest, forgetful of all ill.

He will awake no more, oh, never more!—
Within the twilight chamber spreads apace   65
The shadow of white Death, and at the door
Invisible Corruption waits to trace
His extreme way to her dim dwelling-place;
The eternal Hunger sits, but pity and awe
Soothe her pale rage, nor dares she to deface   70
So fair a prey, till darkness, and the law
Of change, shall o'er his sleep the mortal curtain draw.

Oh, weep for Adonais!—The quick Dreams,
The passion-wingèd Ministers of thought,
Who were his flocks, whom near the living streams   75
Of his young spirit he fed, and whom he taught
The love which was its music, wander not,—
Wander no more, from kindling brain to brain,
But droop there, whence they sprung; and mourn their lot
Round the cold heart, where, after their sweet pain,   80
They ne'er will gather strength, or find a home again.

And one with trembling hands clasps his cold head,
And fans him with her moonlight wings, and cries;
'Our love, our hope, our sorrow, is not dead;
See, on the silken fringe of his faint eyes,   85
Like dew upon a sleeping flower, there lies

A tear some Dream has loosened from his brain.'
Lost Angel of a ruined Paradise!
She knew not 'twas her own; as with no stain
She faded, like a cloud which had outwept its rain.   90

One from a lucid urn of starry dew
Washed his light limbs as if embalming them;
Another clipped her profuse locks, and threw
The wreath upon him, like an anadem,
Which frozen tears instead of pearls begem;   95
Another in her wilful grief would break
Her bow and wingèd reeds, as if to stem
A greater loss with one which was more weak:
And dull the barbèd fire against his frozen cheek

Another Splendour on his mouth alit,   100
That mouth, whence it was wont to draw the breath
Which gave it strength to pierce the guarded wit,
And pass into the panting heart beneath
With lightning and with music: the damp death
Quenched its caress upon his icy lips;   105
And, as a dying meteor stains a wreath
Of moonlight vapour, which the cold night clips,
It flushed through his pale limbs, and passed to its eclipse.

And others came . . . Desires and Adorations,
Wingèd Persuasions and veiled Destinies,   110
Splendours, and Glooms, and glimmering Incarnations
Of hopes and fears, and twilight Phantasies;
And Sorrow, with her family of Sighs,
And Pleasure, blind with tears, led by the gleam
Of her own dying smile instead of eyes,   115
Came in slow pomp;—the moving pomp might seem
Like pageantry of mist on an autumnal stream.

All he had loved, and moulded into thought,
From shape, and hue, and odour, and sweet sound,
Lamented Adonais. Morning sought   120
Her eastern watch-tower, and her hair unbound,
Wet with the tears which should adorn the ground,
Dimmed the aëreal eyes that kindle day;
Afar the melancholy thunder moaned,
Pale Ocean in unquiet slumber lay,   125
And the wild Winds flew round, sobbing in their dismay.

Lost Echo sits amid the voiceless mountains,
And feeds her grief with his remembered lay,
And will no more reply to winds or fountains,
Or amorous birds perched on the young green spray,   130
Or herdsman's horn, or bell at closing day;
Since she can mimic not his lips, more dear
Than those for whose disdain she pined away
Into a shadow of all sounds:—a drear
Murmur, between their songs, is all the woodmen hear.   135

Grief made the young Spring wild, and she threw down
Her kindling buds, as if she Autumn were,
Or they dead leaves; since her delight is flown,
For whom should she have waked the sullen year?
To Phoebus was not Hyacinth so dear   140
Nor to himself Narcissus, as to both
Thou, Adonais: wan they stand and sere
Amid the faint companions of their youth,
With dew all turned to tears; odour, to sighing ruth.

Thy spirit's sister, the lorn nightingale   145
Mourns not her mate with such melodious pain;
Not so the eagle, who like thee could scale
Heaven, and could nourish in the sun's domain
Her mighty youth with mourning, doth complain,
Soaring and screaming round her empty nest,   150
As Albion wails for thee: the curse of Cain
Light on his head who pierced thy innocent breast,
And scared the angel soul that was its earthly guest!

Ah, woe is me! Winter is come and gone,
But grief returns with the revolving year;   155
The airs and streams renew their joyous tone;
The ants, the bees, the swallows reappear;
Fresh leaves and flowers deck the dead Seasons' bier;
The amorous birds now pair in every brake,
And build their mossy homes in field and brere;   160
And the green lizard, and the golden snake,
Like unimprisoned flames, out of their trance awake.

Through wood and stream and field and hill and Ocean
A quickening life from the Earth's heart has burst

---

152. *pierced:* (Shelley believed that an unsigned hostile review of a poem
of Keats's had helped cause Keats's death).

As it has ever done, with change and motion,   165
From the great morning of the world when first
God dawned on Chaos; in its stream immersed,
The lamps of Heaven flash with a softer light;
All baser things pant with life's sacred thirst;
Diffuse themselves; and spend in love's delight,   170
The beauty and the joy of their renewèd might.

The leprous corpse, touched by this spirit tender,
Exhales itself in flowers of gentle breath;
Like incarnations of the stars, when splendour
Is changed to fragrance, they illumine death   175
And mock the merry worm that wakes beneath;
Nought we know, dies. Shall that alone which knows
Be as a sword consumed before the sheath
By sightless lightning?—the intense atom glows
A moment, then is quenched in a most cold repose.   180

Alas! that all we loved of him should be,
But for our grief, as if it had not been,
And grief itself be mortal! Woe is me!
Whence are we, and why are we? of what scene
The actors or spectators? Great and mean   185
Meet massed in death, who lends what life must borrow.
As long as skies are blue, and fields are green,
Evening must usher night, night urge the morrow,
Month follow month with woe, and year wake year to sorrow.

He will awake no more, oh, never more!   190
'Wake thou,' cried Misery, 'childless Mother, rise
Out of thy sleep, and slake, in thy heart's core,
A wound more fierce than his, with tears and sighs.'
And all the Dreams that watched Urania's eyes,
And all the Echoes whom their sister's song   195
Had held in holy silence, cried: 'Arise!'
Swift as a Thought by the snake Memory stung,
From her ambrosial rest the fading Splendour sprung.

She rose like an autumnal Night, that springs
Out of the East, and follows wild and drear   200
The golden Day, which, on eternal wings,
Even as a ghost abandoning a bier,
Had left the Earth a corpse. Sorrow and fear
So struck, so roused. so rapped Urania:

So saddened round her like an atmosphere   205
  Of stormy mist; so swept her on her way
Even to the mournful place where Adonais lay.

  Out of her secret Paradise she sped,
  Through camps and cities rough with stone, and steel,
  And human hearts, which to her aery tread   210
  Yielding not, wounded the invisible
  Palms of her tender feet where'er they fell:
  And barbèd tongues, and thoughts more sharp than they,
  Rent the soft Form they never could repel,
  Whose sacred blood, like the young tears of May,   215
Paved with eternal flowers that undeserving way.

  In the death-chamber for a moment Death,
  Shamed by the presence of that living Might,
  Blushed to annihilation, and the breath
  Revisited those lips, and Life's pale light   220
  Flashed through those limbs, so late her dear delight.
  'Leave me not wild and drear and comfortless,
  As silent lightning leaves the starless night!
  Leave me not!' cried Urania: her distress
Roused Death: Death rose and smiled, and met her vain caress. 225

  'Stay yet awhile! speak to me once again;
  Kiss me, so long but as a kiss may live;
  And in my heartless breast and burning brain
  That word, that kiss, shall all thoughts else survive,
  With food of saddest memory kept alive,   230
  Now thou art dead, as if it were a part
  Of thee, my Adonais! I would give
  All that I am to be as thou now art!
But I am chained to Time, and cannot thence depart!

  'O gentle child, beautiful as thou wert,   235
  Why didst thou leave the trodden paths of men
  Too soon, and with weak hands though mighty heart
  Dare the unpastured dragon in his den?
  Defenceless as thou wert, oh, where was then
  Wisdom the mirrored shield, or scorn the spear?   240
  Or hadst thou waited the full cycle, when
  Thy spirit should have filled its crescent sphere,
The monsters of life's waste had fled from thee like deer.

'The herded wolves, bold only to pursue;
The obscene ravens, clamorous o'er the dead;   245
The vultures to the conqueror's banner true
Who feed where Desolation first has fed,
And whose wings rain contagion;—how they fled,
When, like Apollo, from his golden bow
The Pythian of the age one arrow sped   250
And smiled!—The spoilers tempt no second blow,
They fawn on the proud feet that spurn them lying low.

'The sun comes forth, and many reptiles spawn;
He sets, and each ephemeral insect then
Is gathered into death without a dawn,   255
And the immortal stars awake again;
So is it in the world of living men:
A godlike mind soars forth, in its delight
Making earth bare and veiling heaven, and when
It sinks, the swarms that dimmed or shared its light   260
Leave to its kindred lamps the spirit's awful night.'

Thus ceased she: and the mountain shepherds came,
Their garlands sere, their magic mantles rent;
The Pilgrim of Eternity, whose fame
Over his living head like Heaven is bent,   265
An early but enduring monument,
Came, veiling all the lightnings of his song
In sorrow; from her wilds Ierne sent
The sweetest lyrist of her saddest wrong,
And Love taught Grief to fall like music from his tongue.   270

Midst others of less note, came one frail Form,
A phantom among men; companionless
As the last cloud of an expiring storm
Whose thunder is its knell; he, as I guess,
Had gazed on Nature's naked loveliness,   275
Actaeon-like, and now he fled astray
With feeble steps o'er the world's wilderness,
And his own thoughts, along that rugged way,
Pursued, like raging hounds, their father and their prey.

---

244. *wolves:* (critics). 250. *Pythian:* slayer of the monster Python; Shelley refers to an early poem of Byron's attacking the critics. 264. *Pilgrim:* Byron. 268. *Ierne:* Hibernia (Ireland). 271. *Form:* (Shelley). 276. *Actaeon:* hunter killed by his own hounds after he had been changed to a deer for gazing on Diana naked.

A pardlike Spirit beautiful and swift—   280
A Love in desolation masked;—a Power
Girt round with weakness;—it can scarce uplift
The weight of the superincumbent hour;
It is a dying lamp, a falling shower,
A breaking billow;—even whilst we speak   285
Is it not broken? On the withering flower
The killing sun smiles brightly: on a cheek
The life can burn in blood, even while the heart may break.

His head was bound with pansies overblown,
And faded violets, white, and pied, and blue;   290
And a light spear topped with a cypress cone,
Round whose rude shaft dark ivy-tresses grew
Yet dripping with the forest's noonday dew,
Vibrated, as the ever-beating heart
Shook the weak hand that grasped it; of that crew   295
He came the last, neglected and apart;
A herd-abandoned deer struck by the hunter's dart.

All stood aloof, and at his partial moan
Smiled through their tears; well knew that gentle band
Who in another's fate now wept his own,   300
As in the accents of an unknown land
He sung new sorrow; sad Urania scanned
The Stranger's mien, and murmured: 'Who art thou?'
He answered not, but with a sudden hand
Made bare his branded and ensanguined brow,   305
Which was like Cain's or Christ's—oh! that it should be so!

What softer voice is hushed over the dead?
Athwart what brow is that dark mantle thrown?
What form leans sadly o'er the white death-bed,
In mockery of monumental stone,   310
The heavy heart heaving without a moan?
If it be He, who, gentlest of the wise,
Taught, soothed, loved, honoured the departed one,
Let me not vex, with inharmonious sighs,
The silence of that heart's accepted sacrifice.   315

Our Adonais has drunk poison—oh!
What deaf and viperous murderer could crown
Life's early cup with such a draught of woe?
The nameless worm would now itself disown:

It felt, yet could escape, the magic tone   320
Whose prelude held all envy, hate, and wrong,
But what was howling in one breast alone,
Silent with expectation of the song,
Whose master's hand is cold, whose silver lyre unstrung.

Live thou, whose infamy is not thy fame!   325
Live! fear no heavier chastisement from me,
Thou noteless blot on a remembered name!
But be thyself, and know thyself to be!
And ever at thy season be thou free
To spill the venom when thy fangs o'erflow;   330
Remorse and Self-contempt shall cling to thee;
Hot Shame shall burn upon thy secret brow,
And like a beaten hound tremble thou shalt—as now.

Nor let us weep that our delight is fled
Far from these carrion kites that scream below;   335
He wakes or sleeps with the enduring dead;
Thou canst not soar where he is sitting now—
Dust to the dust! but the pure spirit shall flow
Back to the burning fountain whence it came,
A portion of the Eternal, which must glow   340
Through time and change, unquenchably the same,
Whilst thy cold embers choke the sordid hearth of shame.

Peace, peace! he is not dead, he doth not sleep—
He hath awakened from the dream of life—
'Tis we, who lost in stormy visions, keep   345
With phantoms an unprofitable strife,
And in mad trance, strike with our spirit's knife
Invulnerable nothings.—*We* decay
Like corpses in a charnel; fear and grief
Convulse us and consume us day by day,   350
And cold hopes swarm like worms within our living clay.

He has outsoared the shadow of our night;
Envy and calumny and hate and pain,
And that unrest which men miscall delight,
Can touch him not and torture not again;   355
From the contagion of the world's slow stain
He is secure, and now can never mourn
A heart grown cold, a head grown gray in vain;
Nor, when the spirit's self has ceased to burn,
With sparkless ashes load an unlamented urn.   360

He lives, he wakes—'tis Death is dead, not he;
Mourn not for Adonais.—Thou young Dawn,
Turn all thy dew to splendour, for from thee
The spirit thou lamentest is not gone;
Ye caverns and ye forests, cease to moan!   365
Cease, ye faint flowers and fountains, and thou Air,
Which like a mourning veil thy scarf hadst thrown
O'er the abandoned Earth, now leave it bare
Even to the joyous stars which smile on its despair!

He is made one with Nature: there is heard   370
His voice in all her music, from the moan
Of thunder, to the song of night's sweet bird;
He is a presence to be felt and known
In darkness and in light, from herb and stone,
Spreading itself where'er that Power may move   375
Which has withdrawn his being to its own;
Which wields the world with never-wearied love,
Sustains it from beneath, and kindles it above.

He is a portion of the loveliness
Which once he made more lovely: he doth bear   380
His part, while the one Spirit's plastic stress
Sweeps through the dull dense world, compelling there,
All new successions to the forms they wear;
Torturing th' unwilling dross that checks its flight
To its own likeness, as each mass may bear;   385
And bursting in its beauty and its might
From trees and beasts and men into the Heaven's light.

The splendours of the firmament of time
May be eclipsed, but are extinguished not;
Like stars to their appointed height they climb,   390
And death is a low mist which cannot blot
The brightness it may veil. When lofty thought
Lifts a young heart above its mortal lair,
And love and life contend in it, for what
Shall be its earthly doom, the dead live there   395
And move like winds of light on dark and stormy air.

The inheritors of unfulfilled renown
Rose from their thrones, built beyond mortal thought,
Far in the Unapparent. Chatterton
Rose pale,—his solemn agony had not   400

399-404. *Chatterton, Sidney, Lucan:* (all were poets and died young).

Yet faded from him; Sidney, as he fought
And as he fell and as he lived and loved
Sublimely mild, a Spirit without spot,
Arose; and Lucan, by his death approved:
Oblivion as they rose shrank like a thing reproved.   405

And many more, whose names on Earth are dark,
But whose transmitted effluence cannot die
So long as fire outlives the parent spark,
Rose, robed in dazzling immortality.
'Thou are become as one of us,' they cry,   410
'It was for thee yon kingless sphere has long
Swung blind in unascended majesty,
Silent alone amid an Heaven of Song.
Assume thy wingèd throne, thou Vesper of our throng!'

Who mourns for Adonais? Oh, come forth,   415
Fond wretch! and know thyself and him aright.
Clasp with thy panting soul the pendulous Earth;
As from a centre, dart thy spirit's light
Beyond all worlds, until its spacious might
Satiate the void circumference: then shrink   420
Even to a point within our day and night;
And keep thy heart light lest it make thee sink
When hope has kindled hope, and lured thee to the brink.

Or go to Rome, which is the sepulchre,
Oh, not of him, but of our joy: 'tis nought   425
That ages, empires, and religions there
Lie buried in the ravage they have wrought;
For such as he can lend,—they borrow not
Glory from those who made the world their prey;
And he is gathered to the kings of thought   430
Who waged contention with their time's decay,
And of the past are all that cannot pass away.

Go thou to Rome,—at once the Paradise,
The grave, the city, and the wilderness;
And where its wrecks like shattered mountains rise,   435
And flowering weeds, and fragrant copses dress
The bones of Desolation's nakedness
Pass, till the spirit of the spot shall lead
Thy footsteps to a slope of green access
Where, like an infant's smile, over the dead   440
A light of laughing flowers along the grass is spread;

And gray walls moulder round, on which dull Time
Feeds, like slow fire upon a hoary brand;
And one keen pyramid with wedge sublime,
Pavilioning the dust of him who planned   445
This refuge for his memory, doth stand
Like flame transformed to marble; and beneath,
A field is spread, on which a newer band
Have pitched in Heaven's smile their camp of death,
Welcoming him we lose with scarce extinguished breath.   450

Here pause: these graves are all too young as yet
To have outgrown the sorrow which consigned
Its charge to each; and if the seal is set,
Here, on one fountain of a mourning mind,
Break it not thou! too surely shalt thou find   455
Thine own well full, if thou returnest home,
Of tears and gall. From the world's bitter wind
Seek shelter in the shadow of the tomb.
What Adonais is, why fear we to become?

The One remains, the many change and pass;   460
Heaven's light forever shines, Earth's shadows fly;
Life, like a dome of many-coloured glass,
Stains the white radiance of Eternity,
Until Death tramples it to fragments.—Die,
If thou wouldst be with that which thou dost seek!   465
Follow where all is fled!—Rome's azure sky,
Flowers, ruins, statues, music, words, are weak
The glory they transfuse with fitting truth to speak.

Why linger, why turn back, why shrink, my Heart?
Thy hopes are gone before: from all things here   470
They have departed; thou shouldst now depart!
A light is passed from the revolving year,
And man, and woman; and what still is dear
Attracts to crush, repels to make thee wither.
The soft sky smiles,—the low wind whispers near: 475
'Tis Adonais calls! oh, hasten thither,
No more let Life divide what Death can join together.

That Light whose smile kindles the Universe,
That Beauty in which all things work and move,
That Benediction which the eclipsing Curse   480
Of birth can quench not, that sustaining Love
Which through the web of being blindly wove

By man and beast and earth and air and sea,
Burns bright or dim, as each are mirrors of
The fire for which all thirst; now beams on me,   485
Consuming the last clouds of cold mortality.

The breath whose might I have invoked in song
Descends on me; my spirit's bark is driven,
Far from the shore, far from the trembling throng
Whose sails were never to the tempest given;   490
The massy earth and spherèd skies are riven!
I am borne darkly, fearfully, afar;
Whilst, burning through the inmost veil of Heaven,
The soul of Adonais, like a star,
Beacons from the abode where the Eternal are.   495

∾

John Keats

ON FIRST LOOKING INTO CHAPMAN'S HOMER
(1816)

Much have I travelled in the realms of gold,
    And many goodly states and kingdoms seen;
    Round many western islands have I been
Which bards in fealty to Apollo hold.
Oft of one wide expanse had I been told   5
    That deep-browed Homer ruled as his demesne;
    Yet did I never breathe its pure serene
Till I heard Chapman speak out loud and bold:
Then felt I like some watcher of the skies
    When a new planet swims into his ken;   10
Or like stout Cortez when with eagle eyes
    He stared at the Pacific—and all his men
Looked at each other with a wild surmise—
    Silent, upon a peak in Darien.

∾

CHAPMAN'S HOMER: 8. *Chapman:* Elizabethan translator of Homer. 14.
Darien: Panama.

SONNET

(1848; *written* 1817)

When I have fears that I may cease to be
  Before my pen has gleaned my teeming brain,
Before high-pilèd books, in charactery,
  Hold like rich garners the full ripened grain;
When I behold, upon the night's starred face,   5
  Huge cloudy symbols of a high romance,
And think that I may never live to trace
  Their shadows, with the magic hand of chance;
And when I feel, fair creature of an hour,
  That I shall never look upon thee more,   10
Never have relish in the faery power
  Of unreflecting love;—then on the shore
Of the wide world I stand alone, and think
Till love and fame to nothingness do sink.

SONNET

Written on a Blank Page in Shakespeare's Poems, facing "A Lover's Complaint"

(1848; *written* 1819-20)

Bright star, would I were stedfast as thou art—
  Not in lone splendour hung aloft the night
And watching, with eternal lids apart,
  Like nature's patient, sleepless Eremite,
The moving waters at their priestlike task   5
  Of pure ablution round earth's human shores,
Or gazing on the new soft-fallen mask
  Of snow upon the mountains and the moors—
No—yet still stedfast, still unchangeable,
  Pillowed upon my fair love's ripening breast,   10
To feel for ever its soft fall and swell,
  Awake for ever in a sweet unrest,
Still, still to hear her tender-taken breath,
And so live ever—or else swoon to death.

ODE ON MELANCHOLY
(1820)

I

No, no, go not to Lethe, neither twist
  Wolf's bane, tight-rooted, for its poisonous wine;
Nor suffer thy pale forehead to be kissed
  By nightshade, ruby grape of Proserpine;
Make not your rosary of yew-berries,   5
  Nor let the beetle, nor the death-moth be
    Your mournful Psyche, nor the downy owl
A partner in your sorrow's mysteries;
  For shade to shade will come too drowsily,
    And drown the wakeful anguish of the soul.   10

II

But when the melancholy fit shall fall
  Sudden from heaven like a weeping cloud,
That fosters the droop-headed flowers all,
  And hides the green hill in an April shroud;
Then glut thy sorrow on a morning rose,   15
  Or on the rainbow of the salt sand-wave,
    Or on the wealth of globèd peonies;
Or if thy mistress some rich anger shows,
  Emprison her soft hand, and let her rave,
    And feed deep, deep upon her peerless eyes.   20

III

She dwells with Beauty—Beauty that must die;
  And Joy, whose hand is ever at his lips
Bidding adieu; and aching Pleasure nigh,
  Turning to Poison while the bee-mouth sips:
Ay, in the very temple of delight   25
  Veiled Melancholy has her sovran shrine,
    Though seen of none save him whose strenuous tongue

ODE ON MELANCHOLY: 1. *Lethe:* underworld river of forgetfulness. 4.
Proserpine: goddess of underworld. 7. *Psyche:* object of desire.

Can burst Joy's grape against his palate fine;
His soul shall taste the sadness of her might,
And be among her cloudy trophies hung.   30

&

ODE ON A GRECIAN URN
(1820)

I

Thou still unravished bride of quietness,
    Thou foster-child of silence and slow time,
Sylvan historian, who canst thus express
    A flowery tale more sweetly than our rhyme:
What leaf-fringed legend haunts about thy shape   5
    Of deities or mortals, or of both,
        In Tempe or the dales of Arcady?
    What men or gods are these? What maidens loth?
What mad pursuit? What struggle to escape?
        What pipes and timbrels? What wild ecstasy?   10

II

Heard melodies are sweet, but those unheard
    Are sweeter; therefore, ye soft pipes, play on;
Not to the sensual ear, but, more endeared,
    Pipe to the spirit ditties of no tone:
Fair youth, beneath the trees, thou canst not leave   15
    Thy song, nor ever can those trees be bare;
        Bold Lover, never, never canst thou kiss,
Though winning near the goal—yet, do not grieve;
    She cannot fade, though thou hast not thy bliss,
        For ever wilt thou love, and she be fair!   20

III

Ah, happy, happy boughs! that cannot shed
    Your leaves, nor ever bid the Spring adieu;

_____

ODE ON A GRECIAN URN: 7. *Tempe, Arcady:* idealized pastoral valleys of
Greece.

And, happy melodist, unwearièd,
  For ever piping songs for ever new;
More happy love! more happy, happy love!   25
  For ever warm and still to be enjoyed,
    For ever panting, and for ever young;
All breathing human passion far above,
  That leaves a heart high-sorrowful and cloyed,
    A burning forehead, and a parching tongue.   30

IV

Who are these coming to the sacrifice?
  To what green altar, O mysterious priest,
Lead'st thou that heifer lowing at the skies,
  And all her silken flanks with garlands drest?
What little town by river or sea shore,   35
  Or mountain-built with peaceful citadel,
    Is emptied of this folk, this pious morn?
And, little town, thy streets for evermore
  Will silent be; and not a soul to tell
    Why thou art desolate, can e'er return.   40

V

O Attic shape! Fair attitude! with brede
  Of marble men and maidens overwrought,
With forest branches and the trodden weed;
  Thou, silent form, dost tease us out of thought
As doth eternity: Cold Pastoral!   45
  When old age shall this generation waste,
    Thou shalt remain, in midst of other woe
Than ours, a friend to man, to whom thou say'st,
  "Beauty is truth, truth beauty,"—that is all
    Ye know on earth, and all ye need to know.   50

_____

41. *Attic:* (Attica was the region of which Athens was the capital city).

ODE TO PSYCHE

(1820)

O Goddess! hear these tuneless numbers, wrung
   By sweet enforcement and remembrance dear,
And pardon that thy secrets should be sung
   Even into thine own soft-conchèd ear:
Surely I dreamt to-day, or did I see   5
   The winged Psyche with awakened eyes?
I wandered in a forest thoughtlessly,
   And, on the sudden, fainting with surprise,
Saw two fair creatures, couchèd side by side
   In deepest grass, beneath the whispering roof   10
   Of leaves and trembled blossoms, where there ran
      A brooklet, scarce espied:

'Mid hushed, cool-rooted flowers, fragrant-eyed,
   Blue, silver-white, and budded Tyrian,
They lay calm-breathing on the bedded grass;   15
   Their arms embracèd, and their pinions too;
   Their lips touched not, but had not bade adieu,
As if disjoinèd by soft-handed slumber,
And ready still past kisses to outnumber
   At tender eye-dawn of aurorean love: 20
      The wingèd boy I knew;
But who wast thou, O happy, happy dove?
      His Psyche true!

O latest born and loveliest vision far
   Of all Olympus' faded hierarchy!   25
Fairer than Phœbe's sapphire-regioned star,
   Or Vesper, amorous glow-worm of the sky;
Fairer than these, though temple thou hast none,
    Nor altar heaped with flowers;
Nor virgin-choir to make delicious moan   30

ODE TO PSYCHE: *Psyche:* the soul (often personified as a maiden with butterfly wings; supposed to have been loved by Eros [desire], son of Venus). 14. *Tyrian:* (Tyre was famous for its purple dyes). 25. *Olympus:* mountain home of the Greek gods. 26. *Phoebe:* Diana (moon goddess). 27. *Vesper:* Venus as evening star.

Upon the midnight hours;
No voice, no lute, no pipe, no incense sweet
  From chain-swung censer teeming;
No shrine, no grove, no oracle, no heat
  Of pale-mouthed prophet dreaming.   35

O brightest! though too late for antique vows,
  Too, too late for the fond believing lyre,
When holy were the haunted forest boughs,
  Holy the air, the water, and the fire;
Yet even in these days so far retired   40
  From happy pieties, thy lucent fans,
  Fluttering among the faint Olympians,
I see, and sing, by my own eyes inspired.
So let me be thy choir, and make a moan
        Upon the midnight hours;   45
Thy voice, thy lute, thy pipe, thy incense sweet
  From swinged censer teeming;
Thy shrine, thy grove, thy oracle, thy heat
  Of pale-mouthed prophet dreaming.

Yes, I will be thy priest, and build a fane   50
  In some untrodden region of my mind,
Where branchèd thoughts, new grown with pleasant pain,
  Instead of pines shall murmur in the wind:
Far, far around shall those dark-clustered trees
  Fledge the wild-ridged mountains steep by steep;   55
And there by zephyrs, streams, and birds, and bees,
  The moss-lain Dryads shall be lulled to sleep;
And in the midst of this wide quietness
A rosy sanctuary will I dress

With the wreathed trellis of a working brain,   60
  With buds, and bells, and stars without a name,
With all the gardener Fancy e'er could feign,
  Who breeding flowers, will never breed the same:
And there shall be for thee all soft delight
  That shadowy thought can win,   65
A bright torch, and a casement ope at night,
  To let the warm Love in!

---

57. *Dryads:* wood nymphs.

ODE TO A NIGHTINGALE
(1819)

I

My heart aches, and a drowsy numbness pains
  My sense, as though of hemlock I had drunk,
Or emptied some dull opiate to the drains
  One minute past, and Lethe-wards had sunk:
'Tis not through envy of thy happy lot,   5
  But being too happy in thine happiness,—
    That thou, light-winged Dryad of the trees,
      In some melodious plot
Of beechen green, and shadows numberless,
  Singest of summer in full-throated ease.   10

II

O, for a draught of vintage! that hath been
  Cooled a long age in the deep-delvèd earth,
Tasting of Flora and the country green,
  Dance, and Provençal song, and sunburnt mirth!
O for a beaker full of the warm South,   15
  Full of the true, the blushful Hippocrene,
    With beaded bubbles winking at the brim,
      And purple-stainèd mouth;
That I might drink, and leave the world unseen,
  And with thee fade away into the forest dim: 20

III

Fade far away, dissolve, and quite forget
  What thou among the leaves hast never known,
The weariness, the fever, and the fret
  Here, where men sit and hear each other groan;
Where palsy shakes a few, sad, last gray hairs,   25
  Where youth grows pale, and spectre-thin, and dies;
    Where but to think is to be full of sorrow
      And leaden-eyed despairs,

ODE TO A NIGHTINGALE: 4. *Lethe-wards:* into oblivion. 7. *Dryad:* wood
nymph. 13. *Flora:* the Spring. 14. *Provençal:* (the troubadours came from
Provence). 16. *Hippocrene:* a fountain whose waters inspired poetic crea-
tion.

Where Beauty cannot keep her lustrous eyes,
  Or new Love pine at them beyond to-morrow.   30

IV

Away! away! for I will fly to thee,
  Not charioted by Bacchus and his pards,
But on the viewless wings of Poesy,
  Though the dull brain perplexes and retards:
Already with thee! tender is the night,   35
    And haply the Queen-Moon is on her throne,
      Cluster'd around by all her starry Fays;
        But here there is no light,
    Save what from heaven is with the breezes blown
      Through verdurous glooms and winding mossy ways.   40

V

I cannot see what flowers are at my feet,
  Nor what soft incense hangs upon the boughs,
But, in embalmèd darkness, guess each sweet
  Wherewith the seasonable month endows
The grass, the thicket, and the fruit-tree wild;   45
    White hawthorn, and the pastoral eglantine;
      Fast fading violets covered up in leaves;
        And mid-May's eldest child,
    The coming musk-rose, full of dewy wine,
      The murmurous haunt of flies on summer eves.   50

VI

Darkling I listen; and, for many a time
  I have been half in love with easeful Death,
Called him soft names in many a mused rhyme,
  To take into the air my quiet breath;
Now more than ever seems it rich to die,   55
    To cease upon the midnight with no pain,
      While thou art pouring forth thy soul abroad
        In such an ecstasy!
    Still wouldst thou sing, and I have ears in vain—
    To thy high requiem become a sod.   60

VII

Thou wast not born for death, immortal Bird!
  No hungry generations tread thee down;

---

32. *pards:* leopards.

The voice I hear this passing night was heard
    In ancient days by emperor and clown:
Perhaps the self-same song that found a path   65
    Through the sad heart of Ruth, when, sick for home,
        She stood in tears amid the alien corn;
            The same that oft-times hath
Charmed magic casements, opening on the foam
    Of perilous seas, in faery lands forlorn.   70

                        VIII

Forlorn! the very word is like a bell
    To toll me back from thee to my sole self!
Adieu! the fancy cannot cheat so well
    As she is famed to do, deceiving elf.
Adieu! adieu! thy plaintive anthem fades   75
    Past the near meadows, over the still stream,
        Up the hill-side; and now 'tis buried deep
            In the next valley-glades:
Was it a vision, or a waking dream?
    Fled is that music:—Do I wake or sleep?   80

                        ❧

                    TO AUTUMN

                     (1820)

                         I

Season of mists and mellow fruitfulness,
    Close bosom-friend of the maturing sun;
Conspiring with him how to load and bless
    With fruit the vines that round the thatch-eves run;
To bend with apples the mossed cottage-trees,   5
    And fill all fruit with ripeness to the core;
        To swell the gourd, and plump the hazel shells
    With a sweet kernel; to set budding more,
And still more, later flowers for the bees,
Until they think warm days will never cease,   10
    For Summer has o'er-brimmed their clammy cells.

_____

66. *Ruth:* (after the death of her husband, an Israelite, she accompanied his
mother back to his native land). 67. *corn:* grain.

II

Who hath not seen thee oft amid thy store?
  Sometimes whoever seeks abroad may find
Thee sitting careless on a granary floor,
  Thy hair soft-lifted by the winnowing wind;   15
Or on a half-reaped furrow sound asleep,
  Drowsed with the fume of poppies, while thy hook
  Spares the next swath and all its twinèd flowers:
And sometimes like a gleaner thou dost keep
  Steady thy laden head across a brook;   20
  Or by a cyder-press, with patient look,
  Thou watchest the last oozings hours by hours.

III

Where are the songs of Spring? Ay, where are they?
  Think not of them, thou hast thy music too,—
While barrèd clouds bloom the soft-dying day,   25
  And touch the stubble-plains with rosy hue;
Then in a wailful choir the small gnats mourn
  Among the river sallows, borne aloft
  Or sinking as the light wind lives or dies;
And full-grown lambs loud bleat from hilly bourn;   30
  Hedge-crickets sing; and now with treble soft
  The red-breast whistles from a garden-croft;
  And gathering swallows twitter in the skies.

LA BELLE DAME SANS MERCI

(1820)

Ah, what can ail thee, wretched wight,
  Alone and palely loitering;
The sedge is withered from the lake,
  And no birds sing.

Ah, what can ail thee, wretched wight,   5
  So haggard and so woe-begone?
The squirrel's granary is full,
  And the harvest's done.

I see a lily on thy brow,
  With anguish moist and fever dew;   10

And on thy cheek a fading rose
Fast withereth too.

I met a lady in the meads
Full beautiful, a faery's child;
Her hair was long, her foot was light,   15
And her eyes were wild.

I set her on my pacing steed,
And nothing else saw all day long;
For sideways would she lean, and sing
A faery's song.   20

I made a garland for her head,
And bracelets too, and fragrant zone;
She looked at me as she did love,
And made sweet moan.

She found me roots of relish sweet,   25
And honey wild, and manna dew;
And sure in language strange she said,
I love thee true.

She took me to her elfin grot,
And there she gazed and sighèd deep,   30
And there I shut her wild sad eyes—
So kissed to sleep.

And there we slumbered on the moss,
And there I dreamed, ah woe betide,
The latest dream I ever dreamed   35
On the cold hill side.

I saw pale kings, and princes too,
Pale warriors, death-pale were they all;
Who cried—"La belle Dame sans merci
Hath thee in thrall!"   40

I saw their starved lips in the gloam
With horrid warning gapèd wide,
And I awoke, and found me here
On the cold hill side.

LA BELLE DAME: ll. 30-33. An earlier version reads: "And there she wept
and sighed full sore;/And there I shut her wild, wild eyes/With kisses
four./And there she lullèd me asleep. . . ."

And this is why I sojourn here   45
   Alone and palely loitering,
Though the sedge is withered from the lake,
   And no birds sing.

~❧~

THE EVE OF ST. AGNES
(1820)

St. Agnes' Eve—Ah, bitter chill it was!
The owl, for all his feathers, was a-cold;
The hare limped trembling through the frozen grass,
And silent was the flock in woolly fold:
Numb were the Beadsman's fingers, while he told   5
His rosary, and while his frosted breath,
Like pious incense from a censer old,
Seemed taking flight for heaven, without a death,
Past the sweet Virgin's picture, while his prayer he saith.

His prayer he saith, this patient, holy man;   10
Then takes his lamp, and riseth from his knees,
And back returneth, meagre, barefoot, wan,
Along the chapel aisle by slow degrees:
The sculptured dead, on each side, seem to freeze,
Emprisoned in black, purgatorial rails: 15
Knights, ladies, praying in dumb orat'ries,
He passeth by; and his weak spirit fails
To think how they may ache in icy hoods and mails.

Northward he turneth through a little door,
And scarce three steps, ere Music's golden tongue   20
Flattered to tears this aged man and poor;
But no—already had his deathbell rung:
The joys of all his life were said and sung:
His was harsh penance on St. Agnes' Eve:
Another way he went, and soon among   25
Rough ashes sat he for his soul's reprieve,
And all night kept awake, for sinners' sake to grieve.

That ancient Beadsman heard the prelude soft;
And so it chanced, for many a door was wide,

EVE OF ST. AGNES: 4. *Beadsman:* poor man supported by charity in return
for his prayers. 16. *orat'ries:* prayer chapels.

From hurry to and fro. Soon, up aloft,   30
The silver, snarling trumpets 'gan to chide:
The level chambers, ready with their pride,
Were glowing to receive a thousand guests:
The carvèd angels, ever eager-eyed,
Stared, where upon their heads the cornice rests,   35
With hair blown back, and wings put cross-wise on their breasts.

At length burst in the argent revelry,
With plume, tiara, and all rich array,
Numerous as shadows haunting faerily
The brain, new stuffed, in youth, with triumphs gay   40
Of old romance. These let us wish away,
And turn, sole-thoughted, to one Lady there,
Whose heart had brooded, all that wintry day,
On love, and winged St. Agnes' saintly care,
As she had heard old dames full many times declare.   45

They told her how, upon St. Agnes' Eve,
Young virgins might have visions of delight,
And soft adorings from their loves receive
Upon the honeyed middle of the night,
If ceremonies due they did aright;   50
As, supperless to bed they must retire,
And couch supine their beauties, lily white;
Nor look behind, nor sideways, but require
Of Heaven with upward eyes for all that they desire.

Full of this whim was thoughtful Madeline: 55
The music, yearning like a God in pain,
She scarcely heard: her maiden eyes divine,
Fixed on the floor, saw many a sweeping train
Pass by—she heeded not at all: in vain
Came many a tiptoe, amorous cavalier,   60
And back retired; not cooled by high disdain,
But she saw not: her heart was otherwhere:
She sighed for Agnes' dreams, the sweetest of the year.

She danced along with vague, regardless eyes,
Anxious her lips, her breathing quick and short: 65
The hallowed hour was near at hand: she sighs
Amid the timbrels, and the thronged resort
Of whisperers in anger, or in sport;

'Mid looks of love, defiance, hate, and scorn,
Hoodwinked with faery fancy; all amort,   70
Save to St. Agnes and her lambs unshorn,
And all the bliss to be before to-morrow morn.

So, purposing each moment to retire,
She lingered still. Meantime, across the moors,
Had come young Porphyro, with heart on fire   75
For Madeline. Beside the portal doors,
Buttressed from moonlight, stands he, and implores
All saints to give him sight of Madeline,
But for one moment in the tedious hours,
That he might gaze and worship all unseen;   80
Perchance speak, kneel, touch, kiss—in sooth such things have been.

He ventures in: let no buzzed whisper tell:
All eyes be muffled, or a hundred swords
Will storm his heart, Love's fev'rous citadel:
For him, those chambers held barbarian hordes,   85
Hyena foemen, and hot-blooded lords,
Whose very dogs would execrations howl
Against his lineage: not one breast affords
Him any mercy, in that mansion foul,
Save one old beldame, weak in body and in soul.   90

Ah, happy chance! the agèd creature came,
Shuffling along with ivory-headed wand,
To where he stood, hid from the torch's flame,
Behind a broad hall-pillar, far beyond
The sound of merriment and chorus bland: 95
He startled her; but soon she knew his face,
And grasped his fingers in her palsied hand,
Saying, "Mercy, Porphyro! hie thee from this place:
"They are all here to-night, the whole blood-thirsty race!

"Get hence! get hence! there's dwarfish Hildebrand;   100
"He had a fever late, and in the fit
"He cursèd thee and thine, both house and land:
"Then there's that old Lord Maurice, not a whit
"More tame for his gray hairs— Alas me! flit!
"Flit like a ghost away."—"Ah, Gossip dear,   105
"We're safe enough; here in this arm-chair sit,

---

70. *amort*: listless, benumbed.

"And tell me how"— "Good Saints! not here, not here;
"Follow me, child, or else these stones will be thy bier."

He followed through a lowly archèd way,
Brushing the cobwebs with his lofty plume,   110
And as she muttered "Well-a—well-a-day!"
He found him in a little moonlight room,
Pale, latticed, chill, and silent as a tomb.
"Now tell me where is Madeline," said he,
"O tell me, Angela, by the holy loom   115
"Which none but secret sisterhood may see,
"When they St. Agnes' wool are weaving piously."

"St. Agnes! Ah! it is St. Agnes' Eve—
"Yet men will murder upon holy days:
"Thou must hold water in a witch's sieve,   120
"And be liege-lord of all the Elves and Fays,
"To venture so: it fills me with amaze
"To see thee, Porphyro!—St. Agnes' Eve!
"God's help! my lady fair the conjuror plays
"This very night: good angels her deceive!   125
"But let me laugh awhile, I've mickle time to grieve."

Feebly she laugheth in the languid moon,
While Porphyro upon her face doth look,
Like puzzled urchin on an agèd crone
Who keepeth closed a wond'rous riddle-book,   130
As spectacled she sits in chimney nook.
But soon his eyes grew brilliant, when she told
His lady's purpose; and he scarce could brook
Tears, at the thought of those enchantments cold,
And Madeline asleep in lap of legends old.   135

Sudden a thought came like a full-blown rose,
Flushing his brow, and in his painèd heart
Made purple riot: then doth he propose
A stratagem, that makes the beldame start:
"A cruel man and impious thou art: 140
"Sweet lady, let her pray, and sleep, and dream
"Alone with her good angels, far apart
"From wicked men like thee. Go, go!—I deem
"Thou canst not surely be the same that thou didst seem."

---

115. *loom:* (it was a medieval practice to sacrifice two lambs on St. Agnes'
Day, January 21; their wool was later woven by nuns).

"I will not harm her, by all saints I swear,"   145
Quoth Porphyro: "O may I ne'er find grace
"When my weak voice shall whisper its last prayer,
"If one of her soft ringlets I displace,
"Or look with ruffian passion in her face:
"Good Angela, believe me by these tears;   150
"Or I will, even in a moment's space,
"Awake, with horrid shout, my foemen's ears,
"And beard them, though they be more fanged than wolves and
      bears."

"Ah! why wilt thou affright a feeble soul?
"A poor, weak, palsy-stricken, churchyard thing,   155
"Whose passing-bell may ere the midnight toll;
"Whose prayers for thee, each morn and evening,
"Were never missed."—Thus plaining, doth she bring
A gentler speech from burning Porphyro;
So woful, and of such deep sorrowing,   160
That Angela gives a promise she will do
Whatever he shall wish, betide her weal or woe.

Which was, to lead him, in close secrecy,
Even to Madeline's chamber, and there hide
Him in a closet, of such privacy   165
That he might see her beauty unespied,
And win perhaps that night a peerless bride,
While legioned faeries paced the coverlet,
And pale enchantment held her sleepy-eyed.
Never on such a night have lovers met,   170
Since Merlin paid his Demon all the monstrous debt.

"It shall be as thou wishest," said the Dame:
"All cates and dainties shall be stored there
"Quickly on this feast-night: by the tambour frame
"Her own lute thou wilt see: no time to spare,   175
"For I am slow and feeble, and scarce dare
"On such a catering trust my dizzy head.
"Wait here, my child, with patience; kneel in prayer
"The while: Ah! thou must needs the lady wed,
"Or may I never leave my grave among the dead."   180

So saying, she hobbled off with busy fear.
The lover's endless minutes slowly passed;

---

171. *paid . . . debt:* i.e.. died (he was begotten by demons).

The dame returned, and whispered in his ear
To follow her; with agèd eyes aghast
From fright of dim espial. Safe at last,   185
Through many a dusky gallery, they gain
The maiden's chamber, silken, hushed, and chaste;
Where Porphyro took covert, pleased amain.
His poor guide hurried back with agues in her brain.

Her faltering hand upon the balustrade,   190
Old Angela was feeling for the stair,
When Madeline, St. Agnes' charmèd maid,
Rose, like a missioned spirit, unaware:
With silver taper's light, and pious care,
She turned, and down the aged gossip led   195
To a safe level matting. Now prepare,
Young Porphyro, for gazing on that bed;
She comes, she comes again, like ring-dove frayed and fled.

Out went the taper as she hurried in;
Its little smoke, in pallid moonshine, died: 200
She closed the door, she panted, all akin
To spirits of the air, and visions wide:
No uttered syllable, or, woe betide!
But to her heart, her heart was voluble,
Paining with eloquence her balmy side;   205
As though a tongueless nightingale should swell
Her throat in vain, and die, heart-stifled, in her dell.

A casement high and triple-arched there was,
All garlanded with carven imag'ries
Of fruits, and flowers, and bunches of knot-grass,   210
And diamonded with panes of quaint device,
Innumerable of stains and splendid dyes,
As are the tiger-moth's deep-damasked wings;
And in the midst, 'mong thousand heraldries,
And twilight saints, and dim emblazonings,   215
A shielded scutcheon blushed with blood of queens and kings.

Full on this casement shone the wintry moon,
And threw warm gules on Madeline's fair breast,
As down she knelt for heaven's grace and boon;
Rose-bloom fell on her hands, together prest,   220

---

218. *gules:* red light.

And on her silver cross soft amethyst,
And on her hair a glory, like a saint:
She seemed a splendid angel, newly drest,
Save wings, for heaven:—Porphyro grew faint:
She knelt, so pure a thing, so free from mortal taint.   225

Anon his heart revives: her vespers done,
Of all its wreathèd pearls her hair she frees;
Unclasps her warmèd jewels one by one;
Loosens her fragrant bodice; by degrees
Her rich attire creeps rustling to her knees: 230
Half-hidden, like a mermaid in sea-weed,
Pensive awhile she dreams awake, and sees,
In fancy, fair St. Agnes in her bed,
But dares not look behind, or all the charm is fled.

Soon, trembling in her soft and chilly nest,   235
In sort of wakeful swoon, perplexed she lay,
Until the poppied warmth of sleep oppressed
Her soothèd limbs, and soul fatigued away;
Flown, like a thought, until the morrow-day;
Blissfully havened both from joy and pain;   240
Clasped like a missal where swart Paynims pray;
Blinded alike from sunshine and from rain,
As though a rose should shut, and be a bud again.

Stolen to this paradise, and so entranced,
Porphyro gazed upon her empty dress,   245
And listened to her breathing, if it chanced
To wake into a slumberous tenderness;
Which when he heard, that minute did he bless,
And breathed himself: then from the closet crept,
Noiseless as fear in a wide wilderness,   250
And over the hushed carpet, silent, stept,
And 'tween the curtains peeped, where, lo!—how fast she slept.

Then by the bed-side, where the faded moon
Made a dim, silver twilight, soft he set
A table, and, half anguished, threw thereon   255
A cloth of woven crimson, gold, and jet:—
O for some drowsy Morphean amulet!

---

241. *clasped . . . pray:* i.e., unopened: Pagans [Paynims] have no need
for missals [Christian prayer books]. 257. *Morphean:* (Morpheus was the
god of sleep).

The boisterous, midnight, festive clarion,
The kettle-drum, and far-heard clarinet,
Affray his ears, though but in dying tone:—   260
The hall door shuts again, and all the noise is gone.

And still she slept an azure-lidded sleep,
In blanchèd linen, smooth, and lavendered,
While he from forth the closet brought a heap
Of candied apple, quince, and plum, and gourd;   265
With jellies soother than the creamy curd,
And lucent syrops, tinct with cinnamon;
Manna and dates, in argosy transferred
From Fez; and spicèd dainties, every one,
From silken Samarcand to cedared Lebanon.   270

These delicates he heaped with glowing hand
On golden dishes and in baskets bright
Of wreathèd silver: sumptuous they stand
In the retired quiet of the night,
Filling the chilly room with perfume light.—   275
"And now, my love, my seraph fair, awake!
"Thou art my heaven, and I thine eremite:
"Open thine eyes, for meek St. Agnes' sake,
"Or I shall drowse beside thee, so my soul doth ache."

Thus whispering, his warm, unnervèd arm   280
Sank in her pillow. Shaded was her dream
By the dusk curtains:—'twas a midnight charm
Impossible to melt as icèd stream:
The lustrous salvers in the moonlight gleam;
Broad golden fringe upon the carpet lies: 285
It seemed he never, never could redeem
From such a stedfast spell his lady's eyes;
So mused awhile, entoiled in woofèd phantasies.

Awakening up, he took her hollow lute,—
Tumultuous,—and, in chords that tenderest be,   290
He played an ancient ditty, long since mute,
In Provence called, "La belle dame sans mercy:"
Close to her ear touching the melody;—
Wherewith disturbed, she uttered a soft moan:
He ceased—she panted quick—and suddenly   295
Her blue affrayèd eyes wide open shone:
Upon his knees he sank, pale as smooth-sculptured stone.

---

296. *affrayèd:* frightened.

Her eyes were open, but she still beheld,
Now wide awake, the vision of her sleep:
There was a painful change, that nigh expelled   300
The blisses of her dream so pure and deep
At which fair Madeline began to weep,
And moan forth witless words with many a sigh;
While still her gaze on Porphyro would keep;
Who knelt, with joinèd hands and piteous eye,   305
Fearing to move or speak, she looked so dreamingly.

"Ah, Porphyro!" said she, "but even now
"Thy voice was at sweet tremble in mine ear,
"Made tuneable with every sweetest vow;
"And those sad eyes were spiritual and clear: 310
"How changed thou art! how pallid, chill, and drear!
"Give me that voice again, my Porphyro,
"Those looks immortal, those complainings dear!
"Oh, leave me not in this eternal woe,
"For if thou diest, my Love, I know not where to go."   315

Beyond a mortal man impassioned far
At these voluptuous accents, he arose,
Ethereal, flushed, and like a throbbing star
Seen mid the sapphire heaven's deep repose;
Into her dream he melted, as the rose   320
Blendeth its odor with the violet,—
Solution sweet: meantime the frost wind blows
Like Love's alarum pattering the sharp sleet
Against the window panes; St. Agnes' moon hath set.

'Tis dark: quick pattereth the flaw-blown sleet: 325
"This is no dream, my bride, my Madeline!"
'Tis dark: the icèd gusts still rave and beat:
"No dream! alas! alas! and woe is mine!
"Porphyro will leave me here to fade and pine.—
"Cruel! what traitor could thee hither bring?   330
"I curse not, for my heart is lost in thine,
"Though thou forsakest a deceivèd thing;—
"A dove forlorn and lost with sick unprunèd wing."

"My Madeline! sweet dreamer! lovely bride!
"Say, may I be for aye thy vassal blest?   335
"Thy beauty's shield, heart-shaped and vermeil-dyed?
"Ah, silver shrine, here will I take my rest
"After so many hours of toil and quest,

"A famished pilgrim,—saved by miracle.
"Though I have found, I will not rob thy nest   340
"Saving of thy sweet self; if thou think'st well
"To trust, fair Madeline, to no rude infidel.

"Hark! 'tis an elfin storm from faery land,
"Of haggard seeming, but a boon indeed:
"Arise! arise! the morning is at hand;—   345
"The bloated wassaillers will never heed:—
"Let us away, my love, with happy speed;
"There are no ears to hear, or eyes to see,—
"Drowned all in Rhenish and the sleepy mead:
"Awake! arise! my love, and fearless be,   350
"For o'er the southern moors I have a home for thee."

She hurried at his words, beset with fears,
For there were sleeping dragons all around,
At glaring watch, perhaps, with ready spears—
Down the wide stairs a darkling way they found.—   355
In all the house was heard no human sound.
A chain-drooped lamp was flickering by each door;
The arras, rich with horseman, hawk, and hound,
Fluttered in the besieging wind's uproar;
And the long carpets rose along the gusty floor.   360

They glide, like phantoms, into the wide hall;
Like phantoms, to the iron porch, they glide;
Where lay the Porter, in uneasy sprawl,
With a huge empty flagon by his side:
The wakeful bloodhound rose, and shook his hide,   365
But his sagacious eye an inmate owns:
By one, and one, the bolts full easy slide;—
The chains lie silent on the footworn stones;—
The key turns, and the door upon its hinges groans.

And they are gone: aye, ages long ago   370
These lovers fled away into the storm.
That night the Baron dreamt of many a woe,
And all his warrior-guests, with shade and form
Of witch, and demon, and large coffin-worm,
Were long be-nightmared. Angela the old   375
Died palsy-twitched, with meagre face deform;
The Beadsman, after thousand aves told,
For aye unsought-for slept among his ashes cold.

---

349. *Rhenish:* Rhine wine; *mead:* liquor made by fermenting honey.

The Victorians

The Victorians

Alfred, Lord Tennyson

MARIANA
(1830)

With blackest moss the flower-plots
  Were thickly crusted, one and all:
The rusted nails fell from the knots
  That held the pear to the gable-wall.
The broken sheds looked sad and strange: 5
  Unlifted was the clinking latch;
  Weeded and worn the ancient thatch
Upon the lonely moated grange.
    She only said, 'My life is dreary,
      He cometh not,' she said;   10
    She said, 'I am aweary, aweary,
      I would that I were dead!'

Her tears fell with the dews at even;
  Her tears fell ere the dews were dried;
She could not look on the sweet heaven,   15
  Either at morn or eventide.
After the flitting of the bats,
  When thickest dark did trance the sky,
  She drew her casement-curtain by,
And glanced athwart the glooming flats.   20
    She only said, 'The night is dreary,
      He cometh not,' she said;
    She said, 'I am aweary, aweary,
      I would that I were dead!'

Upon the middle of the night,　　　　　　　25
　　Waking she heard the night-fowl crow:
The cock sung out an hour ere light:
　　From the dark fen the oxen's low
Came to her: without hope of change,
　　In sleep she seemed to walk forlorn,　　30
　　Till cold winds woke the gray-eyed morn
About the lonely moated grange.
　　　　She only said, 'The day is dreary,
　　　　　　He cometh not,' she said;
　　　　She said, 'I am aweary, aweary,　　35
　　　　　　I would that I were dead!'

About a stone-cast from the wall
　　A sluice with blackened waters slept,
And o'er it many, round and small,
　　The clustered marish-mosses crept.
Hard by a poplar shook alway,　　　　　　40
　　All silver-green with gnarlèd bark:
　　For leagues no other tree did mark
The level waste, the rounding gray.
　　　　She only said, 'My life is dreary,　　45
　　　　　　He cometh not,' she said;
　　　　She said, 'I am aweary, aweary,
　　　　　　I would that I were dead!'

And ever when the moon was low,
　　And the shrill winds were up and away,　50
In the white curtain, to and fro,
　　She saw the gusty shadow sway.
But when the moon was very low,
　　And wild winds bound within their cell,
　　The shadow of the poplar fell　　　　　55
Upon her bed, across her brow.
　　　　She only said, 'The night is dreary,
　　　　　　He cometh not,' she said;
　　　　She said, 'I am aweary, aweary.
　　　　　　I would that I were dead!'　　60

All day within the dreamy house,
　　The doors upon their hinges creaked:
The blue fly sung in the pane; the mouse
　　Behind the mouldering wainscot shrieked,
Or from the crevice peered about.　　　　65

Old faces glimmered through the doors,
Old footsteps trod the upper floors,
Old voices called her from without.
　　She only said, 'My life is dreary,
　　　　He cometh not,' she said;   70
　　She said, 'I am aweary, aweary,
　　　　I would that I were dead!'

The sparrow's chirrup on the roof,
　　The slow clock ticking, and the sound
Which to the wooing wind aloof   75
　　The poplar made, did all confound
Her sense; but most she loathed the hour
　　When the thick-moted sunbeam lay
Athwart the chambers, and the day
Was sloping toward his western bower.   80
　　Then, said she, 'I am very dreary,
　　　　He will not come,' she said;
　　She wept, 'I am aweary, aweary,
　　　　O God, that I were dead!'

THE LOTOS-EATERS
(1832)

"Courage!" he said, and pointed toward the land,
"This mounting wave will roll us shoreward soon."
In the afternoon they came unto a land,
In which it seemèd always afternoon.
All round the coast the languid air did swoon,   5
Breathing like one that hath a weary dream.
Full-faced above the valley stood the moon;
And like a downward smoke, the slender stream
Along the cliff to fall and pause and fall did seem.

A land of streams! some, like a downward smoke,   10
Slow-dropping veils of thinnest lawn, did go;
And some through wavering lights and shadows broke,
Rolling a slumbrous sheet of foam below.
They saw the gleaming river seaward flow

THE LOTOS-EATERS: 1. *he:* Ulysses, speaking to his men during the long
voyage home from Troy.

From the inner land: far off, three mountain-tops,   15
Three silent pinnacles of agèd snow,
Stood sunset-flushed: and, dewed with showery drops,
Up-clomb the shadowy pine above the woven copse.

The charmèd sunset lingered low adown
In the red West: through mountain clefts the dale   20
Was seen far inland, and the yellow down
Bordered with palm, and many a winding vale
And meadow, set with slender galingale;
A land where all things always seemed the same!
And round about the keel with faces pale,   25
Dark faces pale against that rosy flame,
The mild-eyed melancholy Lotos-eaters came.

Branches they bore of that enchanted stem,
Laden with flower and fruit, whereof they gave
To each, but whoso did receive of them,   30
And taste, to him the gushing of the wave
Far far away did seem to mourn and rave
On alien shores; and if his fellow spake,
His voice was thin, as voices from the grave;
And deep-asleep he seemed, yet all awake,   35
And music in his ears his beating heart did make.

They sat them down upon the yellow sand,
Between the sun and moon upon the shore;
And sweet it was to dream of Fatherland,
Of child, and wife, and slave; but evermore   40
Most weary seemed the sea, weary the oar,
Weary the wandering fields of barren foam.
Then some one said, "We will return no more";
And all at once they sang, "Our island home
Is far beyond the wave; we will no longer roam."   45

Choric Song

There is sweet music here that softer falls
Than petals from blown roses on the grass,
Or night-dews on still waters between walls
Of shadowy granite, in a gleaming pass;
Music that gentlier on the spirit lies,   50
Than tired eyelids upon tired eyes;

Music that brings sweet sleep down from the blissful skies.
Here are cool mosses deep,
And through the moss the ivies creep,
And in the stream the long-leaved flowers weep,   55
And from the craggy ledge the poppy hangs in sleep.

Why are we weighed upon with heaviness,
And utterly consumed with sharp distress,
While all things else have rest from weariness?
All things have rest: why should we toil alone,   60
We only toil, who are the first of things,
And make perpetual moan,
Still from one sorrow to another thrown:
Nor ever fold our wings,
And cease from wanderings,   65
Nor steep our brows in slumber's holy balm;
Nor harken what the inner spirit sings,
'There is no joy but calm!'—
Why should we only toil, the roof and crown of things?

Lo! in the middle of the wood,   70
The folded leaf is wooed from out the bud
With winds upon the branch, and there
Grows green and broad, and takes no care,
Sun-steeped at noon, and in the moon
Nightly dew-fed; and turning yellow   75
Falls, and floats adown the air.
Lo! sweetened with the summer light,
The full-juiced apple, waxing over-mellow,
Drops in a silent autumn night.
All its allotted length of days,   80
The flower ripens in its place,
Ripens and fades, and falls, and hath no toil,
Fast-rooted in the fruitful soil.

Hateful is the dark-blue sky,
Vaulted o'er the dark-blue sea.   85
Death is the end of life; ah, why
Should life all labour be?
Let us alone. Time driveth onward fast,
And in a little while our lips are dumb.
Let us alone. What is it that will last?   90
All things are taken from us, and become
Portions and parcels of the dreadful Past.

Let us alone. What pleasure can we have
To war with evil? Is there any peace
In ever climbing up the climbing wave?
All things have rest, and ripen toward the grave   9�
In silence; ripen, fall and cease:
Give us long rest or death, dark death, or dreamful ease.

How sweet it were, hearing the downward stream,
With half-shut eyes ever to seem   100
Falling asleep in a half-dream!
To dream and dream, like yonder amber light,
Which will not leave the myrrh-bush on the height;
To hear each other's whispered speech;
Eating the Lotos day by day,   105
To watch the crisping ripples on the beach,
And tender curving lines of creamy spray;
To lend our hearts and spirits wholly
To the influence of mild-minded melancholy;
To muse and brood and live again in memory,   110
With those old faces of our infancy
Heaped over with a mound of grass,
Two handfuls of white dust, shut in an urn of brass!

Dear is the memory of our wedded lives,
And dear the last embraces of our wives   115
And their warm tears: but all hath suffered change;
For surely now our household hearths are cold:
Our sons inherit us: our looks are strange:
And we should come like ghosts to trouble joy.
Or else the island princes over-bold   120
Have eat our substance, and the minstrel sings
Before them of the ten years' war in Troy,
And our great deeds, as half-forgotten things.
Is there confusion in the little isle?
Let what is broken so remain.   125
The Gods are hard to reconcile:
'Tis hard to settle order once again.
There *is* confusion worse than death,
Trouble on trouble, pain on pain,
Long labour unto agèd breath,   130
Sore task to hearts worn out with many wars
And eyes grown dim with gazing on the pilot-stars
But, propt on beds of amaranth and moly,

How sweet (while warm airs lull us, blowing lowly)
With half-dropt eyelids still,   135
Beneath a heaven dark and holy,
To watch the long bright river drawing slowly
His waters from the purple hill—
To hear the dewy echoes calling
From cave to cave through the thick-twinèd vine—   140
To watch the emerald-coloured water falling
Through many a woven acanthus-wreath divine!
Only to hear and see the far-off sparkling brine,
Only to hear were sweet, stretched out beneath the pine.
The Lotos blooms below the barren peak: 145
The Lotos blows by every winding creek:
All day the wind breathes low with mellower tone:
Through every hollow cave and alley lone
Round and round the spicy downs the yellow Lotos-dust is blown.
We have had enough of action, and of motion we,   150
Rolled to starboard, rolled to larboard, when the surge was seething
    free,
Where the wallowing monster spouted his foam-fountains in the sea.
Let us swear an oath, and keep it with an equal mind,
In the hollow Lotos-land to live and lie reclined
On the hills like gods together, careless of mankind.   155
For they lie beside their nectar, and the bolts are hurled
Far below them in the valleys, and the clouds are lightly curled
Round their golden houses, girdled with the gleaming world:
Where they smile in secret, looking over wasted lands,
Blight and famine, plague and earthquake, roaring deeps and fiery
    sands,   160
Clanging fights, and flaming towns, and sinking ships, and praying
    hands.
But they smile, they find a music centred in a doleful song
Steaming up, a lamentation and an ancient tale of wrong,
Like a tale of little meaning though the words are strong;
Chanted from an ill-used race of men that cleave the soil,   165
Sow the seed, and reap the harvest with enduring toil,
Storing yearly little dues of wheat, and wine and oil;
Till they perish and they suffer—some, 'tis whispered—down in hell
Suffer endless anguish, others in Elysian valleys dwell,
Resting weary limbs at last on beds of asphodel.   170
Surely, surely, slumber is more sweet than toil, the shore

---

156. *they:* i.e., the gods.

Than labour in the deep mid-ocean, wind and wave and oar;
O rest ye, brother mariners, we will not wander more.

THE LADY OF SHALOTT
(1832)

I

On either side the river lie
Long fields of barley and of rye,
That clothe the wold and meet the sky;
And thro' the field the road runs by
    To many-tower'd Camelot;   5
And up and down the people go,
Gazing where the lilies blow
Round an island there below,
    The island of Shalott.

Willows whiten, aspens quiver,   10
Little breezes dusk and shiver
Thro' the wave that runs for ever
By the island in the river
    Flowing down to Camelot,
Four grey walls, and four grey towers,   15
Overlook a space of flowers,
And the silent isle imbowers
    The Lady of Shalott.

By the margin, willow-veil'd,
Slide the heavy barges trail'd   20
By slow horses; and unhail'd
The shallop flitteth silken-sail'd
    Skimming down to Camelot:
But who hath seen her wave her hand?
Or at the casement seen her stand?   25
Or is she known in all the land,
    The Lady of Shalott?

Only reapers, reaping early
In among the bearded barley,
Hear a song that echoes cheerly   30
From the river winding clearly,

Down to tower'd Camelot:
And by the moon the reaper weary,
Piling sheaves in uplands airy,
Listening, whispers " 'Tis the fairy   35
    Lady of Shalott."

II

There she weaves by night and day
A magic web with colours gay.
She has heard a whisper say,
A curse is on her if she stay   40
        To look down to Camelot.
She knows not what the curse may be,
And so she weaveth steadily,
And little other care hath she,
        The Lady of Shalott.   45

And moving thro' a mirror clear
That hangs before her all the year,
Shadows of the world appear.
There she sees the highway near
        Winding down to Camelot: 50
There the river eddy whirls,
And there the surly village-churls,
And the red cloaks of market girls,
        Pass onward from Shalott.

Sometimes a troop of damsels glad,   55
An abbot on an ambling pad,
Sometimes a curly shepherd-lad,
Or long-hair'd page in crimson clad,
        Goes by to tower'd Camelot;
And sometimes thro' the mirror blue   60
The knights come riding two and two:
She hath no loyal knight and true,
        The Lady of Shalott.

But in her web she still delights
To weave the mirror's magic sights,   65
For often thro' the silent nights
A funeral, with plumes and lights
        And music, went to Camelot:
Or when the moon was overhead,
Came two young lovers lately wed;   70

"I am half sick of shadows," said
   The Lady of Shalott.

III

A bow-shot from her bower-eaves,
He rode between the barley-sheaves,
The sun came dazzling thro' the leaves,   75
And flamed upon the brazen greaves
   Of bold Sir Lancelot.
A red-cross knight for ever kneel'd
To a lady in his shield,
That sparkled on the yellow field,   80
   Beside remote Shalott.

The gemmy bridle glitter'd free,
Like to some branch of stars we see
Hung in the golden Galaxy.
The bridle bells rang merrily   85
   As he rode down to Camelot:
And from his blazon'd baldric slung
A mighty silver bugle hung,
And as he rode his armour rung,
   Beside remote Shalott.   90

All in the blue unclouded weather
Thick-jewell'd shone the saddle-leather,
The helmet and the helmet-feather
Burn'd like one burning flame together,
   As he rode down to Camelot.   95
As often thro' the purple night,
Below the starry clusters bright,
Some bearded meteor, trailing light,
   Moves over still Shalott.

His broad clear brow in sunlight glow'd;   100
On burnish'd hooves his war-horse trode;
From underneath his helmet flow'd
His coal-black curls as on he rode,
   As he rode down to Camelot.
From the bank and from the river   105
He flash'd into the crystal mirror,
"Tirra lirra," by the river
   Sang Sir Lancelot.

She left the web, she left the loom,
She made three paces thro' the room,   110
She saw the water-lily bloom,
She saw the helmet and the plume,
    She look'd down to Camelot.
Out flew the web and floated wide;
The mirror crack'd from side to side;   115
"The curse is come upon me," cried
    The Lady of Shalott.

IV

In the stormy east-wind straining,
The pale yellow woods were waning,
The broad stream in his banks complaining,   120
Heavily the low sky raining
    Over tower'd Camelot;
Down she came and found a boat
Beneath a willow left afloat,
And round about the prow she wrote   125
    The Lady of Shalott.

And down the river's dim expanse
Like some bold seër in a trance,
Seeing all his own mischance—
With a glassy countenance   130
    Did she look to Camelot.
And at the closing of the day
She loosed the chain, and down she lay;
The broad stream bore her far away,
    The Lady of Shalott.   135

Lying, robed in snowy white
That loosely flew to left and right—
The leaves upon her falling light—
Thro' the noises of the night
    She floated down to Camelot: 140
And as the boat-head wound along
The willowy hills and fields among,
They heard her singing her last song,
    The Lady of Shalott.

Heard a carol, mournful, holy,   145
Chanted loudly, chanted lowly,

Till her blood was frozen slowly,
And her eyes were darken'd wholly,
   Turn'd to tower'd Camelot.
For ere she reach'd upon the tide   150
The first house by the water-side,
Singing in her song she died,
   The Lady of Shalott.

Under tower and balcony,
By garden-wall and gallery,   155
A gleaming shape she floated by,
Dead-pale between the houses high,
   Silent into Camelot.
Out upon the wharfs they came,
Knight and burgher, lord and dame,   160
And round the prow they read her name,
   The Lady of Shalott.

Who is this? and what is here?
And in the lighted palace near
Died the sound of royal cheer;   165
And they cross'd themselves for fear,
   All the knights at Camelot:
But Lancelot mused a little space;
He said, "She has a lovely face;
God in His mercy lend her grace,   170
   The Lady of Shalott."

                ⨀

From LOCKSLEY HALL

(1842)

Comrades, leave me here a little, while as yet 't is early morn;
Leave me here, and when you want me, sound upon the bugle horn.

'T is the place, and all around it, as of old, the curlews call,
Dreary gleams about the moorland flying over Locksley Hall;

Locksley Hall, that in the distance overlooks the sandy tracts,   5
And the hollow ocean-ridges roaring into cataracts.

Many a night from yonder ivied casement, ere I went to rest,
Did I look on great Orion sloping slowly to the west.

Many a night I saw the Pleiads, rising thro' the mellow shade,
Glitter like a swarm of fireflies tangled in a silver braid.   10

Here about the beach I wander'd, nourishing a youth sublime
With the fairy tales of science, and the long result of time;

When the centuries behind me like a fruitful land reposed;
When I clung to all the present for the promise that it closed;

When I dipt into the future far as human eye could see,   15
Saw the vision of the world and all the wonder that would be.—

In the spring a fuller crimson comes upon the robin's breast;
In the spring the wanton lapwing gets himself another crest;

In the spring a livelier iris changes on the burnish'd dove;   19
In the spring a young man's fancy lightly turns to thoughts of love.

.   .   .   .

Can I but relive in sadness? I will turn that earlier page
Hide me from my deep emotion, O thou wondrous Mother-Age!

Make me feel the wild pulsation that I felt before the strife,
When I heard my days before me, and the tumult of my life;

Yearning for the large excitement that the coming years would
        yield,   111
Eager-hearted as a boy when first he leaves his father's field,

And at night along the dusky highway near and nearer drawn,
Sees in heaven the light of London flaring like a dreary dawn;

And his spirit leaps within him to be gone before him then,   115
Underneath the light he looks at, in among the throngs of men;

Men, my brothers, men the workers, ever reaping something
        new;
That which they have done but earnest of the things that they
        shall do.

For I dipt into the future, far as human eye could see,   119
Saw the Vision of the world, and all the wonder that would be;

Saw the heavens fill with commerce, argosies of magic sails,
Pilots of the purple twilight, dropping down with costly bales;

---

9. *Pleiads:* star cluster in the constellation Taurus.
118. *earnest:* earnest money, token, pledge.

Heard the heavens fill with shouting, and there rain'd a ghastly
    dew
From the nations' airy navies grappling in the central blue;

Far along the world-wide whisper of the south-wind rushing
    warm,   125
With the standards of the peoples plunging thro' the thunder
    storm;

Till the war-drum throbb'd no longer, and the battle flags were
    furl'd
In the Parliament of man, the Federation of the world.

There the common sense of most shall hold a fretful realm in
    awe,
And the kindly earth shall slumber, lapt in universal law.   130

So I triumphed, ere my passion sweeping thro' me left me dry,
Left me with the palsied heart, and left me with the jaundiced
    eye;

Eye, to which all order festers, all things here are out of joint,
Science moves, but slowly slowly, creeping on from point to
    point:

Slowly comes a hungry people, as a lion, creeping nigher,   135
Glares at one that nods and winks behind a slowly-dying fire.

Yet I doubt not thro' the ages one increasing purpose runs,
And the thoughts of men are widen'd with the process of the
    suns.

What is that to him that reaps not harvest of his youthful joys,
Tho' the deep heart of existence beat for ever like a boy's?   140

Knowledge comes, but wisdom lingers, and I linger on the
    shore,
And the individual withers, and the world is more and more.

Knowledge comes, but wisdom lingers, and he bears a laden
    breast,
Full of sad experience, moving toward the stillness of his rest.

Hark, my merry comrades call me, sounding on the bugle-horn,
They to whom my foolish passion were a target for their scorn: 146

Shall it not be scorn to me to harp on such a moulder'd string?
I am shamed thro' all my nature to have loved so slight a thing.

Weakness to be wroth with weakness! woman's pleasure,
    woman's pain—
Nature made them blinder motions bounded in a shallower
    brain: 150

Woman is the lesser man, and all thy passions, match'd with
    mine,
Are as moonlight unto sunlight, and as water unto wine—

Here at least, where nature sickens, nothing. Ah, for some
    retreat
Deep in yonder shining Orient, where my life began to beat;

Where in wild Mahratta-battle fell my father evil-starr'd;—   155
I was left a trampled orphan, and a selfish uncle's ward.

Or to burst all links of habit—there to wander far away,
On from island unto island at the gateways of the day.

Larger constellations burning, mellow moons and happy skies,
Breadths of tropic shade and palms in cluster, knots of Para-
    dise.   160

Never comes the trader, never floats an European flag,
Slides the bird o'er lustrous woodland, swings the trailer from
    the crag;

Droops the heavy-blossom'd bower, hangs the heavy-fruited
    tree—
Summer isles of Eden lying in dark-purple spheres of sea.

There methinks would be enjoyment more than in this march
    of mind.   165
In the steamship, in the railway, in the thoughts that shake
    mankind.

There the passions cramp'd no longer shall have scope and
    breathing space;
I will take some savage woman, she shall rear my dusky race.

Iron-jointed, supple-sinew'd, they shall dive, and they shall run,
Catch the wild goat by the hair, and hurl their lances in the sun;

148. *so slight a thing:* the speaker's cousin Amy, who has jilted him. 155.
Mahratta: a people of south central India.

Whistle back the parrot's call, and leap the rainbows of the
    brooks,   171
Not with blinded eyesight poring over miserable books—

Fool, again the dream, the fancy! but I *know* my words are
    wild,
But I count the gray barbarian lower than the Christian child.

I, to herd with narrow foreheads, vacant of our glorious gains,   175
Like a beast with lower pleasures, like a beast with lower pains!

Mated with a squalid savage—what to me were sun or clime?
I the heir of all the ages, in the foremost files of time—

I that rather held it better men should perish one by one,   179
Than that earth should stand at gaze like Joshua's moon in Ajalon!

Not in vain the distance beacons. Forward, forward let us range,
Let the great world spin for ever down the ringing grooves of
    change.

Thro' the shadow of the globe we sweep into the younger day;
Better fifty years of Europe than a cycle of Cathay.   184

Mother-age,—for mine I knew not,—help me as when life begun;
Rift the hills, and roll the waters, flash the lightnings,
    weigh the Sun—

O, I see the crescent promise of my spirit hath not set.
Ancient founts of inspiration well thro' all my fancy yet.

Howsoever these things be, a long farewell to Locksley Hall!
Now for me the woods may wither, now for me the rooftree
    fall.   190

Comes a vapour from the margin, blackening over heath and
    holt,
Cramming all the blast before it, in its breast a thunderbolt.

Let it fall on Locksley Hall, with rain or hail, or fire or snow;
For the mighty wind arises, roaring seaward, and I go.

∼∽

---

180. *moon:* see Joshua 10:12-15. 185. *mine:* i.e. my mother.

MORTE D'ARTHUR
(1842)

So all day long the noise of battle roll'd
Among the mountains by the winter sea;
Until King Arthur's table, man by man,
Had fall'n in Lyonnesse about their Lord,
King Arthur: then, because his wound was deep,   5
The bold Sir Bedivere uplifted him,
Sir Bedivere, the last of all his knights,
And bore him to a chapel nigh the field,
A broken chancel with a broken cross,
That stood on a dark strait of barren land.   10
On one side lay the Ocean, and on one
Lay a great water, and the moon was full.
    Then spake King Arthur to Sir Bedivere:
'The sequel of to-day unsolders all
The goodliest fellowship of famous knights   15
Whereof this world holds record. Such a sleep
They sleep—the men I loved. I think that we
Shall never more, at any future time,
Delight our souls with talk of knightly deeds,
Walking about the gardens and the halls   20
Of Camelot, as in the days that were.
I perish by this people which I made,—
Tho' Merlin sware that I should come again
To rule once more—but let what will be, be,
I am so deeply smitten thro' the helm   25
That without help I cannot last till morn.
Thou therefore take my brand Excalibur,
Which was my pride: for thou rememberest how
In those old days, one summer noon, an arm

---

1. *noise of battle:* between Arthur and Modred, his usurping nephew.
See Sir Thomas Malory, *Le Morte D'Arthur* (1470), Book XXI. *Lyonesse:*
land supposed to have existed off the SW tip of Cornwall, and to have
been later covered by the sea. 27. *brand:* sword.

Rose up from out the bosom of the lake,   30
Clothed in white samite, mystic, wonderful,
Holding the sword—and how I row'd across
And took it, and have worn it, like a king:
And, wheresoever I am sung or told
In aftertime, this also shall be known: 35
But now delay not: take Excalibur,
And fling him far into the middle mere:
Watch what thou seëst, and lightly bring me word.'
    To him replied the bold Sir Bedivere:
'It is not meet, Sir King, to leave thee thus,   40
Aidless, alone, and smitten thro' the helm.
A little thing may harm a wounded man.
Yet I thy hest will all perform at full,
Watch what I see, and lightly bring thee word.'
    So saying, from the ruin'd shrine he stept   45
And in the moon athwart the place of tombs,
Where lay the mighty bones of ancient men,
Old knights, and over them the sea-wind sang
Shrill, chill, with flakes of foam. He, stepping down
By zig-zag paths, and juts of pointed rock,   50
Came on the shining levels of the lake.
    There drew he forth the brand Excalibur,
And o'er him, drawing it, the winter moon,
Brightening the skirts of a long cloud, ran forth
And sparkled keen with frost against the hilt: 55
For all the haft twinkled with diamond sparks,
Myriads of topaz-lights, and jacinth-work
Of subtlest jewellery. He gazed so long
That both his eyes were dazzled, as he stood,
This way and that dividing the swift mind,   60
In act to throw: but at the last it seem'd
Better to leave Excalibur conceal'd
There in the many-knotted waterflags,
That whistled stiff and dry about the marge.
So strode he back slow to the wounded King.   65
    Then spake King Arthur to Sir Bedivere:
'Hast thou perform'd my mission which I gave?
What is it thou hast seen? or what hast heard?'
    And answer made the bold Sir Bedivere:
'I heard the ripple washing in the reeds,   70

---

31. *samite:* rich silk fabric. 37. *mere:* lake.

And the wild water lapping on the crag.'
  To whom replied King Arthur, faint and pale:
'Thou hast betray'd thy nature and thy name,
Not rendering true answer, as beseem'd
Thy fëalty, nor like a noble knight: 75
For surer sign had follow'd, either hand,
Or voice, or else a motion of the mere.
This is a shameful thing for men to lie.
Yet now, I charge thee, quickly go again
As thou art lief and dear, and do the thing   80
I bade thee, watch, and lightly bring me word.'
  Then went Sir Bedivere the second time
Across the ridge, and paced beside the mere,
Counting the dewy pebbles, fix'd in thought;
But when he saw the wonder of the hilt,   85
How curiously and strangely chased, he smote
His palms together, and he cried aloud.
  'And if indeed I cast the brand away,
Surely a precious thing, one worthy note,
Should thus be lost for ever from the earth,   90
Which might have pleased the eyes of many men.
What good should follow this, if this were done?
What harm, undone? deep harm to disobey,
Seeing obedience is the bond of rule.
Were it well to obey then, if a king demand   95
An act unprofitable, against himself?
The King is sick, and knows not what he does.
What record, or what relic of my lord
Should be to aftertime, but empty breath
And rumours of a doubt? but were this kept,   100
Stored in some treasure-house of mighty kings,
Some one might show it at a joust of arms,
Saying, "King Arthur's sword, Excalibur,
Wrought by the lonely maiden of the Lake.
Nine years she wrought it, sitting in the deeps   105
Upon the hidden bases of the hills."
So might some old man speak in the aftertime
To all the people, winning reverence.
But now much honour and much fame were lost.'
  So spake he, clouded with his own conceit,   110
And hid Excalibur the second time,
And so strode back slow to the wounded King.
  Then spoke King Arthur, breathing heavily:

'What is it thou hast seen? or what has heard?'
And answer made the bold Sir Bedivere: 115
'I heard the water lapping on the crag,
And the long ripple washing in the reeds.'
　　To whom replied King Arthur, much in wrath:
'Ah, miserable and unkind, untrue,
Unknightly, traitor-hearted! Woe is me! 120
Authority forgets a dying king,
Laid widow'd of the power in his eye
That bow'd the will. I see thee what thou art,
For thou, the latest-left of all my knights,
In whom should meet the offices of all, 125
Thou wouldst betray me for the precious hilt;
Either from lust of gold, or like a girl
Valuing the giddy pleasure of the eyes.
Yet, for a man may fail in duty twice,
And the third time may prosper, get thee hence: 130
But, if thou spare to fling Excalibur,
I will arise and slay thee with my hands.'
　　Then quickly rose Sir Bedivere, and ran,
And, leaping down the ridges lightly, plunged
Among the bulrush-beds, and clutch'd the sword, 135
And strongly wheel'd and threw it. The great brand
Made lightnings in the splendour of the moon,
And flashing round and round, and whirl'd in an arch,
Shot like a streamer of the northern morn,
Seen where the moving isles of winter shock 140
By night, with noises of the northern sea.
So flash'd and fell the brand Excalibur:
But ere he dipt the surface, rose an arm
Clothed in white samite, mystic, wonderful,
And caught him by the hilt, and brandish'd him 145
Three times, and drew him under in the mere.
And lightly went the other to the King.
　　Then spoke King Arthur, drawing thicker breath:
'Now see I by thine eyes that this is done.
Speak out: what is it thou hast heard, or seen?' 150
　　And answer made the bold Sir Bedivere:
'Sir King, I closed mine eyelids, lest the gems
Should blind my purpose, for I never saw,
Nor shall see, here or elsewhere, till I die,
Not tho' I live three lives of mortal men, 155
So great a miracle as yonder hilt.

Then with both hands I flung him, wheeling him;
But when I look'd again, behold an arm,
Clothed in white samite, mystic, wonderful,
That caught him by the hilt, and brandish'd him   160
Three times, and drew him under in the mere.'
  And answer made King Arthur, breathing hard:
'My end draws nigh; 'tis time that I were gone.
Make broad thy shoulders to receive my weight,
And bear me to the margin; yet I fear   165
My wound hath taken cold, and I shall die.'
  So saying, from the pavement he half rose,
Slowly, with pain, reclining on his arm,
And looking wistfully with wide blue eyes
As in a picture. Him Sir Bedivere   170
Remorsefully regarded thro' his tears,
And would have spoken, but he found not words,
Then took with care, and kneeling on one knee,
O'er both his shoulders drew the languid hands,
And rising bore him thro' the place of tombs.   175
  But, as he walk'd, King Arthur panted hard,
Like one that feels a nightmare on his bed
When all the house is mute. So sigh'd the King,
Muttering and murmuring at his ear, 'Quick, quick!
I fear it is too late, and I shall die.'   180
But the other swiftly strode from ridge to ridge,
Clothed with his breath, and looking, as he walk'd,
Larger than human on the frozen hills.
He heard the deep behind him, and a cry
Before. His own thought drove him like a goad.   185
Dry clash'd his harness in the icy caves
And barren chasms, and all to left and right
The bare black cliff clang'd round him, as he based
His feet on juts of slippery crag that rang
Sharp-smitten with the dint of armed heels—   190
And on a sudden, lo! the level lake,
And the long glories of the winter moon.
  Then saw they how there hove a dusky barge,
Dark as a funeral scarf from stem to stern,
Beneath them; and descending they were ware   195
That all the decks were dense with stately forms
Black-stoled, black-hooded, like a dream—by these
Three Queens with crowns of gold—and from them rose
A cry that shiver'd to the tingling stars,

And, as it were one voice, an agony   200
Of lamentation, like a wind, that shrills
All night in a waste land, where no one comes,
Or hath come, since the making of the world.
    Then murmur'd Arthur, 'Place me in the barge,'
And to the barge they came. There those three Queens   205
Put forth their hands, and took the King, and wept.
But she, that rose the tallest of them all
And fairest, laid his head upon her lap,
And loosed the shatter'd casque, and chafed his hands,
And call'd him by his name, complaining loud,   210
And dropping bitter tears against his brow
Striped with dark blood: for all his face was white
And colourless, and like the wither'd moon
Smote by the fresh beam of the springing east;
And all his greaves and cuisses dash'd with drops   215
Of onset; and the light and lustrous curls—
That made his forehead like a rising sun
High from the daïs-throne—were parch'd with dust;
Or, clotted into points and hanging loose,
Mix'd with the knightly growth that fringed his lips.   220
So like a shatter'd column lay the King;
Not like that Arthur who, with lance in rest,
From spur to plume a star of tournament,
Shot thro' the lists at Camelot, and charged
Before the eyes of ladies and of kings.   225
    Then loudly cried the bold Sir Bedivere,
'Ah! my Lord Arthur, whither shall I go?
Where shall I hide my forehead and my eyes?
For now I see the true old times are dead,
When every morning brought a noble chance,   230
And every chance brought out a noble knight.
Such times have been not since the light that led
The holy Elders with the gift of myrrh.
But now the whole ROUND TABLE is dissolved
Which was an image of the mighty world;   235
And I, the last, go forth companionless,
And the days darken round me, and the years,
Among new men, strange faces, other minds.'
    And slowly answered Arthur from the barge:
'The old order changeth, yielding place to new,   240

---

233. *myrrh:* at the nativity.

And God fulfils Himself in many ways,
Lest one good custom should corrupt the world.
Comfort thyself: what comfort is in me?
I have lived my life, and that which I have done
May He within Himself make pure! but thou,   245
If thou shouldst never see my face again,
Pray for my soul. More things are wrought by prayer
Than this world dreams of. Wherefore, let thy voice
Rise like a fountain for me night and day.
For what are men better than sheep or goats   250
That nourish a blind life within the brain,
If, knowing God, they lift not hands of prayer
Both for themselves and those who call them friend?
For so the whole round earth is every way
Bound by gold chains about the feet of God.   255
But now farewell. I am going a long way
With these thou seëst—if indeed I go—
(For all my mind is clouded with a doubt)
To the island-valley of Avilion;
Where falls not hail, or rain, or any snow,   260
Nor ever wind blows loudly; but it lies
Deep-meadow'd, happy, fair with orchard-lawns
And bowery hollows crown'd with summer sea,
Where I will heal me of my grievous wound.'
    So said he, and the barge with oar and sail   265
Moved from the brink, like some full-breasted swan
That, fluting a wild carol ere her death,
Ruffles her pure cold plume, and takes the flood
With swarthy webs. Long stood Sir Bedivere
Revolving many memories, till the hull   270
Look'd one black dot against the verge of dawn,
And on the mere the wailing died away.

❧

---

259. *Avilion*: abode and burial place of Arthur, sometimes identified with
Glastonbury in SW England; the afterlife.

ULYSSES

(1842)

It little profits that an idle king,
By this still hearth, among these barren crags,
Matched with an agèd wife, I mete and dole
Unequal laws unto a savage race,
That hoard, and sleep, and feed, and know not me.   5
I cannot rest from travel. I will drink
Life to the lees. All time I have enjoyed
Greatly, have suffered greatly, both with those
That loved me, and alone; on shore, and when
Through scudding drifts the rainy Hyades   10
Vext the dim sea. I am become a name;
For always roaming with a hungry heart
Much have I seen and known,—cities of men
And manners, climates, councils, governments,
Myself not least, but honored of them all,—   15
And drunk delight of battle with my peers,
Far on the ringing plains of windy Troy.
I am a part of all that I have met;
Yet all experience is an arch where-through
Gleams that untravelled world whose margin fades   20
Forever and forever when I move.
How dull it is to pause, to make an end,
To rust unburnished, not to shine in use!
As though to breathe were life! Life piled on life
Were all too little, and of one to me   25
Little remains; but every hour is saved
From that eternal silence, something more,
A bringer of new things; and vile it were
For some three suns to store and hoard myself,
And this gray spirit yearning in desire   30
To follow knowledge like a sinking star,
Beyond the utmost bound of human thought.

ULYSSES: 1. *king:* Ulysses himself, now home at Ithaca after the voyage.
10. *Hyades:* group of stars.

'This is my son, mine own Telemachus,
To whom I leave the sceptre and the isle—
Well-loved of me, discerning to fulfil   35
This labor, by slow prudence to make mild
A rugged people, and through soft degrees
Subdue them to the useful and the good.
Most blameless is he, centred in the sphere
Of common duties, decent not to fail   40
In offices of tenderness, and pay
Meet adoration to my household gods,
When I am gone. He works his work, I mine.
    There lies the port; the vessel puffs her sail;
There gloom the dark, broad seas. My mariners,   45
Souls that have toiled, and wrought, and thought with me,—
That ever with a frolic welcome took
The thunder and the sunshine, and opposed
Free hearts, free foreheads,—you and I are old:
Old age hath yet his honor and his toil.   50
Death closes all; but something ere the end,
Some work of noble note, may yet be done,
Not unbecoming men that strove with gods.
The lights begin to twinkle from the rocks;
The long day wanes; the slow moon climbs; the deep   55
Moans round with many voices. Come, my friends.
'Tis not too late to seek a newer world.
Push off, and sitting well in order smite
The sounding furrows; for my purpose holds
To sail beyond the sunset, and the baths   60
Of all the western stars, until I die.
It may be that the gulfs will wash us down;
It may be we shall touch the Happy Isles,
And see the great Achilles, whom we knew.
Though much is taken, much abides; and though   65
We are nct now that strength which in old days
Moved earth and heaven, that which we are, we are,—
One equal temper of heroic hearts,
Made weak by time and fate, but strong in will
To strive, to seek, to find, and not to yield.   70

❧

---

63. *Happy Isles:* Heaven in Greek myth.

From IN MEMORIAM
(1850)

Prologue

Strong Son of God, immortal Love,
    Whom we, that have not seen thy face,
    By faith, and faith alone, embrace,
Believing where we cannot prove;

Thine are these orbs of light and shade;   5
    Thou madest Life in man and brute;
    Thou madest Death; and lo, thy foot
Is on the skull which thou hast made.

Thou wilt not leave us in the dust:
    Thou madest man, he knows not why;   10
    He thinks he was not made to die;
And thou hast made him: thou art just.

Thou seemest human and divine,
    The highest, holiest manhood, thou:
    Our wills are ours, we know not how;   15
Our wills are ours, to make them thine.

Our little systems have their day;
    They have their day and cease to be:
    They are but broken lights of thee,
And thou, O Lord, art more than they.   20

We have but faith: we cannot know;
    For knowledge is of things we see;
    And yet we trust it comes from thee,
A beam in darkness: let it grow.

Let knowledge grow from more to more,   25
    But more of reverence in us dwell;
    That mind and soul, according well,
May make one music as before,

But vaster. We are fools and slight;
    We mock thee when we do not fear: 30
    But help thy foolish ones to bear;
Help thy vain worlds to bear thy light.

Forgive what seemed my sin in me;
  What seemed my worth since I began;
  For merit lives from man to man,   35
And not from man, O Lord, to thee.

Forgive my grief for one removed,
  Thy creature, whom I found so fair.
  I trust he lives in thee, and there
I find him worthier to be loved.   40

Forgive these wild and wandering cries,
  Confusions of a wasted youth;
  Forgive them where they fail in truth,
And in thy wisdom make me wise.

II

Old yew, which graspest at the stones
  That name the underlying dead,
  Thy fibres net the dreamless head,
Thy roots are wrapt about the bones.

The seasons bring the flower again,   5
  And bring the firstling to the flock;
  And in the dusk of thee the clock
Beats out the little lives of men.

O, not for thee the glow, the bloom,
  Who changest not in any gale,   10
  Nor branding summer suns avail
To touch thy thousand years of gloom;

And gazing on thee, sullen tree,
  Sick for thy stubborn hardihood,
  I seem to fail from out my blood   15
And grow incorporate into thee.

III

O Sorrow, cruel fellowship,
  O Priestess in the vaults of Death,
  O sweet and bitter in a breath,
What whispers from thy lying lip?

'The stars,' she whispers, 'blindly run;   5
  A web is woven across the sky;

From out waste places comes a cry,
And murmurs from the dying sun;

'And all the phantom, Nature, stands—
    With all the music in her tone,   10
    A hollow echo of my own,—
A hollow form with empty hands.'

And shall I take a thing so blind,
    Embrace her as my natural good;
    Or crush her, like a vice of blood,   15
Upon the threshold of the mind?

VII

Dark house, by which once more I stand
    Here in the long unlovely street,
    Doors, where my heart was used to beat
So quickly, waiting for a hand,

A hand that can be clasped no more—   5
    Behold me, for I cannot sleep,
    And like a guilty thing I creep
At earliest morning to the door.

He is not here; but far away
    The noise of life begins again,   10
    And ghastly through the drizzling rain
On the bald street breaks the blank day.

XI

Calm is the morn without a sound,
    Calm as to suit a calmer grief,
    And only through the faded leaf
The chestnut pattering to the ground;

Calm and deep peace on this high wold,   5
    And on these dews that drench the furze.
    And all the silvery gossamers
That twinkle into green and gold;

Calm and still light on yon great plain
    That sweeps with all its autumn bowers,   10
    And crowded farms and lessening towers,
To mingle with the bounding main;

Calm and deep peace in this wide air,
  These leaves that redden to the fall,
  And in my heart, if calm at all,   15
If any calm, a calm despair;

Calm on the seas, and silver sleep,
  And waves that sway themselves in rest,
  And dead calm in that noble breast
Which heaves but with the heaving deep.   20

xv

To-night the winds begin to rise
  And roar from yonder dropping day;
  The last red leaf is whirled away,
The rooks are blown about the skies;

The forest cracked, the waters curled,   5
  The cattle huddled on the lea;
  And wildly dashed on tower and tree
The sunbeam strikes along the world:

And but for fancies, which aver
  That all thy motions gently pass   10
  Athwart a plane of molten glass,
I scarce could brook the strain and stir

That makes the barren branches loud;
  And but for fear it is not so,
  The wild unrest that lives in woe   15
Would dote and pore on yonder cloud

That rises upward always higher,
  And onward drags a laboring breast,
  And topples round the dreary west,
A looming bastion fringed with fire.   20

XXIV

And was the day of my delight
  As pure and perfect as I say?
  The very source and fount of day
Is dashed with wandering isles of night.

If all was good and fair we met,   5
  This earth had been the Paradise
  It never looked to human eyes
Since our first sun arose and set.

And is it that the haze of grief
  Makes former gladness loom so great?   10
  The lowness of the present state,
That sets the past in this relief?

Or that the past will always win
  A glory from its being far,
  And orb into the perfect star   15
We saw not when we moved therein?

XXXIX

Old warder of these buried bones,
  And answering now my random stroke
  With fruitful cloud and living smoke,
Dark yew, that graspest at the stones

And dippest toward the dreamless head,   5
  To thee too comes the golden hour
  When flower is feeling after flower;
But Sorrow,—fixt upon the dead,

And darkening the dark graves of men,—
  What whispered from her lying lips?   10
  Thy gloom is kindled at the tips,
And passes into gloom again.

LXVII

When on my bed the moonlight falls,
  I know that in thy place of rest
  By that broad water of the west
There comes a glory on the walls:

Thy marble bright in dark appears,   5
  As slowly steals a silver flame
  Along the letters of thy name,
And o'er the number of thy years.

The mystic glory swims away,
  From off my bed the moonlight dies;   10
  And closing eaves of wearied eyes
I sleep till dusk is dipt in gray;

And then I know the mist is drawn
  A lucid veil from coast to coast,
  And in the dark church like a ghost   15
Thy tablet glimmers in the dawn.

LIV

O, yet we trust that somehow good
  Will be the final goal of ill,
  To pangs of nature, sins of will,
Defects of doubt, and taints of blood;

That nothing walks with aimless feet;   5
  That not one life shall be destroyed,
  Or cast as rubbish to the void,
When God hath made the pile complete;

That not a worm is cloven in vain;
  That not a moth with vain desire   10
  Is shrivelled in a fruitless fire,
Or but subserves another's gain.

Behold, we know not anything;
  I can but trust that good shall fall
  At last—far off—at last, to all,   15
And every winter change to spring.

So runs my dream; but what am I?
  An infant crying in the night;
  An infant crying for the light,
And with no language but a cry.   20

LV

The wish, that of the living whole
  No life may fail beyond the grave,
  Derives it not from what we have
The likest God within the soul?

Are God and Nature then at strife,   5
  That Nature lends such evil dreams?
  So careful of the type she seems,
So careless of the single life,

That I, considering everywhere
  Her secret meaning in her deeds,   10
  And finding that of fifty seeds
She often brings but one to bear,

I falter where I firmly trod,
  And falling with my weight of cares

Upon the great world's altar-stairs   15
    That slope through darkness up to God,

I stretch lame hands of faith, and grope,
    And gather dust and chaff, and call
    To what I feel is Lord of all,
And faintly trust the larger hope.   20

LVI

"So careful of the type?" but no,
    From scarped cliff and quarried stone
    She cries, "A thousand types are gone:
I care for nothing, all shall go.

"Thou makest thine appeal to me: 5
    I bring to life, I bring to death:
    The spirit does but mean the breath
I know no more." And he, shall he,

Man, her last work, who seemed so fair,
    Such splendid purpose in his eyes,   10
    Who rolled the psalm to wintry skies,
Who built him fanes of fruitless prayer,

Who trusted God was love indeed
    And love Creation's final law—
    Though Nature, red in tooth and claw   15
With ravine, shrieked against his creed—

Who loved, who suffered countless ills,
    Who battled for the True, the Just,
    Be blown about the desert dust,
Or sealed within the iron hills?   20

No more? A monster then, a dream,
    A discord. Dragons of the prime,
    That tare each other in their slime,
Were mellow music match'd with him.

O life as futile, then, as frail!   25
    O for thy voice to soothe and bless!
    What hope of answer, or redress?
Behind the veil, behind the veil.

CXXI

Sad Hesper o'er the buried sun
    And ready, thou, to die with him,

Thou watchest all things ever dim
And dimmer, and a glory done:

The team is loosened from the wain, 5
   The boat is drawn upon the shore;
   Thou listenest to the closing door,
And life is darkened in the brain.

Bright Phosphor, fresher for the night,
   By thee the world's great work is heard 10
   Beginning, and the wakeful bird;
Behind thee comes the greater light:

The market boat is on the stream,
   And voices hail it from the brink;
   Thou hear'st the village hammer clink, 15
And see'st the moving of the team.

Sweet Hesper-Phosphor, double name
   For what is one, the first, the last,
   Thou, like my present and my past,
Thy place is changed; thou art the same. 20

CXXVI

Love is and was my Lord and King,
   And in his presence I attend
   To hear the tidings of my friend,
Which every hour his couriers bring.

Love is and was my King and Lord, 5
   And will be, though as yet I keep
   Within his court on earth, and sleep
Encompassed by his faithful guard,

And hear at times a sentinel
   Who moves about from place to place, 10
   And whispers to the worlds of space,
In the deep night, that all is well.

CXXXI

O living will that shalt endure
   When all that seems shall suffer shock,
   Rise in the spiritual rock,
Flow through our deeds and make them pure,

That we may lift from out of dust 5
   A voice as unto him that hears,

A cry above the conquered years
To one that with us works, and trust,

With faith that comes of self-control,
   The truths that never can be proved   10
   Until we close with all we loved,
And all we flow from, soul in soul.

                ❧

From *The Epilogue*

. . . And rise, O moon, from yonder down,
   Till over down and over dale
   All night the shining vapor sail
And pass the silent-lighted town,

The white-faced halls, the glancing rills,   5
   And catch at every mountain head,
   And o'er the friths that branch and spread
Their sleeping silver through the hills;

And touch with shade the bridal doors,
   With tender gloom the roof, the wall;   10
   And breaking let the splendor fall
To spangle all the happy shores

By which they rest, and ocean sounds,
   And, star and system rolling past,
   A soul shall draw from out the vast   15
And strike his being into bounds,

And, moved through life of lower phase,
   Result in man, be born and think,
   And act and love, a closer link
Betwixt us and the crowning race   20

Of those that, eye to eye, shall look
   On knowledge; under whose command
   Is Earth and Earth's, and in their hand
Is Nature like an open book;

---

17. *moved* . . *phase:* (refers to the metamorphoses of the foetus).

No longer half-akin to brute,   25
   For all we thought and loved and did,
   And hoped, and suffered, is but seed
Of what in them is flower and fruit;

Whereof the man that with me trod
   This planet was a noble type   30
   Appearing ere the times were ripe,
That friend of mine who lives in God,

That God, which ever lives and loves,
   One God, one law, one element,
   And one far-off divine event,   35
To which the whole creation moves.

From *The Princess*

(1850)

OUR ENEMIES HAVE FALLEN

"Our enemies have fallen, have fallen; the seed,
The little seed they laughed at in the dark,
Has risen and cleft the soil, and grown a bulk
Of spanless girth, that lays on every side
A thousand arms and rushes to the Sun.   5

  "Our enemies have fallen, have fallen: they came;
The leaves were wet with women's tears: they heard
A noise of songs they would not understand:
They marked it with the red cross to the fall,
And would have strown it, and are fall'n themselves.   10

  "Our enemies have fallen, have fallen: they came,
The woodmen with their axes: lo the tree!
But we will make it fagots for the hearth,
And shape it plank and beam for roof and floor,
And boats and bridges for the use of men.   15

  "Our enemies have fallen, have fallen: they struck;
With their own blows they hurt themselves, nor knew

There dwelt an iron nature in the grain:
The glittering axe was broken in their arms,
Their arms were shattered to the shoulder blade.   20

"Our enemies have fallen, but this shall grow
A night of Summer from the heat, a breadth
Of Autumn, dropping fruits of power; and rolled
With music in the growing breeze of Time,
The tops shall strike from star to star, the fangs   25
Shall move the stony bases of the world.

TEARS, IDLE TEARS

Tears, idle tears, I know not what they mean,
Tears from the depth of some divine despair
Rise in the heart, and gather to the eyes,
In looking on the happy Autumn-fields,
And thinking of the days that are no more.   5

Fresh as the first beam glittering on a sail,
That brings our friends up from the underworld,
Sad as the last which reddens over one
That sinks with all we love below the verge;
So sad, so fresh, the days that are no more.   10

Ah, sad and strange as in dark summer dawns
The earliest pipe of half-awakened birds
To dying ears, when unto dying eyes
The casement slowly grows a glimmering square;
So sad, so strange, the days that are no more.   15

Dear as remembered kisses after death,
And sweet as those by hopeless fancy feigned
On lips that are for others; deep as love,
Deep as first love, and wild with all regret;
O Death in Life, the days that are no more!   20

NOW SLEEPS THE CRIMSON PETAL

Now sleeps the crimson petal, now the white,
Nor waves the cypress in the palace walk;
Nor winks the gold fin in the porphyry font.
The fire-fly wakens; waken thou with me.

Now droops the milk-white peacock like a   5
    ghost,
And like a ghost she glimmers on to me.

Now lies the Earth all Danaë to the stars,
And all thy heart lies open unto me.

Now slides the silent meteor on, and leaves
A shining furrow, as thy thoughts in me.   10

Now folds the lily all her sweetness up,
And slips into the bosom of the lake.
So fold thyself, my dearest, thou, and slip
Into my bosom and be lost in me.

COME DOWN, O MAID

Come down, O maid, from yonder mountain
    height.
What pleasure lives in height (the shepherd
    sang),
In height and cold, the splendor of the hills?
But cease to move so near the heavens, and cease
To glide a sunbeam by the blasted pine,   5
To sit a star upon the sparkling spire;
And come, for Love is of the valley, come,
For Love is of the valley, come thou down
And find him; by the happy threshold, he,
Or hand in hand with Plenty in the maize,   10

Or red with spirted purple of the vats,
Or foxlike in the vine; nor cares to walk
With Death and Morning on the Silver Horns,
Nor wilt thou snare him in the white ravine,
Nor find him dropt upon the firths of ice,   15
That huddling slant in furrow-cloven falls
To roll the torrent out of dusky doors.
But follow; let the torrent dance thee down
To find him in the valley; let the wild
Lean-headed eagles yelp alone, and leave   20
The monstrous ledges there to slope, and spill
Their thousand wreaths of dangling water-
        smoke,
That like a broken purpose waste in air.
So waste not thou, but come; for all the vales
Await thee; azure pillars of the hearth   25
Arise to thee; the children call, and I
Thy shepherd pipe, and sweet is every sound,
Sweeter thy voice, but every sound is sweet;
Myriads of rivulets hurrying through the lawn,
The moan of doves in immemorial elms,   30
And murmuring of innumerable bees.

TITHONUS

(1860)

The woods decay, the woods decay and fall,
The vapors weep their burthen to the ground,
Man comes and tills the field and lies beneath,
And after many a summer dies the swan.
Me only cruel immortality   5
Consumes; I wither slowly in thine arms,
Here at the quiet limit of the world,
A white-haired shadow roaming like a dream
The ever-silent spaces of the East,
Far-folded mists, and gleaming halls of morn.   10

    Alas! for this gray shadow, once a man—
So glorious in his beauty and thy choice,

TITHONUS: mortal husband of Aurora, goddess of dawn, who had pro-
cured for him exemption from death but not from old age.

Who madest him thy chosen, that he seemed
To his great heart none other than a god!
I asked thee, 'Give me immortality.'   15
Then didst thou grant mine asking with a smile,
Like wealthy men who care not how they give.
But thy strong Hours indignant worked their wills,
And beat me down and marred and wasted me,
    And though they could not end me, left me maimed   20
To dwell in presence of immortal youth,
Immortal age beside immortal youth,
And all I was, in ashes. Can thy love,
Thy beauty, make amends, though even now,
Close over us, the silver star, thy guide,   25
Shines in those tremulous eyes that fill with tears
To hear me? Let me go: take back thy gift:
Why should a man desire in any way
To vary from the kindly race of men,
Or pass beyond the goal of ordinance   30
Where all should pause, as is most meet for all?

    A soft air fans the cloud apart; there comes
A glimpse of that dark world where I was born.
Once more the old mysterious glimmer steals
From thy pure brows, and from thy shoulders pure,   35
And bosom beating with a heart renewed.
Thy cheek begins to redden through the gloom,
Thy sweet eyes brighten slowly close to mine,
Ere yet they blind the stars, and the wild team
Which love thee, yearning for thy yoke, arise,   40
And shake the darkness from their loosened manes,
And beat the twilight into flakes of fire.

    Lo! ever thus thou growest beautiful
In silence, then before thine answer given
Departest, and thy tears are on my cheek.   45

    Why wilt thou ever scare me with thy tears,
And make me tremble lest a saying learnt,
In days far-off, on that dark earth, be true?
"The gods themselves cannot recall their gifts."

    Ay me! ay me! with what another heart   50
In days far-off, and with what other eyes
I used to watch—if I be he that watched—
The lucid outline forming round thee; saw

The dim curls kindle into sunny rings;
Changed with thy mystic change, and felt my blood   55
Glow with the glow that slowly crimsoned all
Thy presence and thy portals, while I lay,
Mouth, forehead, eyelids, growing dewy-warm
With kisses balmier than half-opening buds
Of April, and could hear the lips that kissed   60
Whispering I knew not what of wild and sweet,
Like that strange song I heard Apollo sing,
    While Ilion like a mist rose into towers.

    Yet hold me not for ever in thine East;
How can my nature longer mix with thine?   65
Coldly thy rosy shadows bathe me, cold
Are all thy lights, and cold my wrinkled feet
Upon thy glimmering thresholds, when the steam
Floats up from those dim fields about the homes
Of happy men that have the power to die,   70
And grassy barrows of the happier dead.
Release me, and restore me to the ground;
Thou seëst all things, thou wilt see my grave:
Thou wilt renew thy beauty morn by morn;
I earth in earth forget these empty courts,   75
And thee returning on thy silver wheels.

❦

Robert Browning

SOLILOQUY OF THE SPANISH CLOISTER
(1842)

Gr-r-r—there go, my heart's abhorrence!
    Water your damned flower-pots, do!
If hate killed men, Brother Lawrence,
    God's blood, would not mine kill you!
What? your myrtle-bush wants trimming?   5
    Oh, that rose has prior claims—
Needs its leaden vase filled brimming?
    Hell dry you up with its flames!

---

62. *song:* Ilion (Troy) was built to the music of Apollo's (the sun god's)
lyre.

At the meal we sit together:
   Salve tibi! I must hear   10
Wise talk of the kind of weather,
   Sort of season, time of year:
Not a plenteous cork-crop: scarcely
   Dare we hope oak-galls, I doubt:
What's the Latin name for "parsley"?   15
   What's the Greek name for Swine's Snout?

Whew! We'll have our platter burnished,
   Laid with care on our own shelf!
With a fire-new spoon we're furnished,
   And a goblet for ourself,   20
Rinsed like something sacrificial
   Ere 'tis fit to touch our chaps—
Marked with L for our initial!
   (He-he! There his lily snaps!)

Saint, forsooth! While brown Dolores   25
   Squats outside the Convent bank
With Sanchicha, telling stories,
   Steeping tresses in the tank,
Blue-black lustrous, thick like horse-hairs,
   —Can't I see his dead eye glow,   30
Bright as 'twere a Barbary corsair's?
   (That is, if he'd let it show!)

When he finishes refection,
   Knife and fork he never lays
Cross-wise, to my recollection,   35
   As do I, in Jesu's praise.
I the Trinity illustrate,
   Drinking watered orange-pulp
In three sips the Arian frustrate;
   While he drains his at one gulp.   40

Oh, those melons! If he's able
   We're to have a feast! so nice!
One goes to the Abbot's table,
   All of us get each a slice.
How go on your flowers? None double?   45
   Not one fruit-sort can you spy?
Strange!—And I, too, at such trouble
   Keep them close-nipped on the sly!

SOLILOQUY: 10. *Salve tibi!*: Hail to you!

There's a great text in Galatians,
　　Once you trip on it, entails   50
Twenty-nine distinct damnations,
　　One sure, if another fails:
If I trip him just a-dying,
　　Sure of heaven as sure can be,
Spin him round and send him flying   55
　　Off to hell, a Manichee!

Or, my scrofulous French novel
　　On gray paper with blunt type!
Simply glance at it, you grovel
　　Hand and foot in Belial's gripe: 60
If I double down its pages
　　At the woeful sixteenth print,
When he gathers his greengages,
　　Ope a sieve and slip it in't?

Or, there's Satan! one might venture   65
　　Pledge one's soul to him, yet leave
Such a flaw in the indenture
　　As he'd miss till, past retrieve,
Blasted lay that rose-acacia
　　We're so proud of! *Hy, Zy, Hine* . . .   70
'St, there's Vespers! *Plena gratiâ,
Ave, Virgo!* Gr-r-r—you swine!

MY LAST DUCHESS

(1842)

FERRARA

That's my last Duchess painted on the wall,
Looking as if she were alive. I call
That piece a wonder, now: Frà Pandolf's hands
Worked busily a day, and there she stands.

---

56. *Manichee:* one who believes that evil exists independently of God. 60.
Belial: cohort of Satan. 63. *greengages:* plums. 64. *sieve:* small-meshed
basket. 71-72. *Plena . . . Virgo:* Hail, Virgin, full of grace (a prayer).

MY LAST DUCHESS: *Ferrara:* the speaker is Duke of this Italian city. 3.
Frà: brother (the painter was a monk).

Will 't please you sit and look at her? I said
"Frà Pandolf" by design, for never read
Strangers like you that pictured countenance,
The depth and passion of its earnest glance,
But to myself they turned (since none puts by
The curtain I have drawn for you, but I)   10
And seemed as they would ask me, if they durst,
How such a glance came there; so, not the first
Are you to turn and ask thus. Sir, 'twas not
Her husband's presence only, called that spot
Of joy into the Duchess' cheek: perhaps   15
Frà Pandolf chanced to say, "Her mantle laps
Over my lady's wrist too much," or "Paint
Must never hope to reproduce the faint
Half-flush that dies along her throat:" such stuff
Was courtesy, she thought, and cause enough   20
For calling up that spot of joy. She had
A heart—how shall I say?—too soon made glad,
Too easily impressed; she liked whate'er
She looked on, and her looks went everywhere.
Sir, 'twas all one! My favour at her breast,   25
The dropping of the daylight in the West,
The bough of cherries some officious fool
Broke in the orchard for her, the white mule
She rode with round the terrace—all and each
Would draw from her alike the approving speech,   30
Or blush, at least. She thanked men,—good! but thanked
Somehow—I know not how—as if she ranked
My gift of a nine-hundred-years-old name
With anybody's gift. Who'd stoop to blame
This sort of trifling? Even had you skill   35
In speech—(which I have not)—to make your will
Quite clear to such an one, and say, "Just this
Or that in you disgusts me; here you miss,
Or there exceed the mark"—and if she let
Herself be lessoned so, nor plainly set   40
Her wits to yours, forsooth, and made excuse,
—E'en then would be some stooping; and I choose
Never to stoop. Oh sir, she smiled, no doubt,
Whene'er I passed her; but who passed without
Much the same smile? This grew; I gave commands;   45
Then all smiles stopped together. There she stands
As if alive. Will 't please you rise? We'll meet

The company below, then. I repeat,
The Count your master's known munificence
Is ample warrant that no just pretence   50
Of mine for dowry will be disallowed;
Though his fair daughter's self, as I avowed
At starting, is my object. Nay, we'll go
Together down, sir. Notice Neptune, though,
Taming a sea-horse, thought a rarity,   55
Which Claus of Innsbruck cast in bronze for me!

MEETING AT NIGHT

(1845)

The gray sea and the long black land;
And the yellow half-moon large and low;
And the startled little waves that leap
In fiery ringlets from their sleep,
As I gain the cove with pushing prow,   5
And quench its speed i' the slushy sand.

Then a mile of warm sea-scented beach;
Three fields to cross till a farm appears;
A tap at the pane, the quick sharp scratch
And blue spurt of a lighted match,   10
And a voice less loud, through its joys and fears.
Than the two hearts beating each to each!

PARTING AT MORNING

(1845)

Round the cape of a sudden came the sea,
And the sun looked over the mountain's rim:
And straight was a path of gold for him,
And the need of a world of men for me.

PARTING AT MORNING: a sequel to the preceding poem. 3. *him:* the sun.

HOME-THOUGHTS, FROM ABROAD
(1845)

O, to be in England
Now that April's there,
And whoever wakes in England
Sees, some morning, unaware,
That the lowest boughs and the brushwood sheaf   5
Round the elm-tree bole are in tiny leaf,
While the chaffinch sings on the orchard bough
In England—now!

And after April, when May follows,
And the whitethroat builds, and all the swallows!   10
Hark, where my blossomed pear-tree in the hedge
Leans to the field and scatters on the clover
Blossoms and dewdrops—at the bent spray's edge—
That's the wise thrush; he sings each song twice over,
Lest you should think he never could recapture   15
The first fine careless rapture!
And though the fields look rough with hoary dew,
All will be gay when noontide wakes anew
The buttercups, the little children's dower
—Far brighter than this gaudy melon-flower!   20

THE BISHOP ORDERS HIS TOMB AT
SAINT PRAXED'S CHURCH
(1845)
ROME, 15—

Vanity, saith the preacher, vanity!
Draw round my bed: is Anselm keeping back?
Nephews—sons mine . . . ah God, I know not! Well—

THE BISHOP ORDERS HIS TOMB: 1. *Vanity:* emptiness. *preacher:* the author
of Ecclesiastes.

She, men would have to be your mother once,
Old Gandolf envied me, so fair she was!   5
What's done is done, and she is dead beside,
Dead long ago, and I am Bishop since,
And as she died so must we die ourselves,
And thence ye may perceive the world's a dream.
Life, how and what is it? As here I lie   10
In this state-chamber, dying by degrees,
Hours and long hours in the dead night, I ask
"Do I live, am I dead?" Peace, peace seems all.
Saint Praxed's ever was the church for peace;
And so, about this tomb of mine. I fought   15
With tooth and nail to save my niche, ye know:
—Old Gandolf cozened me, despite my care;
Shrewd was that snatch from out the corner south
He graced his carrion with, God curse the same!
Yet still my niche is not so cramped but thence   20
One sees the pulpit o' the epistle-side,
And somewhat of the choir, those silent seats,
And up into the aëry dome where live
The angels, and a sunbeam's sure to lurk.
And I shall fill my slab of basalt there,   25
And 'neath my tabernacle take my rest,
With those nine columns round me, two and two,
The odd one at my feet where Anselm stands,
Peach-blossom marble all, the rare, the ripe,
As fresh-poured red wine of a mighty pulse.   30
—Old Gandolf with his paltry onion-stone,
Put me where I may look at him! True peach,
Rosy and flawless; how I earned the prize!
Draw close. That conflagration of my church
—What then? So much was saved if aught were missed!   35
My sons, ye would not be my death? Go dig
The white-grape vineyard where the oil-press stood,
Drop water gently till the surface sinks,
And if ye find . . . ah God, I know not, I! . . .
Bedded in store of rotten fig-leaves soft,   40
And corded up in a tight olive-frail,
Some lump, ah God, of *lapis lazuli,*

---

5. *Gandolf:* the Bishop's predecessor. 21. *epistle-side:* (the right as one faces
the altar). 31. *onion-stone:* an inferior greenish marble. 41. *-frail:* -basket.
42. *lapis lazuli:* valuable blue stone.

Big as a Jew's head cut off at the nape,
Blue as a vein o'er the Madonna's breast—
Sons, all have I bequeathed you, villas, all,   45
That brave Frascati villa with its bath—
So, let the blue lump poise between my knees,
Like God the Father's globe on both his hands
Ye worship in the Jesu Church so gay,
For Gandolf shall not choose but see and burst!   50
Swift as a weaver's shuttle fleet our years;
Man goeth to the grave, and where is he?
Did I say basalt for my slab, sons? Black—
'Twas ever antique-black I meant! How else
Shall ye contrast my frieze to come beneath?   55
The bas-relief in bronze ye promised me,
Those Pans and Nymphs ye wot of, and perchance
Some tripod, thyrsus, with a vase or so,
The Saviour at his sermon on the mount,
St. Praxed in a glory, and one Pan   60
Ready to twitch the Nymph's last garment off,
And Moses with the tables . . . but I know
Ye mark me not! What do they whisper thee,
Child of my bowels, Anselm? Ah, ye hope
To revel down my villas while I gasp   65
Bricked o'er with beggar's moldy travertine
Which Gandolf from his tomb-top chuckles at!
Nay, boys, ye love me—all of jasper, then!
'Tis jasper ye stand pledged to, lest I grieve
My bath must needs be left behind, alas!   70
One block, pure green as a pistachio-nut,
There's plenty jasper somewhere in the world—
And have I not St. Praxed's ear to pray
Horses for ye, and brown Greek manuscripts,
And mistresses with great smooth marbly limbs?   75
—That's if ye carve my epitaph aright,
Choice Latin, picked phrase, Tully's every word,
No gaudy ware like Gandolf's second line—
Tully, my masters? Ulpian serves his need!

---

46. *Frascati:* resort near Rome. 54. *antique-black:* type of fine marble. 57.
Pans: pagan nature-gods. 58. *tripod, thyrsus:* stool and staff used in ancient
Greek ritual. 62. *tables:* stone tablets inscribed with the ten commandments.
66. *travertine:* kind of limestone. 68. *jasper:* smooth green stone. 77. *Tully:*
Cicero. 79. *Ulpian:* Roman jurist (whose Latin is inferior to Cicero's).

And then how I shall lie through centuries,   80
And hear the blessed mutter of the Mass,
And see God made and eaten all day long,
And feel the steady candle-flame, and taste
Good strong, thick, stupefying incense-smoke!
For as I lie here, hours of the dead night,   85
Dying in state and by such slow degrees,
I fold my arms as if they clasped a crook,
And stretch my feet forth straight as stone can point,
And let the bedclothes for a mort-cloth drop
Into great laps and folds of sculptor's-work.   90
And as yon tapers dwindle, and strange thoughts
Grow, with a certain humming in my ears,
About the life before I lived this life,
And this life too, popes, cardinals, and priests,
St. Praxed at his sermon on the mount,   95
Your tall pale mother with her talking eyes,
And new-found agate urns as fresh as day,
And marble's language, Latin pure, discreet,
—Aha, ELUCESCEBAT quoth our friend?
No Tully, said I, Ulpian at the best!   100
Evil and brief hath been my pilgrimage.
All *lapis*, all, sons! Else I give the Pope
My villas. Will ye ever eat my heart?
Ever your eyes were as a lizard's quick;
They glitter like your mother's for my soul,   105
Or ye would heighten my impoverished frieze,
Piece out its starved design, and fill my vase
With grapes, and add a vizor and a term,
And to the tripod ye would tie a lynx
That in his struggle throws the thyrsus down,   110
To comfort me on my entablature
Whereon I am to lie till I must ask
"Do I live, am I dead?" There, leave me, there!
For ye have stabbed me with ingratitude
To death—ye wish it—God, ye wish it! Stone—   115
Gritstone, a-crumble! Clammy squares which sweat
As if the corpse they keep were oozing through—
And no more *lapis* to delight the world!
Well, go! I bless ye. Fewer tapers there,

---

99. *Elucescebat:* "he was famous." 108. *vizor:* mask. *term:* bust and
pedestal.

But in a row. And, going, turn your backs   120
—Aye, like departing altar-ministrants,
And leave me in my church, the church for peace,
That I may watch at leisure if he leers—
Old Gandolf—at me, from his onion-stone,
As still he envied me, so fair she was.   125

LOVE AMONG THE RUINS

(1855)

Where the quiet-colored end of evening smiles
        Miles and miles
On the solitary pastures where our sheep
        Half-asleep
Tinkle homeward through the twilight, stray or stop   5
        As they crop—
Was the site once of a city great and gay,
        (So they say)
Of our country's very capital, its prince
        Ages since   10
Held his court in, gathered councils, wielding far
        Peace or war.

Now,—the country does not even boast a tree,
        As you see,
To distinguish slopes of verdure, certain rills   15
        From the hills
Intersect and give a name to, (else they run
        Into one)
Where the domed and daring palace shot its spires
        Up like fires   20
O'er the hundred-gated circuit of a wall
        Bounding all,
Made of marble, men might march on nor be pressed,
        Twelve abreast.

And such plenty and perfection, see, of grass   25
        Never was!
Such a carpet as, this summer-time, o'erspreads
        And imbeds

Every vestige of the city, guessed alone,
   Stock or stone—   30
Where a multitude of men breathed joy and woe
   Long ago:
Lust of glory pricked their hearts up, dread of shame
   Struck them tame;
And that glory and that shame alike, the gold   35
   Bought and sold.

Now,—the single little turret that remains
   On the plains,
By the caper overrooted, by the gourd
   Overscored,   40
While the patching houseleek's head of blossom winks
   Through the chinks—
Marks the basement whence a tower in ancient time
   Sprang sublime,
And a burning ring, all round, the chariots traced   45
   As they raced,
And the monarch and his minions and his dames
   Viewed the games.

And I know, while thus the quiet-colored eve
   Smiles to leave   50
To their folding, all our many-tinkling fleece
   In such peace.
And the slopes and rills in undistinguished grey
   Melt away—
That a girl with eager eyes and yellow hair   55
   Waits me there
In the turret whence the charioteers caught soul
   For the goal,
When the king looked, where she looks now, breathless, dumb
   Till I come.   6o

But he looked upon the city, every side,
   Far and wide,
All the mountains topped with temples, all the glades'
   Colonnades,
All the causeys, bridges, aqueducts,—and then,   65
   All the men!
When I do come, she will speak not, she will stand,
   Either hand
On my shoulder, give her eyes the first embrace
   Of my face,   70

Ere we rush, ere we extinguish sight and speech
    Each on each.

In one year they sent a million fighters forth
    South and North,
And they built their gods a brazen pillar high   75
    As the sky,
Yet reserved a thousand chariots in full force—
    Gold, of course.
Oh, heart! oh, blood that freezes, blood that burns!
    Earth's returns   80
For whole centuries of folly, noise and sin!
    Shut them in,
With their triumphs and their glories and the rest!
    Love is best.

A TOCCATA OF GALUPPI'S
(1855)

Oh, Galuppi, Baldassare, this is very sad to find!
I can hardly misconceive you; it would prove me deaf and blind;
But although I take your meaning, 'tis with such a heavy mind!

Here you come with your old music, and here's all the good it brings.
What, they lived once thus at Venice, where the merchants were the
    kings,   5
Where St. Mark's is, where the Doges used to wed the sea with rings?

Ay, because the sea's the street there; and 'tis arched by . . . what
    you call
. . . Shylock's bridge with houses on it, where they kept the carnival:
I was never out of England—it's as if I saw it all.

Did young people take their pleasure when the sea was warm in
    May?   10
Balls and masks begun at midnight, burning ever to mid-day,
When they made up fresh adventures for the morrow, do you say?

A TOCCATA OF GALUPPI'S: *Toccata:* musical form, somewhat like prelude,
once used for organ or harpsichord. *Galuppi:* eighteenth-century Italian
composer; organist at St. Mark's cathedral in Venice. 6. *Doges:* Venetian
magistrates. 8. *Shylock's bridge:* the Rialto.

Was a lady such a lady, cheeks so round and lips so red,—
On her neck the small face buoyant, like a bell-flower on its bed,
O'er the breast's superb abundance where a man might base his
    head?   15

Well, and it was graceful of them—they'd break talk off and afford
—She, to bite her mask's black velvet—he, to finger on his sword,
While you sat and played Toccatas, stately at the clavichord?

What? Those lesser thirds so plaintive, sixths diminished, sigh on
    sigh,
Told them something? Those suspensions, those solutions—"Must we
    die?"   20
Those commiserating sevenths—"Life might last! we can but try!"

"Were you happy?"—"Yes."—"And are you still as happy?"—"Yes.
    And you?"
—"Then more kisses!"—"Did *I* stop them, when a million seemed so
    few?"
Hark, the dominant's persistence till it must be answered to!

So, an octave struck the answer. Oh, they praised you, I dare say! 25
"Brave Galuppi! that was music! good alike at grave and gay!
I can always leave off talking when I hear a master play!"

Then they left you for their pleasure: till in due time, one by one,
Some with lives that came to nothing, some with deeds as well undone,
Death stepped tacitly and took them where they never see the sun. 30

But when I sit down to reason, think to take my stand nor swerve,
Till I triumph o'er a secret wrung from nature's close reserve,
In you come with your cold music, till I creep through every nerve,

Yes, you, like a ghostly cricket, creaking where a house was burned:
"Dust and ashes, dead and done with, Venice spent what Venice
    earned.   35
The soul, doubtless, is immortal—where a soul can be discerned.

"Yours for instance: you know physics, something of geology,
Mathematics are your pastime; souls shall rise in their degree;
Butterflies may dread extinction,—you'll not die, it cannot be!

"As for Venice and her people, merely born to bloom and drop,   40
Here on earth they bore their fruitage, mirth and folly were the crop:
What of soul was left, I wonder, when the kissing had to stop?

"Dust and ashes!" So you creak it, and I want the heart to scold.
Dear dead women, with such hair, too—what's become of all the gold
Used to hang and brush their bosoms? I feel chilly and grown
    old.   45

TWO IN THE CAMPAGNA

(1855)

I wonder do you feel to-day
    As I have felt since, hand in hand,
We sat down on the grass, to stray
    In spirit better through the land,
This morn of Rome and May?   5

For me, I touched a thought, I know,
    Has tantalized me many times,
(Like turns of thread the spiders throw
    Mocking across our path) for rhymes
To catch at and let go.   10

Help me to hold it! First it left
    The yellowing fennel, run to seed
There, branching from the brickwork's cleft,
    Some old tomb's ruin: yonder weed
Took up the floating weft,   15

Where one small orange cup amassed
    Five beetles—blind and green they grope
Among the honey-meal: and last,
    Everywhere on the grassy slope
I traced it. Hold it fast!   20

The champaign with its endless fleece
    Of feathery grasses everywhere!
Silence and passion, joy and peace,
    An everlasting wash of air—
Rome's ghost since her decease.   25

TWO IN THE CAMPAGNA: *Campagna:* plain surrounding Rome.

Such life here, through such lengths of hours,
   Such miracles performed in play,
Such primal naked forms of flowers,
   Such letting nature have her way
While heaven looks from its towers!   30

How say you? Let us, O my dove,
   Let us be unashamed of soul,
As earth lies bare to heaven above!
   How is it under our control
To love or not to love?   35

I would that you were all to me,
   You that are just so much, no more.
Nor yours nor mine, nor slave nor free!
   Where does the fault lie? What the core
O' the wound, since wound must be?   40

I would I could adopt your will,
   See with your eyes, and set my heart
Beating by yours, and drink my fill
   At your soul's springs,—your part my part
In life, for good and ill.   45

No. I yearn upward, touch you close,
   Then stand away. I kiss your cheek,
Catch your soul's warmth,—I pluck the rose
   And love it more than tongue can speak—
Then the good minute goes.   50

Already how am I so far
   Out of that minute? Must I go
Still like the thistle-ball, no bar,
   Onward, whenever light winds blow,
Fixed by no friendly star?   55

Just when I seemed about to learn!
   Where is the thread now? Off again!
The old trick! Only I discern—
   Infinite passion, and the pain
Of finite hearts that yearn.   60

MEMORABILIA

(1855)

Ah, did you once see Shelley plain,
    And did he stop and speak to you,
And did you speak to him again?
    How strange it seems and new!

But you were living before that,   5
    And also you are living after;
And the memory I started at—
    My starting moves your laughter!

I crossed a moor, with a name of its own
    And a certain use in the world no doubt,   10
Yet a hand's-breath of it shines alone
    'Mid the blank miles round about:

For there I picked up on the heather
    And there I put inside my breast
A moulted feather, an eagle-feather!   15
    Well, I forget the rest.

FRA LIPPO LIPPI

(1855)

I am poor brother Lippo, by your leave!
You need not clap your torches to my face.
Zooks, what's to blame? you think you see a monk!
What, 'tis past midnight, and you go the rounds,
And here you catch me at an alley's end   5
Where sportive ladies leave their doors ajar?
The Carmine's my cloister; hunt it up,
Do—harry out, if you must show your zeal,
Whatever rat, there, haps on his wrong hole,
And nip each softling of a wee white mouse,   10

FRA LIPPO LIPPI: 1. *Lippo:* Fra Lippo Lippi, fifteenth-century Florentine painter, is addressing the police.

Weke, weke, that's crept to keep him company!
Aha, you know your betters? Then, you'll take
Your hand away that's fiddling on my throat,
And please to know me likewise. Who am I?
Why, one, sir, who is lodging with a friend   15
Three streets off—he's a certain . . . how d' ye call?
Master—a . . . Cosimo of the Medici,
I' the house that caps the corner. Boh! you were best!
Remember and tell me, the day you're hanged,
How you affected such a gullet's-gripe!   20
But you, sir, it concerns you that your knaves
Pick up a manner nor discredit you:
Zooks, are we pilchards, that they sweep the streets
And count fair prize what comes into their net?
He's Judas to a tittle, that man is!   25
Just such a face! Why, sir, you make amends.
Lord, I'm not angry! Bid your hangdogs go
Drink out this quarter-florin to the health
Of the munificent House that harbors me
(And many more beside, lads! more beside!)   30
And all's come square again. I'd like his face—
His, elbowing on his comrade in the door
With the pike and lantern,—for the slave that holds
John Baptist's head a-dangle by the hair
With one hand ("Look you, now," as who should say)   35
And his weapon in the other, yet unwiped!
It's not your chance to have a bit of chalk,
A wood-coal or the like? or you should see!
Yes, I'm the painter, since you style me so.
What, brother Lippo's doings, up and down,   40
You know them and they take you? like enough!
I saw the proper twinkle in your eye—
'Tell you, I liked your looks at very first.
Let's sit and set things straight now, hip to haunch.
Here's spring come, and the nights one makes up bands   45
To roam the town and sing out carnival,
And I've been three weeks shut within my mew,
A-painting for the great man, saints and saints
And saints again. I could not paint all night—
Ouf! I leaned out of window for fresh air.   50

---

17. *Cosimo . . . Medici:* wealthy banker, statesman, art patron.

There came a hurry of feet and little feet,
A sweep of lute-strings, laughs, and whiffs of song,—
Flower o' the broom,
Take away love, and our earth is a tomb!
Flower o' the quince,   55
I let Lisa go, and what good in life since?
Flower o' the thyme—and so on. Round they went.
Scarce had they turned the corner when a titter
Like the skipping of rabbits by moonlight,—three slim shapes—
And a face that looked up . . . zooks, sir, flesh, and blood,   60
That's all I'm made of! Into shreds it went,
Curtain and counterpane and coverlet,
All the bed-furniture—a dozen knots,
There was a ladder! Down I let myself,
Hands and feet, scrambling somehow, and so dropped,   65
And after them. I came up with the fun
Hard by Saint Laurence, hail fellow, well met,—
Flower o' the rose,
If I've been merry, what matter who knows?
And so as I was stealing back again   70
To get to bed and have a bit of sleep
Ere I rise up to-morrow and go work
On Jerome knocking at his poor old breast
With his great round stone to subdue the flesh,
You snap me of the sudden. Ah, I see!   75
Though your eye twinkles still, you shake your head—
Mine's shaved,—a monk, you say—the sting's in that!
If Master Cosimo announced himself,
Mum's the word naturally; but a monk!
Come, what am I a beast for? tell us, now!   80
I was a baby when my mother died
And father died and left me in the street.
I starved there, God knows how, a year or two
On fig skins, melon-parings, rinds and shucks,
Refuse and rubbish. One fine frosty day,   85
My stomach being empty as your hat,
The wind doubled me up and down I went.
Old Aunt Lapaccia trussed me with one hand,
(Its fellow was a stinger as I knew)

---

52. *song:* the interspersed lyrics imitate improvised Italian folk songs. 67.
Saint Laurence: church (San Lorenzo). 73. *Jerome:* early Christian saint
and ascetic.

And so along the wall, over the bridge,   90
By the straight cut to the convent. Six words there,
While I stood munching my first bread that month:
"So, boy, you're minded," quoth the good fat father
Wiping his own mouth, 'twas refection-time,—
"To quit this very miserable world?   95
Will you renounce" . . . "the mouthful of bread?" thought I;
By no means! Brief, they made a monk of me;
I did renounce the world, its pride and greed,
Palace, farm, villa, shop, and banking-house,
Trash, such as these poor devils of Medici   100
Have given their hearts to—all at eight years old.
Well, sir, I found in time, you may be sure,
'Twas not for nothing—the good bellyful,
The warm serge and the rope that goes all round,
And day-long blessed idleness beside!   105
"Let's see what the urchin's fit for"—that came next.
Not overmuch their way, I must confess.
Such a to-do! They tried me with their books;
Lord, they'd have taught me Latin in pure waste!
Flower o' the clove,   110
All the Latin I construe is, "amo" I love!
But, mind you, when a boy starves in the streets
Eight years together, as my fortune was,
Watching folk's faces to know who will fling
The bit of half-stripped grape-bunch he desires,   115
And who will curse or kick him for his pains,—
Which gentleman processional and fine,
Holding a candle to the Sacrament
Will wink and let him lift a plate and catch
The droppings of the wax to sell again,   120
Or holla for the Eight and have him whipped,—
How say I?—nay, which dog bites, which lets drop
His bone from the heap of offal in the street,—
Why, soul and sense of him grow sharp alike,
He learns the look of things, and none the less   125
For admonition from the hunger-pinch.
I had a store of such remarks, be sure,
Which, after I found leisure, turned to use.
I drew men's faces on my copy-books,
Scrawled them within the antiphonary's marge,   130

---

117. *processional:* marching in a (religious) procession. 121. *Eight:* (Florentine magistrates). 130. *antiphonary's marge:* margin of music-book.

Joined legs and arms to the long music-notes,
Found eyes and nose and chin for A's and B's,
And made a string of pictures of the world
Betwixt the ins and outs of verb and noun,
On the wall, the bench, the door. The monks looked black.   135
"Nay," quoth the prior, "turn him out, d' ye say?
In no wise. Lose a crow and catch a lark.
What if at last we get our man of parts,
We Carmelites, like those Camaldolese
And Preaching Friars, to do our church up fine   140
And put the front on it that ought to be!"
And hereupon he bade me daub away.
Thank you! my head being crammed, the walls a blank,
Never was such prompt disemburdening.
First, every sort of monk, the black and white,   145
I drew them, fat and lean: then, folk at church,
From good old gossips waiting to confess
Their cribs of barrel-droppings, candle-ends,—
To the breathless fellow at the altar-foot,
Fresh from his murder, safe and sitting there   150
With the little children round him in a row
Of admiration, half for his beard and half
For that white anger of his victim's son
Shaking a fist at him with one fierce arm,
Signing himself with the other because of Christ   155
(Whose sad face on the cross sees only this
After the passion of a thousand years)
Till some poor girl, her apron o'er her head
(Which the intense eyes looked through,) came at eve
On tiptoe, said a word, dropped in a loaf,   160
Her pair of earrings and a bunch of flowers
(The brute took growling), prayed, and so was gone.
I painted all, then cried, " 'Tis ask and have—
Choose, for more's ready!"—laid the ladder-flat,
And showed my covered bit of cloister-wall.   165
The monks closed in a circle and praised loud
Till checked, taught what to see and not to see,
Being simple bodies,—"That's the very man!
Look at the boy who stoops to pat the dog!
That woman's like the prior's niece who comes   170
To care about his asthma: it's the life!"

139-40. *Camaldolese, Friars:* rival orders. 148. *cribs:* thefts.

But there my triumph's straw-fire flared and funked;
Their betters took their turn to see and say:
The prior and the learnèd pulled a face
And stopped all that in no time. "How? what's here?   175
Quite from the mark of painting, bless us all!
Faces, arms, legs, and bodies like the true
As much as pea and pea! it's devil's-game!
Your business is not to catch men with show,
With homage to the perishable clay,   180
But lift them over it, ignore it all,
Make them forget there's such a thing as flesh.
Your business is to paint the souls of men—
Man's soul, and it's a fire, smoke . . . no it's not . . .
It's vapor done up like a new-born babe—   185
(In that shape when you die it leaves your mouth)
It's . . . well, what matters talking, it's the soul!
Give us no more of body than shows soul!
Here's Giotto, with his saint a-praising God,
That sets us praising,—why not stop with him?   190
Why put all thoughts of praise out of our head
With wonder at lines, colors, and what not?
Paint the soul, never mind the legs and arms!
Rub all out, try at it a second time.
Oh, that white smallish female with the breasts,   195
She's just my niece . . . Herodias, I would say,—
Who went and danced and got men's heads cut off!
Have it all out!" Now, is this sense, I ask?
A fine way to paint soul, by painting body
So ill, the eye can't stop there, must go further   200
And can't fare worse! Thus, yellow does for white
When what you put for yellow's simply black,
And any sort of meaning looks intense
When all beside itself means and looks naught.
Why can't a painter lift each foot in turn,   205
Left foot and right foot, go a double step,
Make his flesh liker and his soul more like,
Both in their order? Take the prettiest face,
The prior's niece . . . patron-saint—is it so pretty
You can't discover if it means hope, fear,   210
Sorrow, or joy? won't beauty go with these?
Suppose I've made her eyes all right and blue,

---

189. *Giotto:* Florentine painter of preceding century. 196. *Herodias:* Herod's wife (who procured John the Baptist's death).

Can't I take breath and try to add life's flash,
And then add soul and heighten them three-fold?
Or say there's beauty with no soul at all—   215
(I never saw it—put the case the same—)
If you get simple beauty and naught else,
You get about the best thing God invents:
That's somewhat; and you'll find the soul you have missed,
Within yourself when you return him thanks,   220
"Rub all out!" Well, well, there's my life, in short,
And so the thing has gone on ever since.
I'm grown a man no doubt; I've broken bounds—
You should not take a fellow eight years old
And make him swear to never kiss the girls.   225
I'm my own master, paint now as I please—
Having a friend, you see, in the corner-house!
Lord, it's fast holding by the rings in front—
Those great rings serve more purposes than just
To plant a flag in, or tie up a horse!   230
And yet the old schooling sticks, the old grave eyes
Are peeping o'er my shoulder as I work,
The heads shake still— "It's art's decline, my son!
You're not of the true painters, great and old;
Brother Angelico's the man, you'll find;   235
Brother Lorenzo stands his single peer:
Fag on at flesh, you'll never make the third!"
Flower o' the pine,
You keep your mistr . . . manners, and I'll stick to mine!
I'm not the third, then: bless us, they must know!   240
Don't you think they're the likeliest to know,
They with their Latin? So, I swallow my rage,
Clench my teeth, suck my lips in tight, and paint
To please them—sometimes do, and sometimes don't;
For, doing most, there's pretty sure to come   245
A turn, some warm eve finds me at my saints—
A laugh, a cry, the business of the world—
(*Flower o' the peach,*
Death for us all, and his own life for each!)
And my whole soul revolves, the cup runs over,   250
The world and life's too big to pass for a dream,
And I do these wild things in sheer despite,
And play the fooleries you catch me at,

235-36. *Angelico, Lorenzo:* painters a generation older than Lippo; and less
realistic in style

In pure rage! The old mill-horse, out at grass
After hard years, throws up his stiff heels so,   255
Although the miller does not preach to him
The only good of grass is to make chaff.
What would men have? Do they like grass or no—
May they or mayn't they? all I want's the thing
Settled for ever one way. As it is,   260
You tell too many lies and hurt yourself;
You don't like what you only like too much,
You do like what, if given you at your word,
You find abundantly detestable.
For me, I think I speak as I was taught;   265
I always see the garden and God there
A-making man's wife: and, my lesson learned,
The value and significance of flesh,
I can't unlearn ten minutes afterwards.
     You understand me: I'm a beast, I know.   270
But see, now—why, I see as certainly
As that the morning-star's about to shine,
What will hap some day. We've a youngster here
Comes to our convent, studies what I do,
Slouches and stares and lets no atom drop: 275
His name is Guidi—he'll not mind the monks—
They call him Hulking Tom, he lets them talk—
He picks my practice up—he'll paint apace,
I hope so—though I never live so long,
I know what's sure to follow. You be judge!   280
You speak no Latin more than I, belike;
However, you're my man, you've seen the world—
The beauty and the wonder and the power,
The shapes of things, their colors, lights and shades,
Changes, surprises,—and God made it all!   285
—For what? do you feel thankful, ay or no,
For this fair town's face, yonder river's line,
The mountain round it and the sky above,
Much more the figures of man, woman, child,
These are the frame to? What's it all about?   290
To be passed over, despised? or dwelt upon,
Wondered at? oh, this last of course!—you say.
But why not do as well as say,—paint these
Just as they are, careless what comes of it?
God's works—paint any one, and count it crime   295

---

276. *Guidi:* (perhaps the first Italian artist to paint a nude figure).

To let a truth slip. Don't object, "His works
Are here already—nature is complete:
Suppose you reproduce her—(which you can't)
There's no advantage! you must beat her, then."
For, don't you mark, we're made so that we love   300
First when we see them painted, things we have passed
Perhaps a hundred times nor cared to see;
And so they are better, painted—better to us,
Which is the same thing. Art was given for that;
God uses us to help each other so,   305
Lending our minds out. Have you noticed, now,
Your cullion's hanging face? A bit of chalk,
And trust me but you should, though! How much more,
If I drew higher things with the same truth!
That were to take the prior's pulpit-place,   310
Interpret God to all of you! Oh, oh,
It makes me mad to see what men shall do
And we in our graves! This world's no blot for us,
Nor blank: it means intensely, and means good:
To find its meaning is my meat and drink   315
"Ay, but you don't so instigate to prayer!"
Strikes in the prior; "when your meaning's plain
It does not say to folk—remember matins,
Or, mind you fast next Friday." Why, for this
What need of art at all? A skull and bones   320
Two bits of stick nailed crosswise, or, what's best,
A bell to chime the hour with, does as well.
I painted a Saint Laurence six months since
At Prato, splashed the fresco in fine style:
"How looks my painting, now the scaffold's down?"   325
I ask a brother: "Hugely," he returns—
"Already not one phiz of your three slaves
Who turn the deacon off his toasted side,
But's scratched and prodded to our heart's content,
The pious people have so eased their own   330
With coming to say prayers there in a rage:
We get on fast to see the bricks beneath.
Expect another job this time next year,
For pity and religion grow i' the crowd—
Your painting serves its purpose!" Hang the fools!   335

---

323. *Laurence:* (roasted to death, A.D. 258). 324. *Prato:* town near Flor-
ence.

—That is—you'll not mistake an idle word
Spoke in a huff by a poor monk, God wot,
Tasting the air this spicy night which turns
The unaccustomed head like Chianti wine!
Oh, the church knows! don't misreport me, now!   340
It's natural a poor monk out of bounds
Should have his apt word to excuse himself:
And hearken how I plot to make amends.
I have bethought me: I shall paint a piece
. . . There's for you! Give me six months, then go, see   345
Something in Sant' Ambrogio's! Bless the nuns!
They want a cast o' my office. I shall paint
God in the midst, Madonna and her babe,
Ringed by a bowery, flowery angel-brood,
Lilies and vestments and white faces, sweet   350
As puff on puff of grated orris-root
When ladies crowd to church at midsummer.
And then i' the front, of course a saint or two—
Saint John, because he saves the Florentines,
Saint Ambrose, who puts down in black and white   355
The convent's friends and gives them a long day,
And Job, I must have him there past mistake,
The man of Uz (and Us without the z,
Painters who need his patience). Well, all these
Secured at their devotion, up shall come   36o
Out of a corner when you least expect,
As one by a dark stair into a great light,
Music and talking, who but Lippo! I!—
Mazed, motionless, and moon-struck—I'm the man!
Back I shrink—what is this I see and hear?   365
I, caught up with my monk's things by mistake,
My old serge gown and rope that goes all round,
I, in this presence, this pure company!
Where's a hole, where's a corner for escape?
Then steps a sweet angelic slip of a thing   370
Forward, puts out a soft palm—"Not so fast!"
—Addresses the celestial presence, "nay—
He made you and devised you, after all,

---

346. *Sant' Ambrogio's:* church in Florence, named for St. Ambrose (l. 355).
347. *cast . . . office:* example of my work [?]. 354. *saves:* (is patron saint
of). 361. *corner:* (where Lippo painted in his own head).

Though he's none of you! Could Saint John there, draw—
His camel-hair make up a painting-brush?   375
We come to brother Lippo for all that,
Iste perfecit opus!" So, all smile—
I shuffle sideways with my blushing face
Under the cover of a hundred wings
Thrown like a spread of kirtles when you're gay   380
And play hot cockles, all the doors being shut,
Till, wholly unexpected, in there pops
The hothead husband! Thus I scuttle off
To some safe bench behind, not letting go
The palm of her, the little lily thing   385
That spoke the good word for me in the nick,
Like the prior's niece . . . Saint Lucy, I would say.
And so all's saved for me, and for the church
A pretty picture gained. Go, six months hence!
Your hand, sir, and good-bye: no lights, no lights!   390
The street's hushed, and I know my own way back,
Don't fear me! There's the grey beginning. Zooks!

❧

ANDREA DEL SARTO
Called "The Faultless Painter"
(1855)

But do not let us quarrel any more,
No, my Lucrezia! bear with me for once:
Sit down and all shall happen as you wish.
You turn your face, but does it bring your heart?
I'll work then for your friend's friend, never fear,   5
Treat his own subject after his own way,
Fix his own time, accept too his own price,
And shut the money into this small hand
When next it takes mine. Will it? tenderly?
Oh, I'll content him,—but to-morrow, Love!   10

---

375. *camel-hair:* (garment). 377. *Iste . . . opus:* this man made the work.
381. *hot cockles:* (children's game in which blindfolded player tries to
guess who strikes him).
ANDREA DEL SARTO: sixteenth-century Italian painter.

I often am much wearier than you think,
This evening more than usual: and it seems
As if—forgive now—should you let me sit
Here by the window, with your hand in mine,
And look a half hour forth on Fiesolè,   15
Both of one mind, as married people use,
Quietly, quietly the evening through,
I might get up to-morrow to my work
Cheerful and fresh as ever. Let us try.
To-morrow, how you shall be glad for this!   20
Your soft hand is a woman of itself,
And mine, the man's bared breast she curls inside.
Don't count the time lost, neither; you must serve
For each of the five pictures we require:
It saves a model. So! keep looking so—   25
My serpentining beauty, rounds on rounds!
—How could you ever prick those perfect ears,
Even to put the pearl there! oh, so sweet—
My face, my moon, my everybody's moon,
Which everybody looks on and calls his,   30
And, I suppose, is looked on by in turn,
While she looks—no one's: very dear, no less.
You smile? why, there's my picture ready made,
There's what we painters call our harmony!
A common grayness silvers everything,—   35
All in a twilight, you and I alike
—You, at the point of your first pride in me
(That's gone you know),—but I, at every point;
My youth, my hope, my art, being all toned down
To yonder sober pleasant Fiesolè.   40
There's the bell clinking from the chapel-top;
That length of convent-wall across the way
Holds the trees safer, huddled more inside;
The last monk leaves the garden; days decrease,
And autumn grows, autumn in everything.   45
Eh? the whole seems to fall into a shape
As if I saw alike my work and self
And all that I was born to be and do,
A twilight-piece. Love, we are in God's hand.
How strange now looks the life he makes us lead;   50
So free we seem, so fettered fast we are!

15. *Fiesolè:* suburb of Florence.

I feel he laid the fetter: let it lie!
This chamber for example—turn your head—
All that's behind us! You don't understand,
Nor care to understand, about my art,   55
But you can hear at least when people speak:
And that cartoon, the second from the door
—It is the thing, Love! so such thing should be—
Behold Madonna!—I am bold to say.
I can do with my pencil what I know,   60
What I see, what at bottom of my heart
I wish for, if I ever wish so deep—
Do easily, too—when I say, perfectly,
I do not boast, perhaps: yourself are judge,
Who listened to the Legate's talk last week,   65
And just as much they used to say in France.
At any rate, 'tis easy, all of it!
No sketches first, no studies, that's long past:
I do what many dream of all their lives,
—Dream? strive to do, and agonize to do,   70
And fail in doing. I could count twenty such
On twice your fingers, and not leave this town,
Who strive—you don't know how the others strive
To paint a little thing like that you smeared
Carelessly passing with your robes afloat,—   75
Yet do much less, so much less, Someone says,
(I know his name, no matter)—so much less!
Well, less is more, Lucrezia: I am judged.
There burns a truer light of God in them,
In their vexed, beating, stuffed, and stopped-up brain,   80
Heart, or whate'er else, than goes on to prompt
This low-pulsed forthright craftsman's hand of mine.
Their works drop groundward, but themselves, I know,
Reach many a time a heaven that's shut to me,
Enter and take their place there sure enough,   85
Though they come back and cannot tell the world.
My works are nearer heaven, but I sit here.
The sudden blood of these men! at a word—
Praise them, it boils, or blame them, it boils too.
I, painting from myself and to myself,   90
Know what I do, am unmoved by men's blame
Or their praise either. Somebody remarks

---

57. *cartoon:* large sketch, to serve as model for painting. 65. *Legate:* repre-
sentative of Pope.

Morello's outline there is wrongly traced,
His hue mistaken; what of that? or else,
Rightly traced and well ordered; what of that?   95
Speak as they please, what does the mountain care?
Ah, but a man's reach should exceed his grasp,
Or what's a heaven for? All is silver-gray,
Placid and perfect with my art: the worse!
I know both what I want and what might gain;   100
And yet how profitless to know, to sigh
"Had I been two, another and myself,
Our head would have o'erlooked the world!" No doubt.
Yonder's a work now, of that famous youth
The Urbinate who died five years ago.   105
('Tis copied, George Vasari sent it me.)
Well, I can fancy how he did it all,
Pouring his soul, with kings and popes to see,
Reaching, that heaven might so replenish him,
Above and through his art—for it gives way;   110
That arm is wrongly put—and there again—
A fault to pardon in the drawing's lines,
Its body, so to speak: its soul is right,
He means right—that, a child may understand.
Still, what an arm! and I could alter it;   115
But all the play, the insight and the stretch—
Out of me, out of me! And wherefore out?
Had you enjoined them on me, given me soul,
We might have risen to Rafael, I and you.
Nay, Love, you did give all I asked, I think—   120
More than I merit, yes, by many times.
But had you—oh, with the same perfect brow,
And perfect eyes, and more than perfect mouth,
And the low voice my soul hears, as a bird
The fowler's pipe, and follows to the snare—   125
Had you, with these the same, but brought a mind!
Some women do so. Had the mouth there urged
"God and the glory! never care for gain.
The present by the future, what is that?
Live for fame, side by side with Agnolo!   130

---

93. *Morello:* a mountain north of Florence. 105. *The Urbinate:* Raphael.
106. *Vasari:* author of *The Lives of the Most Eminent Painters, Sculptors,
and Architects,* from which Browning took much of the material used in
this poem and in "Fra Lippo Lippi." 130. *Agnolo:* Michelangelo (he
and Raphael are often considered the two greatest Italian artists).

Rafael is waiting: up to God, all three!"
I might have done it for you. So it seems:
Perhaps not. All is as God overrules.
Beside, incentives come from the soul's self;
The rest avail not. Why do I need you?   135
What wife had Rafael, or has Agnolo?
In this world, who can do a thing, will not;
And who would do it, cannot, I perceive:
Yet the will's somewhat—somewhat, too, the power—
And thus we half-men struggle. At the end,   140
God, I conclude, compensates, punishes.
'Tis safer for me, if the award be strict,
That I am something underrated here,
Poor this long while, despised, to speak the truth.
I dared not, do you know, leave home all day,   145
For fear of chancing on the Paris lords.
The best is when they pass and look aside;
But they speak sometimes; I must bear it all.
Well may they speak! That Francis, that first time,
And that long festal year at Fontainebleau!   150
I surely then could sometimes leave the ground,
Put on the glory, Rafael's daily wear,
In that humane great monarch's golden look,—
One finger in his beard or twisted curl
Over his mouth's good mark that made the smile,   155
One arm about my shoulder, round my neck,
The jingle of his gold chain in my ear,
I painting proudly with his breath on me,
All his court round him, seeing with his eyes,
Such frank French eyes, and such a fire of souls   160
Profuse, my hand kept plying by those hearts,—
And, best of all, this, this, this face beyond,
This in the background, waiting on my work,
To crown the issue with a last reward!
A good time, was it not, my kingly days?   165
And had you not grown restless . . . but I know—
'Tis done and past; 'twas right, my instinct said;
Too live the life grew, golden and not gray,
And I'm the weak-eyed bat no sun should tempt
Out of his grange whose four walls make his world.   170
How could it end in any other way?

149. *Francis*: (French king from whom Andrea embezzled money to buy
Lucrezia a house).

You called me, and I came home to your heart.
The triumph was—to reach and stay there; since
I reached it ere the triumph, what is lost?
Let my hands frame your face in your hair's gold,   175
You beautiful Lucrezia that are mine!
"Rafael did this, Andrea painted that;
The Roman's is the better when you pray,
But still the other's Virgin was his wife—"
Men will excuse me. I am glad to judge   180
Both pictures in your presence; clearer grows
My better fortune, I resolve to think.
For, do you know, Lucrezia, as God lives,
Said one day Agnolo, his very self,
To Rafael . . . I have known it all these years . . .   185
(When the young man was flaming out his thoughts
Upon a palace-wall for Rome to see,
Too lifted up in heart because of it)
"Friend, there's a certain sorry little scrub
Goes up and down our Florence, none cares how,   190
Who, were he set to plan and execute
As you are, pricked on by your popes and kings,
Would bring the sweat into that brow of yours!"
To Rafael's!—And indeed the arm is wrong.
I hardly dare . . . yet, only you to see,   195
Give the chalk here—quick, thus the line should go!
Ay, but the soul! he's Rafael! rub it out!
Still, all I care for, if he spoke the truth,
(What he? why, who but Michel Agnolo?
Do you forget already words like those?)   200
If really there was such a chance so lost,—
Is, whether you're—not grateful—but more pleased.
Well, let me think so. And you smile indeed!
This hour has been an hour! Another smile?
If you would sit thus by me every night   205
I should work better, do you comprehend?
I mean that I should earn more, give you more.
See, it is settled dusk now; there's a star;
Morello's gone, the watch-lights show the wall,
The cue-owls speak the name we call them by.   210
Come from the window, love,—come in, at last,
Inside the melancholy little house

---

178. *Roman's:* (Raphael's).

We built to be so gay with. God is just.
King Francis may forgive me: oft at nights
When I look up from painting, eyes tired out,   215
The walls become illumined, brick from brick
Distinct, instead of mortar, fierce bright gold,
That gold of his I did cement them with!
Let us but love each other. Must you go?
That cousin here again? he waits outside?   220
Must see you—you, and not with me? Those loans?
More gaming debts to pay? you smiled for that?
Well, let smiles buy me! have you more to spend?
While hand and eye and something of a heart
Are left me, work's my ware, and what's it worth?   225
I'll pay my fancy. Only let me sit
The grey remainder of the evening out,
Idle, you call it, and muse perfectly
How I could paint, were I but back in France,
One picture, just one more—the Virgin's face,   230
Not yours this time! I want you at my side
To hear them—that is, Michel Agnolo—
Judge all I do and tell you of its worth.
Will you? To-morrow, satisfy your friend.
I take the subjects for his corridor,   235
Finish the portrait out of hand—there, there,
And throw him in another thing or two
If he demurs; the whole should prove enough
To pay for this same cousin's freak. Beside,
What's better and what's all I care about,   240
Get you the thirteen scudi for the ruff!
Love, does that please you? Ah, but what does he,
The cousin! what does he to please you more?
    I am grown peaceful as old age to-night.
I regret little, I would change still less.   245
Since there my past life lies, why alter it?
The very wrong to Francis!—it is true
I took his coin, was tempted and complied,
And built this house and sinned, and all is said.
My father and my mother died of want.   250
Well, had I riches of my own? you see
How one gets rich! Let each one bear his lot.
They were born poor, lived poor, and poor they died:
And I have labored somewhat in my time
And not been paid profusely. Some good son   255

Paint my two hundred pictures—let him try!
No doubt, there's something strikes a balance. Yes,
You loved me quite enough, it seems to-night.
This must suffice me here. What would one have?
In heaven, perhaps, new chances, one more chance—   260
Four great walls in the New Jerusalem
Meted on each side by the angel's reed,
For Leonard, Rafael, Agnolo and me
To cover—the three first without a wife,
While I have mine! So—still they overcome   265
Because there's still Lucrezia,—as I choose.
Again the cousin's whistle! Go, my Love.

Matthew Arnold

TO MARGUERITE

(1854)

Yes: in the sea of life enisled,
   With echoing straits between us thrown.
Dotting the shoreless watery wild,
   We mortal millions live *alone*.
The islands feel the enclasping flow,   5
And then their endless bounds they know.

But when the moon their hollows lights,
   And they are swept by balms of spring,
And in their glens, on starry nights,
   The nightingales divinely sing;   10
And lovely notes, from shore to shore,
Across the sounds and channels pour;

O then a longing like despair
   Is to their farthest caverns sent!
For surely once, they feel, we were   15
   Parts of a single continent.

---

263. *Leonard:* Leonardo da Vinci ("The Last Supper," the "Mona Lisa").

Now round us spreads the watery plain—
O might our marges meet again!

Who ordered that their longing's fire
 Should be, as soon as kindled, cooled?   20
Who renders vain their deep desire?—
 A god, a god their severance ruled;
And bade betwixt their shores to be
The unplumbed, salt, estranging sea.

A SUMMER NIGHT

(1852)

In the deserted, moon-blanched street,
How lonely rings the echo of my feet!
Those windows, which I gaze at, frown,
Silent and white, unopening down,
Repellent as the world; but see,   5
A break between the housetops shows
The moon! and lost behind her, fading dim
Into the dewy dark obscurity
Down at the far horizon's rim,
Doth a whole tract of heaven disclose!   10

And to my mind the thought
Is on a sudden brought
Of a past night, and a far different scene.
Headlands stood out into the moonlit deep
As clearly as at noon;   15
The spring-tide's brimming flow
Heaved dazzlingly between;
Houses, with long white sweep,
Girdled the glistening bay;
Behind, through the soft air,   20
The blue haze-cradled mountains spread away.
That night was far more fair—
But the same restless pacings to and fro,
And the same vainly throbbing heart was there,
And the same bright, calm moon.   25

And the calm moonlight seems to say,—
Hast thou, then, still the old unquiet breast,
Which neither deadens into rest,

Nor ever feels the fiery glow
That whirls the spirit from itself away,   30
But fluctuates to and fro,
Never by passion quite possessed,
And never quite benumbed by the world's sway?
And I, I know not if to pray
Still to be what I am, or yield, and be   35
Like all the other men I see.

For most men in a brazen prison live,
Where, in the sun's hot eye,
With heads bent o'er their toil, they languidly
Their lives to some unmeaning task-work give,   40
Dreaming of naught beyond their prison-wall.
And as, year after year,
Fresh products of their barren labor fall
From their tired hands, and rest
Never yet comes more near,   45
Gloom settles slowly down over their breast.
And while they try to stem
The waves of mournful thought by which they are prest,
Death in their prison reaches them,
Unfreed, having seen nothing, still unblest.   50

And the rest, a few,
Escape their prison, and depart
On the wide ocean of life anew.
There the freed prisoner, where'er his heart
Listeth, will sail;   55
Nor doth he know how there prevail,
Despotic on that sea,
Trade-winds which cross it from eternity.
Awhile he holds some false way, undebarred
By thwarting signs, and braves   60
The freshening wind and blackening waves.
And then the tempest strikes him; and between
The lightning-bursts is seen
Only a driving wreck,
And the pale master on his spar-strewn deck   65
With anguished face and flying hair,
Grasping the rudder hard,
Still bent to make some port, he knows not where,
Still standing for some false, impossible shore.
And sterner comes the roar   70

Of sea and wind; and through the deepening gloom
Fainter and fainter wreck and helmsman loom,
And he too disappears, and comes no more.

Is there no life, but these alone?
Madman or slave, must man be one?   75

Plainness and clearness without shadow of stain!
Clearness divine!
Ye heavens, whose pure dark regions have no sign
Of languor, though so calm, and though so great
Are yet untroubled and unpassionate;   80
Who, though so noble, share in the world's toil,
And, though so tasked, keep free from dust and soil!
I will not say that your mild deeps retain
A tinge, it may be, of their silent pain
Who have longed deeply once, and longed in vain;   85
But I will rather say that you remain
A world above man's head, to let him see
How boundless might his soul's horizons be,
How vast, yet of what clear transparency!
How it were good to live there, and breathe free;   90
How fair a lot to fill
Is left to each man still!

THE SCHOLAR-GIPSY

(1853)

There was very lately a lad in the University of Oxford, who was by his poverty forced to leave his studies there; and at last to join himself to a company of vagabond gypsies. Among these extravagant people, by the insinuating subtilty of his carriage, he quickly got so much of their love and esteem as that they discovered to him their mystery. After he had been a pretty while exercised in the trade, there chanced to ride by a couple of scholars, who had formerly been of his acquaintance. They quickly spied out their old friend among the gypsies; and he gave them an account of the necessity which drove him to that kind of life, and told them that the people he went with were not such impostors as they were taken for, but that they had a traditional kind of learning among them, and could do wonders by the power of imagination, their fancy binding that of others; that himself

had learned much of their art, and when he had compassed the whole secret,
he intended, he said, to leave their company, and give the world an account
of what he had learned.—GLANVIL's Vanity of Dogmatizing, 1661.

Go, for they call you, Shepherd, from the hill;
  Go, Shepherd, and untie the wattled cotes:
    No longer leave thy wistful flock unfed,
  Nor let thy bawling fellows rack their throats,
    Nor the cropped grasses shoot another head.   5
      But when the fields are still,
  And the tired men and dogs all gone to rest,
    And only the white sheep are sometimes seen
    Cross and recross the strips of moon-blanched green:
Come, Shepherd, and again begin the quest.   10

Here, where the reaper was at work of late,
  In this high field's dark corner, where he leaves
    His coat, his basket, and his earthen cruse,
  And in the sun all morning binds the sheaves,
    Then here, at noon, comes back his stores to use: 15
      Here will I sit and wait,
  While to my ear from uplands far away
    The bleating of the folded flocks is borne,
    With distant cries of reapers in the corn—
All the live murmur of a summer's day.   20

Screened is this nook o'er the high, half-reaped field,
  And here till sundown, Shepherd, will I be.
    Through the thick corn the scarlet poppies peep,
  And round green roots and yellowing stalks I see
    Pale blue convolvulus in tendrils creep: 25
      And air-swept lindens yield
  Their scent, and rustle down their perfumed showers
    Of bloom on the bent grass where I am laid,
    And bower me from the August sun with shade;
And the eye travels down to Oxford's towers: 30

And near me on the grass lies Glanvil's book—
  Come, let me read the oft-read tale again:
    The story of that Oxford scholar poor,

THE SCHOLAR-GYPSY: 31. *Glanvil's book:* Joseph Glanvil's *Vanity of Dog-
matizing* (1661), from which Arnold took the anecdote of the poverty-
stricken scholar who went to live with the gypsies.

Of pregnant parts and quick inventive brain,
  Who, tired of knocking at preferment's door, 35
    One summer morn forsook
His friends, and went to learn the gipsy lore,
  And roamed the world with that wild brotherhood,
  And came, as most men deemed, to little good,
But came to Oxford and his friends no more. 40

But once, years after, in the country lanes,
  Two scholars, whom at college erst he knew,
    Met him, and of his way of life inquired.
Whereat he answered that the gipsy crew,
  His mates, had arts to rule as they desired 45
    The workings of men's brains;
And they can bind them to what thoughts they will:
  'And I,' he said 'the secret of their art,
  When fully learned, will to the world impart:
But it needs heaven-sent moments for this skill!' 50

This said, he left them, and returned no more,
  But rumours hung about the country-side,
    That the lost scholar long was seen to stray,
Seen by rare glimpses, pensive and tongue-tied,
  In hat of antique shape, and cloak of grey, 55
    The same the gipsies wore.
Shepherds had met him on the Hurst in spring;
  At some lone alehouse in the Berkshire moors,
  On the warm ingle-bench, the smock-frocked boors
Had found him seated at their entering, 60

But, 'mid their drink and clatter, he would fly:
  And I myself seem half to know thy looks,
    And put the shepherds, wanderer, on thy trace;
And boys who in lone wheatfields scare the rooks
  I ask if thou hast passed their quiet place; 65
    Or in my boat I lie
Moored to the cool bank in the summer heats,
  'Mid wide grass meadows which the sunshine fills,
  And watch the warm green-muffled Cumner hills,
And wonder if thou haunt'st their shy retreats. 70

For most, I know, thou lov'st retired ground.
  Thee, at the ferry, Oxford riders blithe,

---

57. *Hurst:* hill SW of Oxford. 58. *Berkshire:* county S of Oxford. 59.
ingle: fireside. *boors:* farmers. 69. *Cumner:* parish SW of Oxford.

Returning home on summer nights, have met
  Crossing the stripling Thames at Bablock-hithe,
    Trailing in the cool stream thy fingers wet,   75
      As the punt's rope chops round:
  And leaning backward in a pensive dream,
    And fostering in thy lap a heap of flowers
    Plucked in shy fields and distant Wychwood bowers,
  And thine eyes resting on the moonlit stream: 80

And then they land, and thou art seen no more.
  Maidens who from the distant hamlets come
    To dance around the Fyfield elm in May,
  Oft through the darkening fields have seen thee roam,
    Or cross a stile into the public way.   85
      Oft thou hast given them store
  Of flowers—the frail-leafed, white anemone—
    Dark bluebells drenched with dews of summer eves,
    And purple orchises with spotted leaves—
  But none hath words she can report of thee.   90

And, above Godstow Bridge, when hay-time's here
  In June, and many a scythe in sunshine flames,
    Men who through those wide fields of breezy grass
  Where black-winged swallows haunt the glittering Thames,
    To bathe in the abandoned lasher pass,   95
      Have often passed thee near
  Sitting upon the river bank o'ergrown:
    Marked thine outlandish garb, thy figure spare,
    Thy dark vague eyes, and soft abstracted air;
  But, when they came from bathing, thou wast gone.   100

At some lone homestead in the Cumner hills,
  Where at her open door the housewife darns,
    Thou hast been seen, or hanging on a gate
  To watch the threshers in the mossy barns.
    Children, who early range these slopes and late   105
      For cresses from the rills,
  Have known thee eying, all an April day,
    The springing pastures and the feeding kine;
    And marked thee, when the stars come out and shine
  Through the long dewy grass move slow away.   110

---

74. *Bablock-hithe:* site of ferry near Cumner. 79. *Wychwood:* forest NW
of Oxford. 83. *Fyfield:* village six miles SW of Oxford. 91. *Godstow
Bridge:* two miles above Oxford on the Thames. 95. *lasher:* mill pond.

In autumn, on the skirts of Bagley Wood,
   Where most the gipsies by the turf-edged way
     Pitch their smoked tents, and every bush you see
  With scarlet patches tagged and shreds of grey,
     Above the forest-ground called Thessaly—   115
       The blackbird picking food
Sees thee, nor stops his meal, nor fears at all;
   So often has he known thee past him stray
   Rapt, twirling in thy hand a withered spray,
And waiting for the spark from heaven to fall.   120

And once, in winter, on the causeway chill
   Where home through flooded fields foot-travellers go,
     Have I not passed thee on the wooden bridge
  Wrapt in thy cloak and battling with the snow,
     Thy face toward Hinksey and its wintry ridge?   125
       And thou hast climbed the hill
And gained the white brow of the Cumner range;
   Turned once to watch, while thick the snowflakes fall,
   The line of festal light in Christ Church hall—
Then sought thy straw in some sequestered grange.   130

But what—I dream! Two hundred years are flown
   Since first thy story ran through Oxford halls,
     And the grave Glanvil did the tale inscribe
  That thou wert wandered from the studious walls
     To learn strange arts, and join a gipsy tribe: 135
       And thou from earth art gone
Long since, and in some quiet churchyard laid;
   Some country nook, where o'er thy unknown grave
   Tall grasses and white flowering nettles wave—
Under a dark red-fruited yew-tree's shade.   140

—No, no, thou hast not felt the lapse of hours.
   For what wears out the life of mortal men?
     'Tis that from change to change their being rolls:
  'Tis that repeated shocks, again, again,
     Exhaust the energy of strongest souls,   145
       And numb the elastic powers.
Till having used our nerves with bliss and teen,
   And tired upon a thousand schemes our wit,
   To the just-pausing Genius we remit
Our worn-out life, and are—what we have been.   150

---

111. *Bagley Wood:* SW of Oxford. 125. *Hinksey:* village S of Oxford.
129. *Christ Church:* an Oxford college. 149. *Genius:* guardian angel.

Thou hast not lived, why shouldst thou perish, so?
  Thou hadst *one* aim, *one* business, *one* desire:
    Else wert thou long since numbered with the dead—
  Else hadst thou spent, like other men, thy fire.
    The generations of thy peers are fled,   155
      And we ourselves shall go;
  But thou possessest an immortal lot,
    And we imagine thee exempt from age
    And living as thou liv'st on Glanvil's page,
  Because thou hadst—what we, alas, have not!   160

For early didst thou leave the world, with powers
  Fresh, undiverted to the world without,
    Firm to their mark, not spent on other things;
  Free from the sick fatigue, the languid doubt,
    Which much to have tried, in much been baffled, brings.   165
      O life unlike to ours!
  Who fluctuate idly without term or scope,
    Of whom each strives, nor knows for what he strives
    And each half lives a hundred different lives;
  Who wait like thee, but not, like thee, in hope.   170

Thou waitest for the spark from heaven: and we,
  Vague half-believers of our casual creeds,
    Who never deeply felt, nor clearly willed,
  Whose insight never has borne fruit in deeds,
    Whose weak resolves never have been fulfilled;   175
      For whom each year we see
  Breeds new beginnings, disappointments new;
    Who hesitate and falter life away,
    And lose to-morrow the ground won to-day—
  Ah, do not we, wanderer, await it too?   180

Yes, we await it, but it still delays,
  And then we suffer; and amongst us one,
    Who most has suffered, takes dejectedly
  His seat upon the intellectual throne;
    And all his store of sad experience he   185
      Lays bare of wretched days;
  Tells us his misery's birth and growth and signs,
    And how the dying spark of hope was fed,
    And how the breast was soothed, and how the head,
  And all his hourly varied anodynes.   190

---

182. *one:* possibly Tennyson (with reference to "In Memoriam"?).

This for our wisest: and we others pine,
  And wish the long unhappy dream would end,
    And waive all claim to bliss, and try to bear,
  With close-lipped patience for our only friend,
     Sad patience, too near neighbour to despair: 195
      But none has hope like thine.
Thou through the fields and through the woods dost stray,
    Roaming the country-side, a truant boy,
    Nursing thy project in unclouded joy,
  And every doubt long blown by time away.   200

O born in days when wits were fresh and clear,
  And life ran gaily as the sparkling Thames;
    Before this strange disease of modern life,
  With its sick hurry, its divided aims,
     Its heads o'ertaxed, its palsied hearts, was rife—   205
      Fly hence, our contact fear!
Still fly, plunge deeper in the bowering wood!
    Averse, as Dido did with gesture stern
    From her false friend's approach in Hades turn,
Wave us away, and keep thy solitude.   210

Still nursing the unconquerable hope,
  Still clutching the inviolable shade,
    With a free onward impulse brushing through,
  By night, the silvered branches of the glade—
     Far on the forest-skirts, where none pursue,   215
      On some mild pastoral slope
Emerge, and resting on the moonlit pales,
    Freshen thy flowers, as in former years,
    With dew, or listen with enchanted ears,
From the dark dingles, to the nightingales.   220

But fly our paths, our feverish contact fly!
  For strong the infection of our mental strife,
    Which, though it gives no bliss, yet spoils for rest,
  And we should win thee from thy own fair life,
     Like us distracted, and like us unblest.   225
      Soon, soon thy cheer would die,
Thy hopes grow timorous, and unfixed thy powers,
    And thy clear aims be cross and shifting made:
    And then thy glad perennial youth would fade,
Fade, and grow old at last, and die like ours.   230

---

209. *false friend:* Aeneas (because he deserted her, she had committed suicide).

Then fly our greetings, fly our speech and smiles!
 —As some grave Tyrian trader, from the sea,
  Descried at sunrise an emerging prow
 Lifting the cool-haired creepers stealthily,
  The fringes of a southward-facing brow   235
   Among the Ægean isles;
 And saw the merry Grecian coaster come,
  Freighted with amber grapes, and Chian wine,
  Green bursting figs, and tunnies steeped in brine;
 And knew the intruders on his ancient home,   240

The young light-hearted masters of the waves;
 And snatched his rudder, and shook out more sail,
  And day and night held on indignantly
 O'er the blue Midland waters with the gale,
  Betwixt the Syrtes and soft Sicily,   245
   To where the Atlantic raves
 Outside the Western Straits, and unbent sails
  There, where down cloudy cliffs, through sheets of foam,
  Shy traffickers, the dark Iberians come;
 And on the beach undid his corded bales.   250

∾

STANZAS FROM THE GRANDE CHARTREUSE
(1855)

 Through Alpine meadows soft-suffused
 With rain, where thick the crocus blows,
 Past the dark forges long disused,
 The mule-track from Saint Laurent goes.
 The bridge is crossed, and slow we ride,   5
 Through forest, up the mountain side.

 The autumnal evening darkens round,
 The wind is up, and drives the rain;
 While, hark! far down, with strangled sound
 Doth the Dead Guier's stream complain,   10

---

232. *Tyrian:* from Tyre, in Asia Minor. 236. *Aegean:* (near Greece). 238.
Chian: from the island of Chios. 245. *Syrtes:* gulf on N.coast of Africa.
249. *Iberians:* early inhabitants of the Spanish peninsula.
 THE GRANDE CHARTREUSE: Carthusian monastery Arnold visited in 1852.
4, 10. *Saint Laurent, Dead Guier's:* near the monastery.

Where that wet smoke, among the woods,
Over his boiling caldron broods.

Swift rush the spectral vapors white
Past limestone scars with ragged pines,
Showing—then blotting from our sight!—   15
Halt—through the cloud-drift something shines!
High in the valley, wet and drear,
The huts of Courrerie appear.

Strike leftward! cries our guide; and higher
Mounts up the stony forest-way.   20
At last the encircling trees retire;
Look! through the showery twilight gray,
What pointed roofs are these advance?
A palace of the kings of France?

Approach, for what we seek is here!   25
Alight, and sparely sup, and wait
For rest in this outbuilding near;
Then cross the sward, and reach that gate;
Knock; pass the wicket. Thou art come
To the Carthusians' world-famed home.   30

The silent courts, where night and day
Into their stone-carved basins cold
The splashing icy fountains play,
The humid corridors behold,
Where, ghost-like in the deepening night,   35
Cowled forms brush by in gleaming white!

The chapel, where no organ's peal
Invests the stern and naked prayer!
With penitential cries they kneel
And wrestle; rising then, with bare   40
And white uplifted faces stand,
Passing the Host from hand to hand;

Each takes, and then his visage wan
Is buried in his cowl once more.
The cells!—the suffering Son of man   45
Upon the wall; the knee-worn floor;
And where they sleep, that wooden bed,
Which shall their coffin be when dead!

---

8. *Courrerie*: Alpine village.

The library, where tract and tome
Not to feed priestly pride are there,   50
To hymn the conquering march of Rome,
Nor yet to amuse, as ours are:
They paint of souls the inner strife,
Their drops of blood, their death in life.

The garden, overgrown—yet mild,   55
See, fragrant herbs are flowering there;
Strong children of the Alpine wild
Whose culture is the brethren's care;
Of human tasks their only one,
And cheerful works beneath the sun.   60

Those halls, too, destined to contain
Each its own pilgrim-host of old,
From England, Germany, or Spain,—
All are before me! I behold
The house, the brotherhood austere.   65
And what am I, that I am here?

For rigorous teachers seized my youth,
And purged its faith, and trimmed its fire,
Showed me the high, white star of Truth,
There bade me gaze, and there aspire.   70
Even now their whispers pierce the gloom:
What dost thou in this living tomb?

Forgive me, masters of the mind!
At whose behest I long ago
So much unlearned, so much resigned: 75
I come not here to be your foe!
I seek these anchorites, not in ruth,
To curse and to deny your truth;

Not as their friend, or child, I speak!
But as, on some far northern strand,   80
Thinking of his own Gods, a Greek
In pity and mournful awe might stand
Before some fallen Runic stone;
For both were faiths, and both are gone.

Wandering between two worlds, one dead,   85
The other powerless to be born,
With nowhere yet to rest my head,

Like these, on earth I wait forlorn.
Their faith, my tears, the world deride:
I come to shed them at their side. 90

Oh, hide me in your gloom profound,
Ye solemn seats of holy pain!
Take me, cowled forms, and fence me round,
Till I possess my soul again;
Till free my thoughts before me roll, 95
Not chafed by hourly false control!

For the world cries, your faith is now
But a dead time's exploded dream;
My melancholy, sciolists say,
Is a passed mode, an outworn theme.— 100
As if the world had ever had
A faith, or sciolists been sad!

Ah! if it *be* passed, take away,
At least, the restlessness, the pain!
Be man henceforth no more a prey 105
To these out-dated stings again!
The nobleness of grief is gone:
Ah, leave us not the fret alone!

But,—if you cannot give us ease,—
Last of the race of them who grieve, 110
Here leave us to die out with these
Last of the people who believe!
Silent, while years engrave the brow;
Silent—the best are silent now.

Achilles ponders in his tent, 115
The kings of modern thought are dumb;
Silent they are, though not content,
And wait to see the future come.
They have the grief men had of yore,
But they contend and cry no more. 120

Our fathers watered with their tears
This sea of time whereon we sail;
Their voices were in all men's ears
Who passed within their puissant hail.
Still the same ocean round us raves, 125
But we stand mute, and watch the waves.

For what availed it, all the noise
And outcry of the former men?
Say, have their sons achieved more joys?
Say, is life lighter now than then?   130
The sufferers died, they left their pain;
The pangs which tortured them remain.

What helps it now, that Byron bore,
With haughty scorn which mocked the smart,
Through Europe to the Ætolian shore   135
The pageant of his bleeding heart?
That thousands counted every groan,
And Europe made his woe her own?

What boots it, Shelley! that the breeze
Carried thy lovely wail away,   140
Musical through Italian trees
Which fringe thy soft blue Spezzian bay?
Inheritors of thy distress,
Have restless hearts one throb the less?

Or are we easier, to have read,   145
O Obermann! the sad, stern page,
Which tells us how thou hidd'st thy head
From the fierce tempest of thine age
In the lone brakes of Fontainebleau,
Or chalets near the Alpine snow?   150

Ye slumber in your silent grave!—
The world, which for an idle day
Grace to your mood of sadness gave,
Long since hath flung her weeds away.
The eternal trifler breaks your spell;   155
But we—we learnt your lore too well!

Years hence, perhaps, may dawn an age,
More fortunate, alas! than we,
Which without hardness will be sage,

---

135. *Aetolian shore:* (where Byron died, in Greece). 140. *carried . . . away:*
Shelley was drowned in the Gulf of Spezzia, Italy. 146. *Obermann:* the
French novelist de Sénancour (1770-1846); "Obermann" was the title of
his melancholy philosophic romance, set in Switzerland. 149. *Fontaine-
bleau:* city near Paris.

And gay without frivolity. 160
Sons of the world, oh! speed those years;
But, while we wait, allow our tears!

Allow them! We admire with awe
The exulting thunder of your race;
You give the universe your law, 165
You triumph over time and space:
Your pride of life, your tireless powers,
We praise them, but they are not ours.

We are like children reared in shade
Beneath some old-world abbey wall, 170
Forgotten in a forest-glade,
And secret from the eyes of all.
Deep, deep the greenwood round them waves,
Their abbey, and its close of graves!

But, where the road runs near the stream, 175
Oft through the trees they catch a glance
Of passing troops in the sun's beam,—
Pennon, and plume, and flashing lance;
Forth to the world those soldiers fare,
To life, to cities, and to war. 180

And through the woods, another way,
Faint bugle-notes from far are borne,
Where hunters gather, staghounds bay,
Round some old forest-lodge at morn.
Gay dames are there, in sylvan green; 185
Laughter and cries—those notes between!

The banners flashing through the trees
Make their blood dance, and chain their eyes;
That bugle-music on the breeze
Arrests them with a charmed surprise. 190
Banner by turns and bugle woo:
Ye shy recluses, follow too!

O children, what do ye reply?
"Action and pleasure, will ye roam
Through these secluded dells to cry 195
And call us? but too late ye come!
Too late for us your call ye blow,
Whose bent was taken long ago.

"Long since we pace this shadowed nave;
We watch those yellow tapers shine,   200
Emblems of hope over the grave,
In the high altar's depth divine.
The organ carries to our ear
Its accents of another sphere.

"Fenced early in this cloistral round   205
Of revery, of shade, of prayer,
How should we grow in other ground?
How can we flower in foreign air?
—Pass, banners, pass, and bugles, cease;
And leave our desert to its peace!"   210

THYRSIS

(1866)

A MONODY

*To commemorate the author's friend, Arthur Hugh
Clough, who died at Florence, 1861*

How changed is here each spot man makes or fills!
    In the two Hinkseys nothing keeps the same;
        The village-street its haunted mansion lacks,
        And from the sign is gone Sibylla's name,
            And from the roofs the twisted chimney-stacks—   5
            Are ye too changed, ye hills?
        See, 'tis no foot of unfamiliar men
            To-night from Oxford up your pathway strays!
            Here came I often, often, in old days—
        Thyrsis and I; we still had Thyrsis then.   10

Runs it not here, the track by Childsworth Farm,
    Past the high wood, to where the elm-tree crowns

---

2. *two Hinkseys:* See "Scholar-Gipsy," line 125; there are a North and a
South Hinksey. (For a map, see Tinker and Lowry, *Poetry of Arnold*,
1940, p. 350.) 4. *Sibylla:* Sybella Curr (d. 1860), hostess of the Cross Keys
tavern in South Hinksey. 10. *Thyrsis:* Arnold's friend the poet Clough
(b. 1819), who died at Florence 13 November 1861. 11. *Childsworth
Farm:* 2½ miles SW from Oxford.

The hill behind whose ridge the sunset flames?
The signal-elm, that looks on Ilsley Downs,
    The Vale, the three lone weirs, the youthful Thames?—   15
        This winter-eve is warm,
Humid the air! leafless, yet soft as spring,
    The tender purple spray on copse and briers!
And that sweet city with her dreaming spires,
She needs not June for beauty's heightening,   20

Lovely all times she lies, lovely to-night!—
    Only, methinks, some loss of habit's power
    Befalls me wandering through this upland dim.
Once pass'd I blindfold here, at any hour;
    Now seldom come I, since I came with him.   25
        That single elm-tree bright
Against the west—I miss it! is it gone?
    We prized it dearly; while it stood, we said,
    Our friend, the Gipsy-Scholar, was not dead;
While the tree lived, he in these fields lived on.   30

Too rare, too rare, grow now my visits here,
    But once I knew each field, each flower, each stick;
    And with the country-folk acquaintance made
By barn in threshing-time, by new-built rick.
    Here, too, our shepherd-pipes we first assay'd.   35
        Ah me! this many a year
My pipe is lost, my shepherd's holiday!
    Needs must I lose them, needs with heavy heart
    Into the world and wave of men depart;
But Thyrsis of his own will went away.   40

It irk'd him to be here, he could not rest.
He loved each simple joy the country yields,
    He loved his mates; but yet he could not keep,
For that a shadow lower'd on the fields,
    Here with the shepherds and the silly sheep.   45
        Some life of men unblest
He knew, which made him droop, and fill'd his head.
    He went; his piping took a troubled sound
    Of storms that rage outside our happy ground;
He could not wait their passing, he is dead!   50

---

14. *Ilsley Downs:* hills 25 miles S of Oxford.

So, some tempestuous morn in early June,
  When the year's primal burst of bloom is o'er,
    Before the roses and the longest day—
When garden-walks, and all the grassy floor,
    With blossoms red and white of fallen May   55
      And chestnut-flowers are strewn—
So have I heard the cuckoo's parting cry,
  From the wet field, through the vext garden-trees,
  Come with the volleying rain and tossing breeze:
  The bloom is gone, and with the bloom go I!   60

Too quick despairer, wherefore wilt thou go?
  Soon will the high Midsummer pomps come on,
    Soon will the musk carnations break and swell,
Soon shall we have gold-dusted snapdragon,
    Sweet-William with its homely cottage-smell,   65
      And stocks in fragrant blow;
Roses that down the alleys shine afar,
  And open, jasmine-muffled lattices,
  And groups under the dreaming garden-trees,
And the full moon, and the white evening-star.   70

He harkens not! light comer, he is flown!
  What matters it? next year he will return,
    And we shall have him in the sweet spring-days,
With whitening hedges, and uncrumpling fern,
    And blue-bells trembling by the forest-ways,   75
      And scent of hay new-mown.
But Thyrsis never more we swains shall see;
  See him come back, and cut a smoother reed,
  And blow a strain the world at last shall heed—
For Time, not Corydon, hath conquer'd thee!   80

Alack, for Corydon no rival now!—
  But when Sicilian shepherds lost a mate,
    Some good survivor with his flute would go,
Piping a ditty sad for Bion's fate;
    And cross the unpermitted ferry's flow,   85
      And relax Pluto's brow,

---

80. *Corydon:* name of typical shepherd in the music matches of ancient pastoral poetry; a match between a Corydon and a Thyrsis occurs in a Latin poem of Clough's. 81. *Sicilian:* Sicily was the site of Theocritus' idylls, the poems which began the pastoral tradition. 84. *Bion:* Greek pastoral poet, 3rd century B.C.; author of "Lament for Adonis." 86. *Pluto:* God of underworld.

And make leap up with joy the beauteous head
  Of Proserpine, among whose crowned hair
  Are flowers first open'd on Sicilian air,
And flute his friend, like Orpheus, from the dead.   90

O easy access to the hearer's grace
  When Dorian shepherds sang to Proserpine!
    For she herself had trod Sicilian fields,
She knew the Dorian water's gush divine,
    She knew each lily white which Enna yields,   95
      Each rose with blushing face;
She loved the Dorian pipe, the Dorian strain.
    But ah, of our poor Thames she never heard!
    Her foot the Cumner cowslips never stirr'd;
And we should tease her with our plaint in vain!   100

Well! wind-dispersed and vain the words will be,
  Yet, Thyrsis, let me give my grief its hour
    In the old haunt, and find our tree-topp'd hill!
Who, if not I, for questing here hath power?
    I know the wood which hides the daffodil,   105
      I know the Fyfield tree,
  I know what white, what purple fritillaries
    The grassy harvest of the river-fields,
    Above by Ensham, down by Sandford, yields,
And what sedg'd brooks are Thames's tributaries;   110

I know these slopes; who knows them if not I?—
  But many a dingle on the loved hill-side,
    With thorns once studded, old, white-blossom'd trees,
  Where thick the cowslips grew, and, far descried,
    High tower'd the spikes of purple orchises,   115
      Hath since our day put by
  The coronals of that forgotten time.
    Down each green bank hath gone the ploughboy's team,
    And only in the hidden brookside gleam
Primroses, orphans of the flowery prime.   120

---

88. *Proserpine:* Goddess of underworld. 90. *Orpheus:* legendary miracle-working Thracian musician. 92. *Dorian:* from Doris in Greece; connotes directness and simplicity. 95. *Enna:* in Sicily, site of Pluto's kidnapping of Proserpine; see *Paradise Lost,* IV, 268-72. 99, 106. *Cumner, Fyfield:* See "The Scholar-Gipsy," lines 69, 83. 109. *Ensham:* market town 5½ miles NW of Oxford. 110. *Sandford:* on Thames, 3 miles SE of Oxford. 112. *dingle:* narrow valley.

Where is the girl, who, by the boatman's door,
  Above the locks, above the boating throng,
    Unmoor'd our skiff, when, through the Wytham flats,
  Red loosestrife and blond meadow-sweet among,
    And darting swallows, and light water-gnats,   125
      We track'd the shy Thames shore?
  Where are the mowers, who, as the tiny swell
    Of our boat passing heav'd the river-grass,
    Stood with suspended scythe to see us pass?—
  They all are gone, and thou art gone as well.   130

Yes, thou art gone! and round me too the night
  In ever-nearing circle weaves her shade.
    I see her veil draw soft across the day,
  I feel her slowly chilling breath invade
    The cheek grown thin, the brown hair sprent with grey;   135
      I feel her finger light
  Laid pausefully upon life's headlong train;—
    The foot less prompt to meet the morning dew,
    The heart less bounding at emotion new,
  And hope, once crush'd, less quick to spring again.   140

And long the way appears, which seem'd so short
  To the less practised eye of sanguine youth;
    And high the mountain-tops, in cloudy air,
  The mountain-tops where is the throne of Truth,
    Tops in life's morning-sun so bright and bare!   145
      Unbreachable the fort
  Of the long-batter'd world uplifts its wall;
    And strange and vain the earthly turmoil grows,
    And near and real the charm of thy repose,
  And night as welcome as a friend would fall.   150

But hush! the upland hath a sudden loss
  Of quiet!—Look, adown the dusk hill-side,
    A troop of Oxford hunters going home,
  As in old days, jovial and talking, ride!
    From hunting with the Berkshire hounds they come,   155
      Quick! let me fly, and cross
  Into yon farther field!—'Tis done; and see,
    Back'd by the sunset, which doth glorify
    The orange and pale violet evening-sky,
  Bare on its lonely ridge, the Tree! the Tree!   160

---

123. *Wytham:* old village 3 miles NW of Oxford. 155. *Berkshire:* See
"Scholar-Gipsy," l. 158.

I take the omen! Eve lets down her veil,
  The white fog creeps from bush to bush about,
  The west unflushes, the high stars grow bright,
  And in the scatter'd farms the lights come out.
    I cannot reach the Signal-Tree to-night,   165
      Yet, happy omen, hail!
  Hear it from thy broad lucent Arno-vale
  (For there thine earth-forgetting eyelids keep
  The morningless and unawakening sleep
  Under the flowery oleanders pale),   170

Hear it, O Thyrsis, still our tree is there!—
  Ah, vain! These English fields, this upland dim,
  These brambles pale with mist engarlanded,
  That lone, sky-pointing tree, are not for him.
    To a boon southern country he is fled,   175
      And now in happier air,
  Wandering with the great Mother's train divine
  (And purer or more subtle soul than thee,
  I trow, the mighty Mother doth not see!)
  Within a folding of the Apennine,   180

Thou hearest the immortal strains of old.
  Putting his sickle to the perilous grain
  In the hot cornfield of the Phrygian king,
  For thee the Lityerses song again
    Young Daphnis with his silver voice doth sing;   185
      Sings his Sicilian fold,

---

167. *Arno:* river in Italy on which Florence is situated. 177. *great Mother:*
Cybele, earth-goddess worshipped in ancient Italy. 180. *Apennine:* Italian
mountain range. 184. *Lityerses:* Daphnis, the ideal Sicilian shepherd of
Greek pastoral poetry, was said to have followed into Phrygia his mistress
Piplea, who had been carried off by robbers, and to have found her in the
power of the king of Phrygia, Lityerses. Lityerses used to make strangers
try a contest with him in reaping corn, and to put them to death if he
overcame them. Hercules arrived in time to save Daphnis, took upon
himself the reaping contest with Lityerses, overcame him, and slew him.
The Lityerses-song connected with this tradition was, like the Linus-song,
one of the early plaintive strains of Greek popular poetry, and used to be
sung by reapers. Other traditions represented Daphnis as beloved by a
nymph who exacted from him an oath to love no one else. He fell in
love with a princess and was struck blind by the jealous nymph. Mer-
cury, who was his father, raised him to Heaven, and made a fountain
spring up in the place from which he ascended. At this fountain the
Sicilians offered yearly sacrifices.—See SERVIUS, *Comment. in Virgil. Bucol.*
v, 20 and viii, 68. [Arnold]

His sheep, his hapless love, his blinded eyes—
  And how a call celestial round him rang,
  And heavenward from the fountain-brink he sprang,
And all the marvel of the golden skies.   190

There thou art gone, and me thou leavest here
  Sole in these fields! yet will I not despair.
    Despair I will not, while I yet descry
  'Neath the mild canopy of English air
    That lonely tree against the western sky.   195
      Still, still these slopes, 'tis clear,
  Our Gipsy-Scholar haunts, outliving thee!
    Fields where soft sheep from cages pull the hay,
    Woods with anemonies in flower till May,
  Know him a wanderer still; then why not me?   200

A fugitive and gracious light he seeks,
  Shy to illumine; and I seek it too.
    This does not come with houses or with gold,
  With place, with honor, and a flattering crew;
    'Tis not in the world's market bought and sold—   205
      But the smooth-slipping weeks
  Drop by, and leave its seeker still untired;
    Out of the heed of mortals he is gone,
    He wends unfollow'd, he must house alone;
  Yet on he fares, by his own heart inspired.   210

Thou too, O Thyrsis, on like quest wast bound;
  Thou wanderedst with me for a little hour!
    Men gave thee nothing; but this happy quest,
  If men esteemed thee feeble, gave thee power,
    If men procured thee trouble, gave thee rest.   215
      And this rude Cumner ground,
  Its fir-topped Hurst, its farms, its quiet fields,
    Here cam'st thou in thy jocund youthful time,
    Here was thine height of strength, thy golden prime!
  And still the haunt beloved a virtue yields.   220

What though the music of thy rustic flute
  Kept not for long its happy, country tone,
    Lost it too soon, and learnt a stormy note
  Of men contention-tost, of men who groan,
    Which task'd thy pipe too sore, and tired thy throat—   225
      It fail'd, and thou wast mute;

---

217. *Hurst:* See "Scholar-Gipsy," l. 57.

Yet hadst thou alway visions of our light,
  And long with men of care thou couldst not stay,
  And soon thy foot resumed its wandering way,
Left human haunt, and on alone till night.   230

Too rare, too rare, grow now my visits here!
  'Mid city-noise, not, as with thee of yore,
  Thyrsis, in reach of sheep-bells is my home!
—Then through the great town's harsh, heart-wearying roar,
  Let in thy voice a whisper often come,   235
    To chase fatigue and fear:
Why faintest thou? I wander'd till I died.
  Roam on! the light we sought is shining still.
  Dost thou ask proof? Our tree yet crowns the hill,
Our Scholar travels yet the loved hill-side.   240

∾

DOVER BEACH

(1867)

The sea is calm to-night,
The tide is full, the moon lies fair
Upon the Straits;—on the French coast, the light
Gleams, and is gone; the cliffs of England stand,
Glimmering and vast, out in the tranquil bay.   5
Come to the window, sweet is the night air!
Only, from the long line of spray
Where the sea meets the moon-blanched sand,
Listen! you hear the grating roar
Of pebbles which the waves suck back, and fling,   10
At their return, up the high strand,
Begin, and cease, and then again begin,
With tremulous cadence slow, and bring
The eternal note of sadness in.

  Sophocles long ago   15
Heard it on the Ægean, and it brought
Into his mind the turbid ebb and flow
Of human misery; we
Find also in the sound a thought,
Hearing it by this distant northern sea.   20

DOVER BEACH: 15. *Sophocles:* Greek tragic dramatist.

The sea of faith
Was once, too, at the full, and round earth's shore
Lay like the folds of a bright girdle furled;
But now I only hear
Its melancholy, long, withdrawing roar,   25
Retreating to the breath
Of the night-wind down the vast edges drear
And naked shingles of the world.

Ah, love, let us be true
To one another! for the world, which seems   30
To lie before us like a land of dreams,
So various, so beautiful, so new,
Hath really neither joy, nor love, nor light,
Nor certitude, nor peace, nor help for pain;
And we are here as on a darkling plain   35
Swept with confused alarms of struggle and flight,
Where ignorant armies clash by night.

❧

Algernon Charles Swinburne

THE GARDEN OF PROSERPINE
(1866)

Here, where the world is quiet,
    Here, where all trouble seems
Dead winds' and spent waves' riot
    In doubtful dreams of dreams;
I watch the green field growing   5
For reaping folk and sowing,
For harvest-time and mowing,
    A sleepy world of streams.

I am tired of tears and laughter,
    And men that laugh and weep   10
Of what may come hereafter
    For men that sow to reap:

I am weary of days and hours,
Blown buds of barren flowers,

Desires and dreams and powers   15
   And everything but sleep.

Here life has death for neighbour,
   And far from eye or ear
Wan waves and wet winds labour,
   Weak ships and spirits steer;   20
They drive adrift, and whither
They wot not who make thither;
But no such winds blow hither,
   And no such things grow here.

No growth of moor or coppice,   25
   No heather-flower or vine,
But bloomless buds of poppies,
   Green grapes of Proserpine,
Pale beds of blowing rushes
Where no leaf blooms or blushes,   30
Save this whereout she crushes
   For dead men deadly wine.

Pale, without name or number,
   In fruitless fields of corn,
They bow themselves and slumber   35
   All night till light is born;
And like a soul belated,
In hell and heaven unmated,
By cloud and mist abated
   Comes out of darkness morn.   40

Though one were strong as seven,
   He too with death shall dwell,
Nor wake with wings in heaven,
   Nor weep for pains in hell;
Though one were fair as roses,   45
His beauty clouds and closes;
And well though love reposes,
   In the end it is not well.

Pale, beyond porch and portal,
   Crowned with calm leaves, she stands   50
Who gathers all things mortal
   With cold immortal hands:

GARDEN OF PROSERPINE: 34. *corn:* wheat, grain.

Her languid lips are sweeter
Than love's who fears to greet her
To men that mix and meet her
   From many times and lands.   55

She waits for each and other,
   She waits for all men born;
Forgets the earth her mother,
   The life of fruits and corn;   60
And spring and seed and swallow
Take wing for her and follow
Where summer song rings hollow
   And flowers are put to scorn.

There go the loves that wither,   65
   The old loves with wearier wings;
And all dead years draw thither,
   And all disastrous things;
Dead dreams of days forsaken,
Blind buds that snows have shaken,   70
Wild leaves that winds have taken,
   Red strays of ruined springs.

We are not sure of sorrow,
   And joy was never sure;
To-day will die to-morrow;   75
   Time stoops to no man's lure;
And love, grown faint and fretful
With lips but half regretful
Sighs, and with eyes forgetful
   Weeps that no loves endure.   80

From too much love of living,
   From hope and fear set free,
We thank with brief thanksgiving
   Whatever gods may be
That no life lives for ever;   85
That dead men rise up never;
That even the weariest river
   Winds somewhere safe to sea.

Then star nor sun shall waken,
   Nor any change of light: 90
Nor sound of waters shaken,
   Nor any sound or sight:

Nor wintry leaves nor vernal,
Nor days nor things diurnal;
Only the sleep eternal   95
    In an eternal night.

George Meredith

THUS PITEOUSLY LOVE CLOSED WHAT HE BEGAT
(1862)

Thus piteously Love closed what he begat:
The union of this ever-diverse pair!
These two were rapid falcons in a snare,
Condemned to do the flitting of the bat.
Lovers beneath the singing sky of May,   5
They wandered once; clear as the dew on flowers:
But they fed not on the advancing hours:
Their hearts held cravings for the buried day.
Then each applied to each that fatal knife,
Deep questioning, which probes to endless dole.   10
Ah, what a dusty answer gets the soul
When hot for certainties in this our life!—
In tragic hints here see what evermore
Moves dark as yonder midnight ocean's force
Thundering like ramping hosts of warrior horse,   15
To throw that faint thin line upon the shore!

LUCIFER IN STARLIGHT
(1883)

On a starred night Prince Lucifer uprose.
Tired of his dark dominion swung the fiend
Above the rolling ball in cloud part screened,
Where sinners hugged their spectre of repose.
Poor prey to his hot fit of pride were those.   5

And now upon his western wing he leaned,
Now his huge bulk o'er Afric's sands careened,
Now the black planet shadowed Arctic snows.
Soaring through wider zones that pricked his scars
With memory of the old revolt from Awe,   10
He reached the middle height, and at the stars,
Which are the brain of heaven, he looked, and sank.
Around the ancient track marched, rank on rank,
The army of unalterable law.

Biographical and Bibliographical References
GENERAL BIBLIOGRAPHY

For individual poets, and in some instances for individual poems, bibliographical suggestions have been placed at the end of the brief biographies below. For the Romantic, Preromantic. and Victorian periods in general, see Ernest Bernbaum, *Guide through the Romantic Movement* (2nd ed., 1949), especially pp. 317-21; T. M. Raysor, ed., *The English Romantic Poets* (rev. ed., 1956); F. E. Faverty, *The Victorian Poets* (1956); also Irving Babbitt, *Rousseau and Romanticism* (1919); T. S. Eliot, *The Sacred Wood* (1920); F. R. Leavis, *Revaluation: Tradition and Development in English Poetry* (1936); J. W. Beach, *The Concept of Nature in Nineteenth-Century Poetry* (1936); and D. G. James, *The Romantic Comedy* (1948). Annual bibliographies of romantic literature and of the period 1660-1800 appear in the periodical *Philological Quarterly*; of Victorian, in *Victorian Studies*. For recent critical interpretations of romanticism, as well as of poems or poets included in this volume, see W. H. Auden, *The Enchafed Flood* (1950); M. H. Abrams, *The Mirror and the Lamp* (1953); John Bayley, *The Romantic Survival* (1957); Donald Davie, *Purity of Diction in English Verse* (1952); Frank Kermode, *Romantic Image* (1957); David Perkins, *The Quest for Permanence* (1959); and M. H. Abrams, *English Romantic Poets: Modern Essays in Criticism* (1960).

MARK AKENSIDE

LIFE. Born 1721 in Newcastle; father a butcher. School in Newcastle; University of Edinburgh (1739). Became poet, editor, and successful surgeon. Died 1770.

LITERARY CAREER. Published poetry as early as 1737. *Pleasures of Imagination* (1744) to some extent prefigures later romantic ideas and practices. *Odes* (1745).

BIOGRAPHY. C. T. Houpt, *Mark Akenside* (1944).

MATTHEW ARNOLD

LIFE. Born 24 December 1822 at Laleham to Thomas Arnold, headmaster of Rugby, and Mary Penrose Arnold. Educated at Winchester, Rugby, Oxford (1841-44); was secretary to Lord Lansdowne (1847-51), who secured him an inspectorship of schools (1851-83), which enabled him to marry Frances Lucy Wightman. Professor of poetry at Oxford (1857-67). Pensioned by Gladstone (1883); lecture tour of America (1883-84). Died suddenly in Liverpool 15 April 1888.

LITERARY CAREER. Arnold began as a poet (*The Strayed Reveller,*

1849; *Empedocles on Etna*, 1852; *Poems*, 1835-55; *Merope*, 1858); but with his essay *On Translating Homer* (1861) established himself as a literary critic. From literary criticism he went on to general attacks on modern materialistic civilization (*Culture and Anarchy*, 1869), and to attempts to reconcile religious feeling and free thought (*Literature and Dogma*, 1873). It is as a lucid essayist and a poet who caught the sense of isolation characteristic of our time that he lives on today.

BIOGRAPHY. E. K. Chambers, *Matthew Arnold, A Study* (1947).

CRITICISM. George Saintsbury, *Matthew Arnold* (1899); Lionel Trilling, *Matthew Arnold* (1939); C. B. Tinker and H. F. Lowry, *The Poetry of Matthew Arnold* (1940).

WILLIAM BLAKE

LIFE. Born 1757 the son of a London hosier; studied drawing at a local academy; was apprenticed to an engraver; was early influenced by the visionary, apocalyptic Swedenborg and the mystic Jacob Boehme. Married Catherine Boucher (1782). Lived in London, practising engraving with varying success, until his death (1827), except for a brief period (1800-1802) when he was given a cottage in Sussex under the patronage of William Hayley. Won renown, during his life and especially posthumously, for his illustrations of Dante, Milton, Bunyan, the Book of Job, and other works.

LITERARY CAREER. Blake's original writings (which he also illustrated) were little known in his own day. They include *Poetical Sketches* (1783), *Songs of Innocence* (1789), *Songs of Experience* (1794), and a number of works in prose and verse (*The Book of Thel, The Marriage of Heaven and Hell, The French Revolution, America, The Four Zoas, Milton, Jerusalem, The Ghost of Abel*) in which his own complex, difficult, and antirational allegories of the human soul are set forth. In general, they vigorously oppose science, morality, and religious or political institutions of any sort.

BIOGRAPHY. Mona Wilson's *Life* (1927, 1948).

CRITICISM. S. F. Damon, *William Blake: His Philosophy and Symbols* (1924, 1958); Joseph Wicksteed, *Blake's Innocence and Experience* (1928); Mark Schorer, *William Blake: The Politics of Vision* (1946); Northrop Frye, *Fearful Symmetry* (1947, 1958); J. Bronowski, *A Man without a Mask* (1944; Penguin ed., 1955); D. V. Erdman, *Blake, Prophet against Empire* (1953).

ROBERT BROWNING

LIFE. Born 7 May 1812 in Camberwell, son of Robert Browning, a well-to-do banker. Educated privately and at the University of London (1829). Traveled, chiefly to Italy; knew Hunt, Wordsworth, Dickens, Carlyle. Married (1846) the invalid poetess Elizabeth Barrett, had one son (1849).

Plunged into grief by wife's death (1861). Later lived much abroad, chiefly in Venice, where he died at his son's home 12 December 1889.

LITERARY CAREER. His early poems, felt by the public to be learned and obscure, and published at his father's expense, include *Pauline* (1833), *Paracelsus* (1835), and *Sordello* (1840). He had a brief and not too successful career as dramatist (1837-53); and first found his successful, psychological-narrative manner in *Bells and Pomegranates* (1841-46); *Men and Women* (1855); and *Dramatis Personae* (1864). *The Ring and the Book* (1868-69) is his most ambitious work, a series of monologues by the participants in a murder trial in seventeenth-century Florence. With it began his reputation as one of the two chief English poets of his age, a reputation which, after *Dramatic Idylls* (1878-79), continued unabated throughout his lifetime.

BIOGRAPHY. W. H. Griffin and H. C. Minchin, *Life of Browning* (1910; rev. ed., 1938); Betty Miller, *Robert Browning: A Portrait* (1952).

CRITICISM. W. C. DeVane, *A Browning Handbook* (1935).

ROBERT BURNS

LIFE. Born 1759 in Ayrshire, son of a tenant-farmer; educated at home. Farmed in partnership with his brother (1784-88). Feted as "bard of Caledonia" in Edinburgh (1787); married Jean Armour (1788); appointed exciseman (1789); died 1796. From 1785 on, he had a series of affairs with various women, several illegitimate children.

LITERARY CAREER. Burns first published a volume of poems (the Kilmarnock edition) in 1786 in order to raise passage-money to Jamaica, where he had been offered a job; but the instant success of the volume kept him in Scotland and led to a second edition, by subscription (1787). In later life he collected and wrote original songs for various Scottish song-books.

BIOGRAPHY. J. D. Ferguson, *Pride and Passion: Robert Burns, 1759-1796* (1939).

CRITICISM. Thomas Carlyle, *Burns* (1828); David Daiches, *Robert Burns* (1950).

LORD BYRON

LIFE. Born 22 January 1788 to "Mad Jack" and Catherine Gordon Byron (his father's second wife). Inherited (1798) title and estate (Newstead Abbey) from great-uncle ("The Wicked Lord"). Educated at Harrow (1801-05) and Trinity College, Cambridge (1805-08). Traveled in Portugal, Spain, Albania, and the Near East (1809-11). Had love affair with Lady Caroline Lamb (1812-13) and allegedly with his half-sister Augusta. Married Anne Isabella Milbanke, who left him after the birth of their child (1815). Left England permanently (1816); lived mostly in Italy; had liaisons with Clare Clairmont (friend of Shelley's second wife), by whom he had a daughter Allegra; and later with Teresa, Countess Guic-cioli. Went to Greece to aid in rebellion against Turks (1823); died at Missolonghi 19 April 1824.

LITERARY CAREER. Byron first won fame for his autobiographical and sentimental travel-poem *Childe Harold's Pilgrimage* (1812-18); and for a series of self-dramatizing, melodramatic, exotic verse-narratives (*The Giaour, The Corsair*, etc.). Today he is chiefly remembered for his spirited satires: *The Vision of Judgment* (1822) (an anti-Southeyan burlesque of Milton), and *Don Juan* (1819-24).

BIOGRAPHY. E. C. Mayne, *Byron* (1912, rev. 1924); L. A. Marchand, *Byron: A Biography* (1957).

CRITICISM. Matthew Arnold, "Byron" in his *Essays in Criticism, Second Series* (1888); T. S. Eliot, "Byron" in his *On Poetry and Poets* (1957); Bertrand Russell, "Byron" in his *History of Western Philosophy* (1945); W. W. Robson, "Byron as Poet" in *Proceedings of the British Academy*, Vol. 43 (1957).

SAMUEL TAYLOR COLERIDGE

LIFE. Born 21 October 1772 at Ottery St. Mary, son of a clergyman. Charity pupil at Christ's Hospital [school] in London (1782-90); Jesus College, Cambridge (1791-93). Married Sara Fricker (1795), by whom he had three children. Met Wordsworth and sister Dorothy 1797, with whom he toured Germany (1799). Annuity from Wedgewood family. Separated from wife (1804—complete separation after 1810). Became opium addict (*ca.* 1800-1816); was desultory lecturer and magazine editor. Lived with physician James Gillman, who largely cured him, from 1816 on. Died 25 July 1834.

LITERARY CAREER. Coleridge wrote very little poetry, and that mostly during his early life and period of intimacy with Wordsworth. His influential literary, philosophical, and theological theories were most fully expressed in the *Biographia Literaria* (1817), which develops a theory of literature and analyzes the ideas and work of Wordsworth; in his lectures on Shakespeare (1808-1818; ed. T. M. Raysor, 1930); and in his *Aids to Reflection* (1825).

BIOGRAPHY. Laurence Hanson, *Life of S. T. Coleridge: The Early Years* (1938); E. K. Chambers, *S. T. Coleridge: A Biographical Study* (1938).

CRITICISM. Walter Pater, "Coleridge," in his *Appreciations* (1889); J. L. Lowes, *The Road to Xanadu: A Study in the Ways of the Imagination* (1927, 2nd ed., 1930); T. S. Eliot, "Wordsworth and Coleridge" in *The Use of Poetry and the Use of Criticism* (1933); Maud Bodkin, *Archetypal Patterns in Poetry* (1934); R. P. Warren, edition of "Ancient Mariner" (1946) and revised essay ("A Poem of Pure Imagination") in his *Selected Essays* (1958); E. E. Stoll, "Symbolism in Coleridge," *Pub. Mod. Lang. Assoc.* 63 (1948); Humphrey House, *Coleridge* (1953); and Elisabeth Schneider, *Coleridge, Opium, and Kubla Khan* (1953).

WILLIAM COLLINS

LIFE AND WRITINGS. Born 1721 in Chichester; father a hatter. West-minster School (1733); Queen's College, Oxford (1740); Magdalen (1741-43). *Persian Eclogues* (1742). Went to London (1744), where he knew Johnson. *Odes* (1746); *Ode on the Popular Superstitions of the Highlands* (published 1788). Symptoms of insanity (about 1751). Died 1759.

BIOGRAPHY. H. W. Garrod, *Collins* (1928). E. G. Ainsworth, *Poor Collins; His Life, His Art, and His Influence* (1937).

OLIVER GOLDSMITH

LIFE. Goldsmith was born in 1728, the son of a Church of England clergyman in rural Ireland; went to Trinity College, Dublin (1744-49). Vacillated in choice of profession, considering the church, the law, and medicine, which he studied in Scotland (1752) and Leyden (1754); be-came a hack writer and Jack-of-all-trades in London (from 1756 on). Friend and clubmate of Johnson, Reynolds, Burke, Boswell; died in debt (1774).

LITERARY CAREER. Goldsmith was a versatile man of letters: his repu-tation (great in his own day and still considerable) was gained in poetry ("The Traveller" [1764] and "The Deserted Village" [1770]); fiction (*The Vicar of Wakefield* [1766]); the essay (*Citizen of the World* [1762]); and the drama (*She Stoops to Conquer* [1773]).

BIOGRAPHY. Austin Dobson, *Life of Oliver Goldsmith* (1888); Stephen Gwynne, *Oliver Goldsmith* (1935); R. M. Wardle, *Oliver Goldsmith* (1957).

CRITICISM. Austin Dobson, *Eighteenth-Century Vignettes* (1892); *Miscellanies* (1898); *Old Kensington Palace* (1910). Editions: *Works*, ed. J. W. M. Gibbs (1884-86).

THOMAS GRAY

LIFE. Born 1716 in London; his father was a scrivener, his mother a milliner. Eton (1727), Peterhouse, Cambridge (1734-38), toured Europe (1739-41) with his old friend Horace Walpole, son of the famous prime minister. After living with mother at Stoke Poges (possible scene of *Elegy*), returned to Peterhouse to devote the rest of his life to antiquarian scholarship. Also studied at British Museum in London (1759) and took various tours of England and Scotland. Regius Professor of History (1768). Died (1771); buried at Stoke Poges.

LITERARY CAREER. Gray wrote little, but expended upon that little infinite pains. Printed the *Elegy* anonymously (1751); *Six Poems* (1753); *Odes by Mr. Gray* (1757). Was offered (and refused) the poet laureate-ship of England (1757). Besides the *Elegy* and the odes his best-loved poems are the mock-heroic verses on the drowning of a favorite cat [Wal-pole's], and his sonnet on the death of his friend Richard West.

BIOGRAPHY. W. P. Jones, *Thomas Gray, Scholar; the True Tragedy of an Eighteenth-Century Gentleman* (1937); Lord David Cecil, *Two Quiet Lives* (1948); R. W. Ketton-Cremer, *Thomas Gray: A Biography* (1955).

CRITICISM. "Gray's Storied Urn" in Cleanth Brooks, *The Well Wrought Urn* (1947).

JOHN KEATS

LIFE. Born 31 October 1795 in London to Thomas and Frances Keats; father was hostler at Swan and Hoop Inn. Private school at Enfield (1803-11); developed taste for literature under influence of Charles Cowden Clarke. Apprenticed to surgeon and druggist (1811-1814), licensed as apothecary (1816). Joined the literary circle of Leigh Hunt (1816); knew Shelley, Hazlitt, and Lamb. Devoted himself to study and writing. Nursed consumptive brother Thomas, who died 1818. Became engaged to Fanny Brawne (1819). Contracted tuberculosis, to cure which he went to Italy (1820), where he died 23 February 1821.

LITERARY CAREER. Published *Poems* (1817) which were favorably reviewed but had little sale. His mythological and allegorical poem *Endymion* (1818) was vigorously attacked by Tory reviewers who disliked Hunt (a liberal) and his friends. *Lamia, Isabella, The Eve of St. Agnes, Other Poems* (1820) met with a more respectful reception, and includes all his finest work. *The Fall of Hyperion* (1856-57), a Miltonic mythological blank-verse poem, he abandoned without completing. His correspondence is energetic, colorful, and intelligent.

BIOGRAPHY. Sidney Colvin, *John Keats: His Life and Poetry, His Friends, Critics, and After-Fame* (1917); Amy Lowell, *John Keats* (1925); John Keats, *Letters* (ed. by H. E. Rollins, 1958).

CRITICISM. M. R. Ridley, *Keats's Craftsmanship: A Study in Poetic Development* (1934); T. S. Eliot, "Shelley and Keats" in *The Use of Poetry and the Use of Criticism* (1933); W. J. Bate, *The Stylistic Development of Keats* (1945); "Keats's Sylvan Historian" in Cleanth Brooks, *The Well Wrought Urn* (1947); E. R. Wasserman, *The Finer Tone* (1953).

GEORGE MEREDITH

LIFE. Born 1828 in Portsmouth to Augustus and Jane Macnamara Meredith, a tailoring family. Began study of law (1846) but abandoned it for literature. Married (1849) Mrs. Nicolls, widow of naval officer and daughter of the novelist Thomas Love Peacock. Wife deserted him (1858), leaving one surviving son. Lived (1862-64) with the Rossettis and Swinburne in London; after wife's death married Marie Vulliamy (1864). Settled in Surrey (1867). Died 1909.

LITERARY CAREER. Meredith was a journalist, publisher's reader, and successful novelist (*The Ordeal of Richard Feverel*, 1859; *Evan Harrington*, 1861; *The Egoist*, 1879; *Diana of the Crossways*, 1885, and several others). He also published some poetry, including the sonnet-sequence *Modern Love* (1862), inspired by his estrangement from his first wife.

BIOGRAPHY. Lionel Stevenson, *The Ordeal of George Meredith* (1953).

PERCY BYSSHE SHELLEY

LIFE. Born 4 August 1792 in Sussex to Timothy and Elizabeth Pilfold Shelley, members of the squirearchy. Educated at Eton (1804-10) and Oxford (1810-11), from which he was expelled for publishing an atheistical tract. Married Harriet Westbrook 1811; had two children (1813, 1814). Eloped with Mary Godwin (1814), whom he married after the suicide of Harriet (1816), and by whom he had several children, only one of whom (Percy, b. 1819) survived. Left England 1818 and lived in Italy, where he met death by drowning, 8 July 1822. Knew Keats and was closely associated, both in England and Italy, with Byron. Supported public reforms of every sort throughout his life.

LITERARY CAREER. Shelley's principal poems, which were psychological, revolutionary, and autobiographical in character, include the radical Utopian *Queen Mab* (1813), the introspective *Alastor* (1816), the lyrical *Lines Written Among the Euganean Hills* (1819), the satiric *Witch of Atlas* (1820), the philosophical *Prometheus Unbound* (1820), the Platonic-amatory *Epipsychidion* (1821), and the elegiac *Adonais* (1821); he also wrote a verse-play *The Cenci* (1819) and a prose *Defense of Poetry* (1821).

BIOGRAPHY. N. I. White, *Shelley* (1940); Kenneth N. Cameron, *The Young Shelley* (1950).

CRITICISM. Matthew Arnold, "Shelley," in his *Essays in Criticism: Second Series* (1888); T. S. Eliot "Shelley and Keats" in *The Use of Poetry and the Use of Criticism* (1933); C. S. Lewis, "Shelley, Dryden, and Mr. Eliot," in his *Rehabilitations and Other Essays* (1939); Carlos Baker, *Shelley's Major Poetry: The Fabric of a Vision* (1948); E. R. Wasserman, *The Subtler Language* (1959), chap. 8 (for "Adonais"); Harold Bloom, *Shelley's Mythmaking* (1959), chap. 4 (for "Ode to the West Wind"); Milton Wilson, *Shelley's Later Poetry* (1959).

CHRISTOPHER SMART

LIFE AND WRITINGS. Born 1722, educated Durham and Cambridge; published *Poems on Several Occasions* (1752), the *Hilliad* (satiric reply to an attack by Hill) (1753), and various odes, translations, and oratories; confined to asylum for religious mania; wrote "Song to David" (1763); died in debt (1771).

BIOGRAPHY AND CRITICISM. K. A. McKenzie, *Christopher Smart, Sa Vie et Ses Oeuvres* (1925).

ALGERNON CHARLES SWINBURNE

LIFE. Born 1837 in London; his father was an admiral, his mother an earl's daughter. Educated at Eton (1849-54), abroad, and at Balliol College, Oxford (1856-60). Suffered ill health, lived chiefly in retirement; died 1909.

LITERARY CAREER. Besides numerous volumes of verse, some revolutionary in spirit, his best-known surviving work is probably the verse-drama *Atalanta in Calydon* (1865).

BIOGRAPHY. E. W. Gosse, *The Life of Algernon Charles Swinburne* (1917); Harold Nicolson, *Swinburne* (1926); G. Lafourcade, *Swinburne, A Literary Biography* (1932).

ALFRED TENNYSON

LIFE. Born 6 August 1809 in Somersby, son of an Anglican clergyman. Educated at home and at Trinity College, Cambridge (1828-31). Lost his father (1831), and his closest friend, Arthur Hallam (1833). Became engaged to Emily Sellwood (1836) but was prevented by poverty and family responsibilities from marrying her till 1850. Pensioned by Sir Robert Peel (1845); awarded laureateship (1850). Lived at Twickenham and on the Isle of Wight, and after 1868 at Aldworth, near Haslemere. Traveled, chiefly in England and France; created first Baron Tennyson by Gladstone (1884). Had three sons, of whom only the third, Hallam, survived him. Died 6 October 1892.

LITERARY CAREER. Earliest verse was published with his brother Charles (*Poems by Two Brothers*, 1827). Two subsequent volumes of poetry (1830, 1833) were so unfavorably received that Tennyson published nothing for nine years. His earliest efforts were lyrical, but he later turned to verse-drama and Arthurian epic (*Idylls of the King*, 1859). His most famous single volume was *In Memoriam*, published anonymously (1850); others include *Ode on the Death of the Duke of Wellington* (1852), *Maud* (1855) and *Demeter and other Poems* (1889).

BIOGRAPHY. Hallam Tennyson, *Alfred, Lord Tennyson: A Memoir* (1898); H. G. Nicolson, *Tennyson: Aspects of his Life, Character, and Poetry* (1923; 1925); Charles Tennyson, *Alfred Tennyson* (1949).

CRITICISM. A. C. Bradley, *A Commentary on Tennyson's "In Memoriam"* (1907); T. S. Eliot, "In Memoriam" in *Essays Ancient and Modern* (1936); W. H. Auden, Introduction to *A Selection from the Poems of Tennyson* (1944). For a discussion of "Tears, Idle Tears," see Cleanth Brooks, *The Well Wrought Urn* (1947), chap. 9, an essay reprinted in John Killham's *Critical Essays on the Poetry of Tennyson* (1960), which also has an introductory review of modern Tennyson criticism.

JAMES THOMSON

LIFE AND WRITINGS. Born 1700 at Ednam; father a Presbyterian minister. University of Edinburgh (1715); went to London (1725); early version of *Winter* (1726). *The Seasons* (1730). Lived by tutoring and patronage. Various masques, plays, and other poetry. *The Castle of Indolence*, imitative of Spenser (1748). Died 1748.

BIOGRAPHY AND CRITICISM. Leon Morel, *James Thomson, Sa Vie et Ses Oeuvres;* Douglas Grant, *James Thomson: Poet of "The Seasons"* (1951).

WILLIAM WORDSWORTH

LIFE. Born 7 April 1770, at Cockermouth, Cumberland, to John Wordsworth, attorney, and Anne Cookson Wordsworth; had three brothers and one sister (Dorothy). Went to grammar school at Hawkshead (1778); lost mother (1778) and father (1783) in early youth. St John's, Cambridge, 1787-91. European tour 1790. After graduation spent year (1792) in France; affair with Annette Vallon, friendship with Girondists. Returned to England shortly before war (1793) broke out between England and France, separating him from Annette, who gave birth to a daughter, Caroline (Dec. 1792). Inherited £900; met Coleridge (1795). Eventually settled with Dorothy in the Lake country of N. W. England (1799); married Mary Hutchison (1802), by whom he had five children (1803-10). Granted political sinecure (Stamp Distributor) in 1813. Died 23 April 1850.

LITERARY CAREER. First published (1793) the heavily descriptive *An Evening Walk and Descriptive Sketches;* contact with the more metaphysical Coleridge led to the now famous *Lyrical Ballads* (1798, 1800). His spiritual autobiography *The Prelude* was written during the period 1798-1805, but not published till after his death (1850). It and *The Excursion* (1814) were to have been parts of a long, never-completed philosophical poem *The Recluse*. After *Poems in Two Volumes* (1807) and the *Collected Works* of 1815 he wrote little that has survived, though continuing to publish at intervals. He, Coleridge, and Southey were popularly known as the Lake Poets. After Southey's death (1843) he became Poet Laureate. Besides Coleridge, the chief influence on him seems to have been his nature-loving sister Dorothy.

BIOGRAPHY. G. McL. Harper, *William Wordsworth: His Life, Works and Influence* (1916; rev. 1929); Dorothy Wordsworth, *Journals* (ed. E. DeSelincourt, 1941); William and Dorothy Wordsworth, *Letters* (ed. E. DeSelincourt, 1935-38); Mary Moorman, *William Wordsworth: The Early Years, 1770-1803* (1957).

CRITICISM. Coleridge, *Biographia Literaria* (1817; ed. *J. Shawcross*, 1907; see especially chapters 14, 17, 18, 19, 20, 22); Matthew Arnold, "Wordsworth" in his *Essays in Criticism* (1888); Walter Pater, "Wordsworth" in his *Appreciations* (1889); Alfred North Whitehead, "The Romantic Reaction" in his *Science and the Modern World* (1925); Arthur Beatty, *William Wordsworth; His Doctrine and Art* (1927); T. S. Eliot, "Wordsworth and Coleridge" in *The Use of Poetry and the Use of Criticism* (1933); H. J. C. Grierson, *Milton and Wordsworth* (1937); J. R. Sutherland, *Wordsworth and Pope* (1944); Josephine Miles, *The Vocabulary of Poetry* (1947); Helen Darbishire, *The Poet Wordsworth* (1950); D. G. James, "Wordsworth and Tennyson" (on *The Prelude* and *In Memoriam*) in *Proc. of the Brit. Acad.* 36 (1950); Lionel Trilling, "Wordsworth and the Rabbis," in his *Opposing Self* (1955); John Wain, "The Liberation of Wordsworth" in his *Preliminary Essays* (1957); John Jones, *The Egotistical Sublime* (1954). For a discussion of the Intimations Ode, see Cleanth Brooks, "Wordsworth and the Paradox of the Imagination" in his *Well Wrought Urn* (1947); and Lionel Trilling, "The Immortality Ode" in his *Liberal Imagination* (1950). For *The Prelude,* see the edition by E. DeSelincourt (1926); and R. D. Havens, *The Mind of a Poet* (1940).

LaVergne, TN USA
09 September 2009
157237LV00001B/114/A